Lecture Notes in Computer Science 3165

Commenced Publication in 1973
Founding and Former Series Editors:
Gerhard Goos, Juris Hartmanis, and Jan van Leeuwen

Marios D. Dikaiakos (Ed.)

Grid Computing

Second European AcrossGrids Conference, AxGrids 2004
Nicosia, Cyprus, January 28-30, 2004
Revised Papers

 Springer

Volume Editor

Marios D. Dikaiakos
University of Cyprus, Department of Computer Science
P.O. Box 20537, CY 1678, Nicosia, Cyprus
E-mail: mdd@ucy.ac.cy

Library of Congress Control Number: 2004113302

CR Subject Classification (1998): C.2.4, D.1.3, D.2.7, D.2.12, D.4, F.2.2, G.2.1

ISSN 0302-9743
ISBN 3-540-22888-8 Springer Berlin Heidelberg New York

Springer is a part of Springer Science+Business Media

springeronline.com

© Springer-Verlag Berlin Heidelberg 2004
Printed in Germany

Typesetting: Camera-ready by author, data conversion by Olgun Computergrafik
Printed on acid-free paper   SPIN: 11314103   06/3142   5 4 3 2 1 0

General Chairs' Message

As conference co-chairs, we have great pleasure in writing this short foreword to the proceedings of the 2nd European AcrossGrids Conference (AxGrids 2004). The conference clearly demonstrated the need in Europe for an annual event that brings together the grid research community to share experiences and learn about new developments. This year, in addition to the large number of attendees from across the 25 member states of the European Union, we were especially pleased to welcome fellow researchers from the Americas and the Asia – Pacific region. Only by talking and working together will we realize our vision of building truly global grids.

In addition to the main AxGrids 2004 conference, and thanks to the large number of researchers from European Commission-funded projects who were present, we were able to run a series of GRIDSTART Technical Working Group meetings and we are indebted to the conference organizers for helping with the logistics of this parallel activity.

In particular we would like to express our gratitude to Marios Dikaiakos and his team for working tirelessly over many months to make the conference the smooth-running success that it was. Of course, no conference is complete without speakers and an audience and we would like to thank everyone for their interest and engagement in the many sessions over the three days of the event.

AxGrids 2004 once again demonstrated the need in Europe for an event to bring together the research community. As we move forward into Framework 6 we look forward to its continuation and expansion to represent all of the grid research community in Europe.

June 2004   Mark Parsons
                                                                         Michal Turala

Editor's Preface

The 2nd European AcrossGrids Conference (AxGrids 2004) aimed to examine the state of the art in research and technology developments in Grid Computing, and provide a forum for the presentation and exchange of views on the latest grid-related research results and future work. The conference was organized by CrossGrid, a European Union-funded project on Grid research, GRIDSTART, the EU-sponsored initiative for consolidating technical advances in grids in Europe, and the University of Cyprus. It continued on from the successful 1st European Across Grids Conference, held in Santiago de Compostela, Spain, in February 2003. AxGrids 2004 was run in conjunction with the 2nd IST Concertation Meeting on Grid Research, which brought together representatives from all EU-funded projects on Grid research for an exchange of experiences and ideas regarding recent developments in European grid research.

The conference was hosted in Nicosia, the capital of Cyprus, and attracted authors and attendees from all over Europe, the USA, and East Asia. The Program Committee of the conference consisted of 37 people from both academia and industry, and there were 13 external reviewers. Overall, AxGrids 2004 attracted 57 paper submissions (42 full papers and 15 short posters). Papers underwent a thorough review by several Program Committee members and external reviewers. After the review, the Program Chair decided to accept 26 papers (out of 42) for regular presentations, 8 papers for short presentations, and 13 papers for poster presentations. Accepted papers underwent a second review for inclusion this postproceedings volume, published as part of Springer's Lecture Notes in Computer Science series. Eventually, we decided to include 27 long and 3 short papers, which cover a range of important topics of grid research, from computational and data grids to the Semantic Grid and grid applications.

Here, we would like to thank the Program Committee members, the external reviewers, and the conference session chairs for their excellent work, which contributed to the high-quality technical program of the conference. We would also like to thank the University of Cyprus, IBM, GRIDSTART, and the Cyprus Telecommunications Authority (CYTA) for making possible the organization of this event through their generous sponsorship. Special thanks go to Maria Poveda for handling organizational issues, to Dr. Pedro Trancoso for setting up and running the Web management system at the Computer Science Department at the University of Cyprus, and to Kyriacos Neocleous for helping with the preparation of the proceedings.

I hope that you find this volume interesting and useful.

Nicosia, Cyprus, June 2004   Marios D. Dikaiakos

Organizing Committee

Conference General Chairs

Michal Turala   ACC Cyfronet & INP, Krakow, Poland
Mark Parsons   EPCC, Univ. of Edinburgh, UK

Program Committee Chair

Marios Dikaiakos   University of Cyprus

Posters and Demos Chair

Jesus Marco   CSIC, Santander, Spain

Website Chair

Pedro Trancoso   University of Cyprus

Publicity Chair

George Papadopoulos   University of Cyprus

Local Organizing Committee

Marios Dikaiakos   University of Cyprus
Nikos Nikolaou   Cyprus Telecom. Authority
Maria Poveda   University of Cyprus

Steering Committee

Bob Bentley	University College London, UK
Marian Bubak	Inst. of Comp. Science & ACC Cyfronet, Poland
Marios Dikaiakos	Univ. of Cyprus
Dietmar Erwin	Forschungszentrum Jülich GmbH, Germany
Fabrizio Gagliardi	CERN, Geneva, Switzerland
Max Lemke	European Commission
Jesus Marco	CSIC, Spain
Holger Marten	Forschungszentrum Karlsruhe GmbH, Germany
Norbert Meyer	PSNC, Poland
Matthias Mueller	HLRS, Germany
Jarek Nabrzyski	PSNC, Poland
Mark Parsons	EPCC, Univ. of Edinburgh, UK
Yannis Perros	Algosystems, Greece
Peter Sloot	Univ. of Amsterdam, The Netherlands
Michal Turala	ACC Cyfronet & INP, Poland

Program Committee

A. Bogdanov	Inst. for HPCDB, Russian Federation
M. Bubak	Inst. of Comp. Sci. & Cyfronet, Poland
B. Coghlan	Trinity College Dublin, Ireland
M. Cosnard	INRIA, France
Y. Cotronis	Univ. of Athens, Greece
J. Cunha	New University of Lisbon, Portugal
E. Deelman	ISI, Univ. Southern California, USA
M. Delfino	Univ. Autònoma de Barcelona, Spain
M. Dikaiakos	Univ. of Cyprus
B. DiMartino	Second University of Naples, Italy
J. Dongarra	Univ. of Tennessee, USA
T. Fahringer	University of Innsbruck, Austria
I. Foster	ANL and Univ. of Chicago, USA
G. Fox	Univ. of Indiana, USA
W. Gentzsch	Sun Europe, Germany
M. Gerndt	TU Munchen, Germany
A. Gomez	CESGA, Spain
A. Hoekstra	Univ. of Amsterdam, The Netherlands
E. Houstis	University of Thessaly, Greece
B. Jones	CERN, Switzerland
P. Kacsuk	Sztaki, Hungary
J. Labarta	Univ. Polytechnica Catalunya, Spain
D. Laforenza	CNR, Italy
E. Markatos	ICS-FORTH & Univ. of Crete, Greece
L. Matyska	Masaryk University, Czech Republic
N. Meyer	Poznan Supercomputing Center, Poland
B. Miller	Univ. of Wisconsin, USA
L. Moreau	Univ. of Southampton, UK
T. Priol	INRIA/IRISA, France
D. Reed	Univ. of Illinois, Urbana-Champaign, USA
R. Sakellariou	Univ. of Manchester, UK
M. Senar	Univ. Autònoma de Barcelona, Spain
P. Sloot	Univ. of Amsterdam, The Netherlands
L. Snyder	Univ. of Washington, USA
P. Trancoso	Univ. of Cyprus
D. Walker	Univ. of Wales, UK
R. Wismüller	TU Munchen, Germany

Referees

Gabriel Antoniu
Vaggelis Floros
Marilena Georgiadou
Anastasios Gounaris
Alexandru Jugravu

Juri Papay
Christian Perez
Norbert Podhorszki
Gergely Sipos
Nicola Tonellotto

Eleni Tsiakkouri
George Tsouloupas
Alex Villazon

Sponsoring Institutions

University of Cyprus
IBM
GRIDSTART
Cyprus Telecommunications Authority

Table of Contents

EU Funded Grid Development in Europe

Paul Graham[3], Matti Heikkurinen[1], Jarek Nabrzyski[2], Ariel Oleksiak[2],
Mark Parsons[3], Heinz Stockinger[1], Kurt Stockinger[1],
Maciej Stroiński[2], and Jan Węglarz[2]

[1] CERN, European Organization for Nuclear Research, Switzerland
[2] PSNC, Poznan Supercomputing and Networking Center, Poland
[3] EPCC, Edinburgh Parallel Computing Centre, Scotland

Abstract. Several Grid projects have been established that deploy a
"first generation Grid". In order to categorise existing projects in Europe, we have developed a taxonomy and applied it to 20 European Grid
projects funded by the European Commission through the Framework
5 IST programme. We briefly describe the projects and thus provide an
overview of current Grid activities in Europe. Next, we suggest future
trends based on both the European Grid activities as well as progress of
the world-wide Grid community. The work we present here is a source of
information that aims to help to promote European Grid development.

1 Introduction

Since the term "Grid" was first introduced, the Grid community has expanded
greatly in the last five years. Originally, only a few pioneering projects such as
Globus, Condor, Legion and Unicore provided Grid solutions. Now, however,
many countries have their own Grid projects that provide specific Grid middleware and infrastructure.

In this paper, in order to give a comprehensive overview of existing technologies and projects in Europe, we establish a general taxonomy for categorising
Grid services, tools and projects. This taxonomy is then applied to existing
projects in Europe. In particular, within the GRIDSTART [5] framework we
have analysed 20 representative Grid projects funded by the European Commission in order to highlight current European trends in Grid computing. The
guiding principle behind this taxonomy is to enable the identification of trends in
European Grid development and to find out where the natural synergies between
projects exist.

Since the need for this taxonomy was practical – and relatively urgent –
a certain amount of guidance in the form of "pre-classification" was deemed
necessary in the information gathering phase. This meant that rather than asking
open questions about the activities of the projects and creating the classification
based on the answers, the projects themselves were asked to identify which layers
and areas (see later) they worked on according to a classification presented to
them in a series of questionnaires. Thus, it is likely that this taxonomy will evolve
as the contacts and collaboration between projects increases.

M. Dikaiakos (Ed.): AxGrids 2004, LNCS 3165, pp. 1–10, 2004.

This taxonomy is based on the IST Grid Projects Inventory and Roadmap [4] (a 215 page document). In this paper we extract the key aspects of the data presented in that document and refer to the original document for further details.

The paper should also prove of interest to the broader distributed computing community since the results presented provide a clear overview of how European Grid activities are evolving. The paper supersedes previous work reported in [7] (describing the initial work towards this survey) and [1] (reporting on a preliminary overview). The more up-to-date overview provided in this paper covers new trends and Grid services which are rapidly evolving from standardisation work as well as benefiting from insight into the latest developments in the various projects, that have occurred since the initial overviews were prepared.

2   Taxonomy

Development of Grid environments requires effort in a variety of disciplines, from preparing sufficient network infrastructure, through the design of reliable middleware, to providing applications and tailored to the end users.

The comparison of Grid projects is made according to three different categorisation schemes. The first is by different technological *layers* [2, 3] that separate the Grid user from the underlying hardware:

- **Applications and Portals.** Applications such as parameter simulations, and grand-challenge problems, often require considerable computing power, access to remote data sets, and may need to interact with scientific instruments. Grid portals offer web-enabled application services, i.e. users can submit and collect results for their jobs on remote resources through a web interface.
- **Application Environment and Tools.** These offer high-level services that allow programmers to develop applications and test their performance and reliability. Users can then make use of these applications in an efficient and convenient way.
- **Middleware (Generic and Application Specific Services).** This layer offers core services such as remote process management, co-allocation of resources, storage access, information (registry), security, data access and transfer, and Quality of Service (QoS) such as resource reservation and trading.
- **Fabric and Connectivity.** Connectivity defines core communication protocols required for Grid-specific network transactions. The fabric comprises the resources geographically distributed and accessible on the Internet.

The second categorisation scheme concerns technical *areas*, which include topics such as dissemination and testbeds and which address the wider issues the impact of Grid technology. All areas with their projects are listed in Figure 2 which categorises different the aspects of Grid projects.

The third main categorisation scheme in this article focuses on the scientific domain of *applications* as well as the computational approaches used (see Section 3.3). Further related work on an earlier taxonomy of Grid resource management can be found in [6].

3   Major Trends in Grid Development

In the Grid inventory report we analysed the major Grid projects in Europe that are referred to as *Wave 1* ("older" projects that received funding prior to 2001) and *Wave 2* ("younger" projects). Links to all project web-sites can be found at [5].

- Wave 1 projects are formally part of the EU-funded GRIDSTART project and are as follows: AVO, CrossGrid, DAMIEN, DataGrid, DataTAG, EGSO, EUROGRID, GRIA, GridLab and GRIP.
- Wave 2 projects are informal partners of the GRIDSTART project and are as follows: BioGrid, COG, FlowGrid, GEMSS, GRACE, GRASP, MammoGrid, MOSES, OpenMolGRID, SeLeNe.

Apart from these EU-funded projects, there are several other national and multi-national Grid initiatives like INFN Grid (Italy), NorduGrid (Northern European countries) and the e-Science Programme (UK) that each encompasses a range of projects. Most of these projects have informal ties with one or more GRIDSTART projects, but the analysis of these ties is beyond the scope of this document.

The analysis presented in this document is based on a survey, categorised by Grid areas, that has been submitted to each of the projects. For further details on the analysis methodology we refer to [4].

3.1   Development in Grid Layers

Generally, one can observe the following *trend*: projects which started later are biased towards the development of higher-level tools and applications (this trend is continued by Wave 2 projects). This is justified since several projects (such as DataGrid and EuroGrid) are preparing a good basis for further work by developing low-level tools in the Fabric and Middleware layer. However, it is not a general rule. For instance, projects such as DataGrid, DataTAG and Cross-Grid, which are co-operating with each other in order to prepare an environment for data-intensive applications, work on Fabric layer components although they started at different times. This complementary work is beneficial, since the application domains of the projects are different.

In the GRIDSTART cluster there are large projects with activities covering many Grid layers (DataGrid, GridLab, CrossGrid: these projects work on complimentary aspects in the specific layer) and smaller projects focused on particular layers (DataTAG, DAMIEN). All Wave 2 projects belong to this second group. Many of them focus on the highest layer and/or on a single application domain (e.g., COG, OpenMolGRID, SeLeNe). Wave 2 projects rarely work on the fabric layer.

The choice of the underlying Grid system obviously influences the architecture of projects too. The two principle Grid toolkits in this study, Globus and UNICORE, are used (see Figure 1). Globus is a more "horizontal" solution in the form of a toolkit offering much necessary functionality while UNICORE is more "vertical" and provides software up to the Graphical User Interface. The influence of these characteristics on project architecture can be noted, for example, in the case of EUROGRID and GRIP. These projects "Grid-enable" applications through preparing application-specific UNICORE plug-ins. They also add more dynamic functionality through extending the UNICORE system itself.

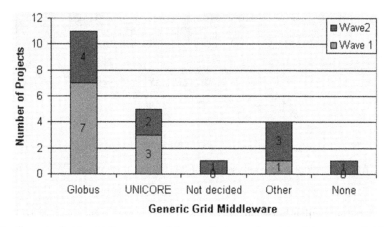

Fig. 1. Generic Grid middleware used by projects analysed in this paper divided into Wave1/Wave2 projects. "Not decided" concerns projects that were in an early stage of development and various solutions were tested. "None" concerns ontology Grid projects and therefore no need for submission of computation jobs has been identified

Generally, one notice that differences between project architectures result from the *different types of Grids* that are being developed. Although the layers defined in Section 2 can still be distinguished, in Data and Information Grids, replication or data search services are placed above various data archives while, in the case of Computational Grids, the global scheduler and job submission systems are built on top of local resource management systems. The next major difference that occurs in the *architectures* of Grid projects results from the trend towards a service-oriented model. Some projects (GEMSS, GRASP, GRIA) represent the service-oriented approach. The difference here is that the stress is put on services (and their performance) rather than specific hardware resources, or a specific scientific application.

3.2   Development in Areas

Development in particular areas is given in Figure 2 which displays the number of projects putting significant effort into a given area. For example, 7 projects develop portals, 17 projects deal with applications, 11 out of the 20 projects focus on Resource Management (for more details see [4]).

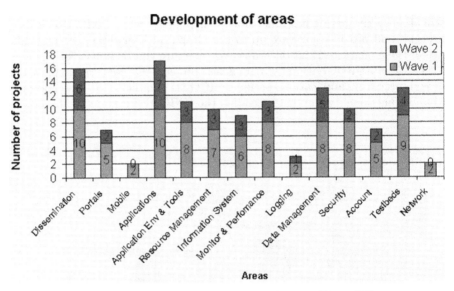

Fig. 2. Areas developed by analysed projects divided into Wave1/Wave2 projects

We also distinguish between Wave 1 and Wave 2 projects in order to indicate the directions and trends of both groups of projects. We can observe the following phenomena:

– Focus on some areas is significantly less for Wave 2 projects, e.g. Resource Management, Information Services, Application Development Environment and Tools, possibly due to the existence of solutions in previous projects.
– Although the scope of development in a certain area in Wave 2 projects may be similar to the one of Wave 1 projects, there is a different level of abstraction. For example, in the case of data management, Wave 2 projects may work on knowledge management rather than low level data access techniques.
– Although Wave 2 projects are more oriented towards high-level Grid functionality, there has been little concentrated, cross-project effort in the development of user friendly access methods such as portals or mobile access. Instead the emphasis is placed on techniques that add semantics to data (and in consequence facilitate access for end users).

Figure 2 does not communicate exactly to the extent of developments in given areas, since projects put different emphasis on specific areas. Furthermore, some technologies belonging to a specific area may be developed to a greater extent than in others.

In Table 1 we give a summary of different solutions provided by the projects. For many of the areas analysed, there are now existing tools that can be incorporated into other projects. Possible examples of existing solutions that may be (or may already have been) applied by other Grid initiatives in order to profit from synergies are:

Table 1. Solutions provided by analysed projects

Dissemination	Industry and research forum	CrossGrid, DataGrid
	Tutorials	DataGrid, GridLab, CrossGrid
Portals	Genius portal, Earth Observation Portal	DataGrid, MammoGrid
	End user support of several existing portals	AVO
	Migrating desktop	CrossGrid
	GridSphere framework, portlets and	GridLab
	portlet development environment	
	UNICORE portal	EUROGRID, GRIP, OpenMolGRID
Applications	Bio-technology applications	EUROGRID, GRIP, GEMSS
	Cactus-based applications (general purpose	GridLab
	framework, large user community	
	in the astrophysics)	
Application env. and tools	PACX-MPI	DAMIEN, CrossGrid (used by)
	Extended Code Coupling Interface	DAMIEN
	MpCCI, MetaVampir, DIMEMAS	
	UNICORE plugins	EuroGrid, OpenMolGRID
	MARMOT MPI verification tool	CrossGrid
	GAT	GridLab
Resource Mgmt and Scheduling	Integration to batch systems	Several of the
	enhanced Job description languages.	Wave 1 projects
	Job submission system	DataGrid
	QoS Manager fro MPI applications	DAMIEN
	Resource Mgmt System (UNICORE based)	EUROGRID
	Use of Globus resources through UNICORE	GRIP
	GridLab Resource Mgmt System (GRMS)	GridLab
Information	GLUE	DataTAG
	UNICORE IDB	EUROGRID, GRIP
	information/knowledge management	BioGrid,COG,MOSES,SeLeNe
Monitoring and Performance	R-GMA, Fabric Monit. & Fault Tolerance	DataGrid
	Monitoring System	GridLab
	MetaVampir, DIMEMAS	DAMIEN
	G-PM	CrossGrid
Logging	Logging and Bookkeeping service	DataGrid
Data Mgmt	Hierarchical Replica Management	DataGrid
	Spitfire	DataGrid
	search or categorisation	EGSO, GRACE
Security	VOMS	DataGrid/DataTAG
	Plug-in for GSI-proxy generation	GRIP
	GridLab Authorisation Service (GAS)	GridLab
Testbeds	(Intercontinental) testbed	DataGrid, DataTAG, GridLab, FlowGrid

- security: VOMS[1] (DataGrid/DataTAG)
- schema for information system : GLUE schema (DataTAG)
- data management: Spitfire (DataGrid)
- developer tools: PACX-MPI (DAMIEN) and MARMOT (CrossGrid)
- framework for portals: GridSphere (GridLab)

Additionally, there are ongoing developments that may provide the basis for further interesting initiatives in the near future. Examples of such solutions are: Resource Management – GRMS (GridLab); Security – GAS (GridLab), CoPS

[1] VOMS: Virtual Organization Membership Service

(AVO); Application Development Environments and Tools – UNICORE plugins (EUROGRID, GRIP), GAT[2] (GridLab); Accounting – Accounting and Billing services (EUROGRID, GRASP).

Despite all these solutions there are several problems yet to be overcome which include:

– Transfer of current solution components to a service based approach.
– Focus on learning from mistakes to build what will become the first reliable, resilient and robust "production" Grids.

3.3   Development in Applications

This section is devoted to applications, as they are the main stimulators of Grid infrastructure development. Their domains, requirements and user communities have a great influence on the structure of many of the current projects.

Figure 3 shows the numbers of applications from particular domains. We have distinguished the following general domains: Earth and Environmental Sciences, Biology and Medicine, Physics and Astronomy, Engineering and Multimedia. All remaining domains fall into the category *other domains*, which includes many commercial and business applications.

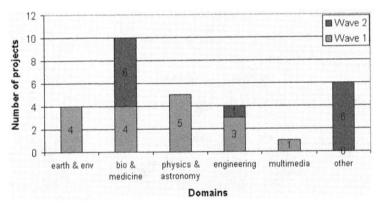

Fig. 3. Areas developed by analysed projects divided into Wave1/Wave2 projects

Although many Grid projects have their roots in physics or are driven by other scientific domains such as biology, medicine or earth sciences, there are also industrial applications including engineering and multimedia. The distribution of application domains has changed considerably between the Wave 1 and Wave 2 projects. Several projects apply Grid technology to the fields of biology and medicine. New applications have also appeared including the ERP sector, e-Learning and solutions such as the semantic web designed for multiple domains. A classification can be found in Figure 4.

---

[2] GAT: Grid Application Toolkit

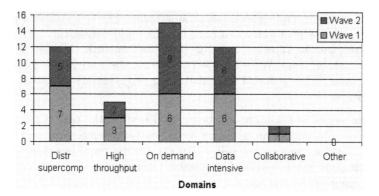

Fig. 4. Applications

The majority of applications for Wave 1 projects deal with large amounts of data (data intensive applications) or require huge computing power (distributed supercomputing applications). However, we should also notice the increasing need, especially in the case of Wave 2 projects, for on demand and collaborative applications, which have additional requirements for higher-level services including mechanisms for controlling quality of service, and sometimes even new architectures (e.g. in the form of distributed services). Additionally, applications that need remote resources for a certain amount of time (on demand applications) often require efficient payment mechanisms. All these trends must be taken into consideration while developing Grid middleware and infrastructure.

Comparing the applications from Wave 2 with those from Wave 1, the following conclusions may be drawn:

- Although present in Wave 1 projects, there is a greater focus on industrial applications in Wave 2.
- Many of of the Wave 2 applications are in the medicine and bio-technology field.
- The trend that about half of the projects deal with data-intensive applications continues, but Wave 2 projects focus on semantics of data and knowledge extraction rather than on low-level data management.
- New applications are emerging for instance in the financial sector (GRASP), ERP (GRASP) and with regard to corporate ontologies targeted to various industries (COG).
- Most Wave 2 projects focus on a single specific area, however, there are also projects such as GRASP or COG targeted to wider communities of users.

There are also areas being developed by only a few projects that might need more consideration in the future:

- Accounting services serve as an example of such an area. Their development is one of the main goals of the GRIA project, which is developing business models for the Grid. ASP services that include accounting and billing are also being implemented in the scope of EUROGRID.

- Mobile access is another example of an activity specific to some of projects. This is one of the objectives of both GridLab and CrossGrid.
- Activities such as knowledge management and semantic Grids do not belong to the goals of "older" Wave 1 projects; however, there are projects concerning these areas in the scope of several Wave 2 projects such as COG, MOSES or BioGrid.

Real industrial applications are being used even in the early Grid projects, which is quite unusual for an emerging technology and demonstrates the validity of the IST funding model. Overall, there is a strong requirement for business involvement since it is increasing the speed of Grid development and is attracting broad communities of end users.

4   Conclusion and Future Trends

In this paper we presented a simple taxonomy of Grid projects based on an inventory of Grid projects in Europe funded in part by the European Union. The main trend is for more recent Wave 2 projects to focus on the high layers of technology, and on biomedical applications in particular. On the other hand, distributed supercomputing and its application has been deemphasised in Wave 2. Based on the current status, we foresee the following future trends:

- International and inter-project collaborations and interoperability will gain more importance. Strong working groups – and organisational support for their work on all the levels involved in the European Grid research – are required in order to profit from synergies and to deal with interoperability.
- There is a strong requirement for quality, reliability, security and above all interoperability for Grid systems. As a result, web services and in particular OGSA will most probably "dominate" the Grid "market" in the short to medium term: we see this tendency already in the newer projects of our survey.

Acknowledgements. This work was partially funded by the European Commission program IST-2001-34808 through the EU GRIDSTART Project. We thank: F. Grey; M. Dolensky, P. Quinn; P. Nowakowski, B. Krammer; R. Badia, P. Lindner, M. Mueller; R. Barbera, F. Bonnassieux, J. van Eldik, S. Fisher, A. Frohner, D. Front, F. Gagliardi, A. Guarise, R. Harakaly, F. Harris, B. Jones, E. Laure, J. Linford, C. Loomis, M. B. Lopez, L. Momtahan, R. Mondardini, J. Montagnat, F. Pacini, M. Reale, T. Roeblitz, Z. Salvet, M. Sgaravatto, J. Templon; R. Cecchini, F. Donno, JP Martin-Flatin, O. Martin, C. Vistoli; R. Bentley, G. Piccinelli; HC Hoppe, D. Breuer, D. Fellows, KD Oertel, R. Ratering; M. Surridge; M. Adamski, M. Chmielewski, Z. Balaton, M. Cafaro, K. Kurowski, J. Novotny, T. Ostwald, T. Schuett, I. Taylor; P. Wieder; E. v.d. Horst; M. Christostalis, K. Votis; N. Baltas, N. F. Diaz; J. Fingberg, G. Lonsdale; M. Cecchi; S. Wesner, K. Giotopulos, T. Dimitrakos, B. Serhan; A. Ricchi; S. Sild, D. McCourt, J. Jing, W. Dubitzky, I. Bagyi and M. Karelson; A. Poulovassilis, P. Wood.

References

1. Marian Bubak, Piotr Nowakowski and Robert Pajak. An Overview of EU-Funded Grid Projects. 1st European Across Grids Conference, Santiago de Compostella, Spain, February 2003.
2. Desplat J.C., Hardy J., Antonioletti M., Nabrzyski J., Stroinski M., Meyer N. Grid Service Requirements, ENACTS report, January 2002.
3. Ian Foster, Carl Kesselman, Steve Tuecke. The Anatomy of the Grid: Enabling Scalable Virtual Organizations, Intl. J. Supercomputer Applications, 15(3), 2001.
4. Fabrizio Gagliardi, Paul Graham, Matti Heikkurinen, Jarek Nabrzyski, Ariel Oleksiak, Mark Parsons, Heinz Stockinger, Kurt Stockinger, Maciej Stroinski, Jan Weglarz. IST Grid Projects Inventory and Roadmap, GRIDSTART-IR-D2.2.1.2-V1.3, 14 August 2003.
5. GRIDSTART project website: http://www.gridstart.org
6. Klaus Krauter, Rajkumar Buyya, and Muthucumaru Maheswaran, A Taxonomy and Survey of Grid Resource Management Systems for Distributed Computing, International Journal of Software: Practice and Experience (SPE), ISSN: 0038-0644, Volume 32, Issue 2, 2002, Wiley Press, USA, February 2002.
7. Jarek Nabrzyski, Ariel Oleksiak. Comparison of Grid Middleware in European Grid Projects, 1st European Across Grids Conference, Santiago de Compostella, Spain, February 2003.

Pegasus:
Mapping Scientific Workflows onto the Grid*

Ewa Deelman[1], James Blythe[1], Yolanda Gil[1], Carl Kesselman[1],
Gaurang Mehta[1], Sonal Patil[1], Mei-Hui Su[1], Karan Vahi[1], and Miron Livny[2]

[1] USC Information Sciences Institute, Marina Del Rey, CA 90292
{deelman,blythe,gil,carl,gmehta,mei,vahi}@isi.edu
[2] Computer Sciences Department, University of Wisconsin, Madison, WI 53706-1685
miron@cs.wisc.edu

Abstract. In this paper we describe the Pegasus system that can map complex workflows onto the Grid. Pegasus takes an abstract description of a workflow and finds the appropriate data and Grid resources to execute the workflow. Pegasus is being released as part of the GriPhyN Virtual Data Toolkit and has been used in a variety of applications ranging from astronomy, biology, gravitational-wave science, and high-energy physics. A deferred planning mode of Pegasus is also introduced.

1 Introduction

Grid technologies are changing the way scientists conduct research, fostering large-scale collaborative endeavors where scientists share their resources, data, applications, and knowledge to pursue common goals. These collaborations, defined as Virtual Organizations (VOs) [17], are formed by many scientists in various fields, from high-energy physics, to gravitational-wave physics to biologists. For example, the gravitational-wave scientists from LIGO and GEO [2] have formed a VO that consists of scientists in the US and Europe, as well as compute, storage and network resources on both continents. As part of this collaboration, the data produced by the LIGO and GEO instruments and calibrated by the scientists are being published to the VO using Grid technologies. Collaborations also extend to Virtual Data, where data refers not only to raw published data, but also data that has been processed in some fashion. Since data processing can be costly, sharing these data products can save the expense of performing redundant computations. The concept of Virtual Data was first introduced within the GriPhyN project (www.griphyn.org). An important aspect of Virtual Data are the applications that produce the desired data products. In order to discover and evaluate the validity of the Virtual Data products, the applications are also published within the VO.

Taking a closer look at the Grid applications, they are no longer monolithic codes, rather they are being built from existing application components. In general, we can think of applications as being defined by workflows, where the

---

* This research was supported in part by the National Science Foundation under grants ITR-0086044(GriPhyN) and EAR-0122464 (SCEC/ITR).

activities in the workflow are individual application components and the dependencies between the activities reflect the data and/or control flow dependencies between components.

A workflow can be described in an abstract form, in which the workflow activities are independent of the Grid resources used to execute the activities. We denote this workflow an abstract workflow. Abstracting away the resource descriptions allows the workflows to be portable. One can describe the workflow in terms of computations that need to take place without identifying particular resources that can perform this computation. Clearly, in a VO environment, this level of abstraction allows for easy sharing of workflow descriptions between VO participants. Abstraction also enables the workflows to be efficiently mapped onto the existing Grid resources at the time that the workflow activities can be executed. It is possible that users may develop workflows ahead of a particular experiment and then execute them during the run of the experiment. Since the Grid environment is very dynamic, and the resources are shared among many users, it is difficult to optimize the workflow from the point of view of execution ahead of time. In fact, one may want to make decisions about the execution locations and the access to a particular (possibly replicated) data set as late as possible.

In this work we refer to the executable workflow as the concrete workflow (CW). In the CW the workflow activities are bound to specific Grid resources. CW also includes the necessary data movement to stage data in and out of the computations. Other nodes in the CW may also include data publication activities, where newly derived data products are published into the Grid environment.

In the paper we focus on the process of mapping abstract workflows to their concrete forms. In particular, we describe Pegasus, which stands for Planning for Execution in Grids. We present the current system and the applications that use it. The current system is semi-dynamic in that the workflows are fully mapped to their concrete form when they are given to Pegasus. We also explore a fully dynamic mode of mapping workflows (termed deferred planning) using a combination of technologies such as Pegasus and the Condor's workflow executioner, DAGMan [19].

2   Pegasus

Pegasus is designed to map abstract workflows onto the Grid environment [15, 14]. The abstract workflows can be constructed by using Chimera [16] or can be written directly by the user. The inputs to the Chimera system are partial workflow descriptions that describe the logical input files, the logical transformations (application components) and their parameters, as well as the logical output files produced by these transformations. The specifications are written in Chimera's Virtual Data Language (VDL). Given a set of partial workflow descriptions and a desired set of logical output filenames, Chimera produces an abstract workflow by matching the names of the input and output files, starting from the user-specified output filenames. An example abstract workflow is shown

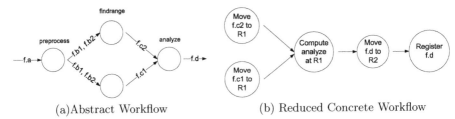

(a)Abstract Workflow   (b) Reduced Concrete Workflow

Fig. 1. Abstract and Concrete Workflows

in Fig. 1a. Some users choose to write the abstract workflow directly, especially if the list of possible VDL definitions is very long. An example of such application is Montage (www.ipac.caltech.edu), an astronomy application, where mosaics of the sky are created based on user requests. In the case of Montage it is not realistic to pre-populate the system with all the possible VDL definitions. Additionally, some preprocessing of the request needs to be performed to pick the appropriate parameters and input files for the montage computation. Whether the input comes through Chimera or is given directly by the user, Pegasus requires that it is specified in a DAX format (a simple XML description of a DAG.) Based on this specification, Pegasus produces a concrete (executable) workflow that can be given to Condor's DAGMan [18] for execution.

Mapping Abstract Workflows onto the Grid. The abstract workflows describe the computation in terms of logical files and logical transformations and indicate the dependencies between the workflow components. Mapping the abstract workflow description to an executable form involves finding: the resources that are available and can perform the computations, the data that is used in the workflow, and the necessary software.

Pegasus consults various Grid information services to find the above information. Pegasus uses the logical filenames referenced in the workflow to query the Globus Replica Location Service (RLS) [9] to locate the replicas of the required data (we assume that data may be replicated in the environment and that the users publish their data products into RLS.) After Pegasus produces new data products (intermediate or final), it registers them into the RLS as well (unless otherwise specified by the user.) In order to be able to find the location of the logical transformations defined in the abstract workflow, Pegasus queries the Transformation Catalog (TC) [12] using the logical transformation names. The catalog returns the physical locations of the transformations (on possibly several systems) and the environment variables necessary for the proper execution of the software. Pegasus queries the Globus Monitoring and Discovery Service (MDS) [11] to find information needed for job scheduling such as the available resources, their characteristics such as the load, the scheduler queue length, and available disk space. The information from the TC is combined with the MDS information to make scheduling decisions. When making resource assignment, Pegasus prefers to schedule the computation where the data already exist, otherwise it makes a random choice or uses a simple scheduling techniques. Additionally, Pegasus uses MDS to find information necessary to execute the workflow such as the location of the gridftp servers [4] that can perform data movement; job managers [10] that can schedule jobs on the remote sites; storage locations, where data can be prestaged; shared execution directories; and the RLS where new data can be registered into, site-wide environment variables. This information is necessary to produce the submit files that describe the necessary data movement, computation and catalog updates.

Pegasus' Workflow Reduction. The information about the available data can be used to optimize the concrete workflow from the point of view of Virtual Data. If data products described within the AW already exist, Pegasus can reuse them and thus reduce the complexity of the CW. In general, the reduction component of Pegasus assumes that it is more costly to execute a component (a job) than to access the results of the component if that data is available. It is possible that someone may have already materialized part of the required dataset and made it available on some storage system. If this information is published into RLS, Pegasus can utilize this knowledge and obtain the data, thus avoiding possibly costly computation. As a result, some components that appear in the abstract workflow do not appear in the concrete workflow. Pegasus also checks for the feasibility of the abstract workflow. It determines the root nodes for the abstract workflow and queries the RLS for the existence of the input files for these components. The workflow can only be executed if the input files for these components can be found to exist somewhere in the Grid and are accessible via a data transport protocol. The final result produced by Pegasus is an executable workflow that identifies the resources where the computation will take place, the data movement for staging data in and out of the computation, and registers the newly derived data products in the RLS. Following the example above, if files $f.c1$ and $f.c2$ have already been computed, then the abstract workflow is reduced to just the analyze activity and a possible concrete workflow is shown in Fig. 1b.

Workflow Execution. The concrete workflow produced by Pegasus is in a form of submit files that are given to DAGMan for execution. The submit files indicate the operations to be performed on given remote systems and the order of the operations. Given the submit files DAGMan submits jobs to Condor-G [18] for execution. DAGMan is responsible for enforcing the dependencies between the jobs defined in the concrete workflow. In case of job failure, DAGMan can be told to retry a job a given number of times or if that fails, DAGMan generates a *rescue* DAG that can be potentially modified and resubmitted at a later time. Job retry is useful for applications that have intermittent software problems. The rescue DAG is useful in cases where the failure was due to lack of disk space that can be reclaimed or in cases where totally new resources need to be assigned for execution.

3   Application Examples

The GriPhyN Virtual Data System (VDS) that consists of Chimera, Pegasus and DAGMan has been used to successfully execute both large workflows with an order of 100,000 jobs with relatively short runtimes [5] and workflows with small number of long-running jobs [15]. Fig. 2 depicts the process of workflow generation, mapping and execution. The user specifies the VDL for the desired data products, Chimera builds the corresponding abstract workflow representation. Pegasus maps this AW to its concrete form and DAGMan executes the jobs specified in the Concrete Workflow. Pegasus and DAGMan were able to map and execute workflows on a variety of platforms: condor pools, clusters managed by LSF or PBS, TeraGrid hosts (www.teragrid.org), and individual hosts. Below, we describe some of the applications that have been run using the VDS.

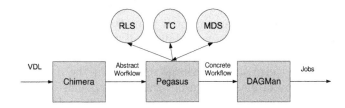

Fig. 2. Components of a Workflow Generation, Mapping and Execution System

Bioinformatics and Biology: One of the most important bioinformatics applications is BLAST, which consists of a set of sequence comparison algorithms that are used to search sequence databases for optimal local alignments to a query. ANL scientists used the VDS to perform two major runs. One consisted of 60 and the other of 450 genomes, each composed of 4,000 sequences. The runs produced on the order of 10,000 jobs and approximately 70GB of data. The execution was performed on a dedicated cluster. A speedup of 5-20 times were achieved using Pegasus and DAGMan not because of algorithmic changes, but because the nodes of the cluster were used efficiently by keeping the submission of the jobs to the cluster constant. Another application that uses the VDS is the tomography application, where 3D structures are derived from a series of 2D electron microscopic projection images. Tomography allows for the reconstruction and detailed structural analysis of complex structures such as synapses and large structures such as dendritic spines. The tomography application is characterized by the acquisition, generation and processing of extremely large amounts of data, upwards of 200GB per run.

Astronomy: Astronomy applications that were executed using the VDS fall into the category of workflows with a large number of small jobs. Among such applications are Montage and Galaxy Morphology. Montage is a grid-capable astronomical mosaicking application. It is used to reproject, background match, and finally mosaic many image plates into a single image. Montage has been used to mosaic image plates from synoptic sky surveys, such as 2MASS in the infrared wavelengths. Fig. 3 shows snapshot of a small Montage workflow that consists of 1200 executable jobs. In the case of Montage, the application scientists produce their own abstract workflows without using Chimera, because they need to tailor the workflow to individual requests [6]. The Galaxy morphology application [13] is used to investigate the dynamical state of galaxy clusters and to explore galaxy evolution inside the context of large-scale structure. Galaxy morphologies are used as a probe of the star formation and stellar distribution history of the galaxies inside the clusters. Galaxy morphology is characterized in terms three parameters that can be calculated directly from an image of the galaxy such as average surface brightness, concentration index, and asymmetry index. The computational requirements for calculating these parameters for a single galaxy are fairly light; however, to statistically characterize a cluster well, the application needs to calculate the parameters for the hundreds or thousands of galaxies that constitute the galaxy cluster.

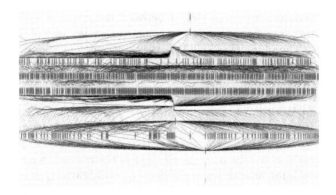

Fig. 3. Montage workflow produced by Pegasus. The light-colored nodes represent data stage-in and the dark-colored nodes, computation

High-Energy Physics: High-energy physics applications such as Atlas and CMS [15] fall into the category of workflows that contain few long running jobs. A variety of different use-cases exist for simulated CMS data production. One of the simpler use-cases is known as an n-tuple-only production that consists of a five stage computational pipeline. These stages consist of a generation stage that simulates the underlying physics of each event and a simulation stage that models the CMS detector's response to the events. Additional stages are geared toward formatting the data and the construction of an "image" of what the physicist would "see" as if the simulated data were actual data recorded by the experimental apparatus. In one of the CMS runs, over the course of 7 days, 678 jobs of 250 events each were submitted using the VDS. From these jobs, 167,500 events were successfully produced using approximately 350 CPU/days of computing power and producing approximately 200GB of simulated data.

Gravitational-Wave Physics: The Laser Interferometer Gravitational-Wave Observatory (LIGO) [2, 15] is a distributed network of interferometers whose mission is to detect and measure gravitational waves predicted by general relativity,

Einstein's theory of gravity. Gravitational waves interact extremely weakly with matter, and the measurable effects produced in terrestrial instruments by their passage are expected to be miniscule. In order to establish a confident detection or measurement, a large amount of auxiliary data is acquired and analyzed along with the strain signal that measures the passage of gravitational waves. The LIGO workflows aimed at detecting gravitational waves emitted by pulsars are characterized by many medium and small jobs. In a Pegasus run conducted at SC 2002, over 58 pulsar searches were performed resulting in a total of 330 tasks, 469 data transfers executed and 330 output files. The total runtime was over 11 hours.

4 Deferred Planning

In the Grid, resources are often shared between users within a VO and across VOs as well. Additionally, resources can come and go, because of failure or local policy changes. Therefore, the Grid is a very dynamic environment, where the availability of the resources and their load can change dramatically from one moment to the next. Even if a particular environment is changing slowly, the duration of the execution of the workflow components can be quite large and by the time a component finishes execution, the data locations may have changed as well as the availability of the resources. Choices made ahead of time even if still feasible may be poor. Clearly, software that deals with executing jobs on the Grid needs to be able to adjust to the changes in the environment. In this work, we focus on providing adaptivity at the level of workflow activities. We assume that once an activity is scheduled on a resource, it will not be preempted and its execution will either fail or succeed.

Up to now, Pegasus was generating fully specified, executable workflows based on an abstract workflow description. The new generation of Pegasus takes a more "lazy" approach to workflow mapping and produces partial executable workflows based on already executed tasks and the currently available Grid resources. In order to provide this level of deferred planning we added a new component to the Pegasus system: the partitioner that partitions the abstract workflow into smaller partial workflows. The dependencies between the partial workflows reflect the original dependencies between the tasks of the abstract workflow. Pegasus then schedules the partial workflows following these dependencies. The assumption, similar to assumption made in the original version of Pegasus is that the workflow does not contain any cycles. Fig. 4 illustrates the partitioning process, where the original workflow is partitioned into partial workflows according to a specified partitioning algorithm. The particular partitioning algorithms shown in Fig. 4 simply partitions the workflow based on the level of the node in the Abstract Workflow. Investigating various partitioning strategies is the focus of our future work.

Once the partitioning is performed, Pegasus maps and submits the partial workflows to the Grid. If there is a dependency between two partial workflows, Pegasus is made to wait (by DAGMan) to map the dependent workflow until

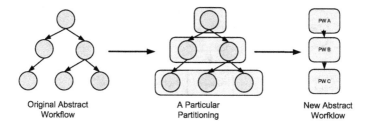

Original Abstract   A Particular   New Abstract
Workflow   Partitioning   Worfklow

Fig. 4. The New Abstract to Concrete Workflow Mapping

the preceding workflow has finished executing. DAGMan is used to drive the deferred planning process by making sure that Pegasus does not refine a partial workflow until the previous partial workflow successfully finished execution. Fig. 5 shows the DAG that is submitted to DAGMan for execution. Given this DAG, DAGMan (instance nr.1) first calls Pegasus on one partition of the abstract workflow, partition A. Pegasus then generates the concrete workflow and produces the submit files necessary for the execution of that workflow through DAGMan, these files are named $Su(A)$. Now the first instance of DAGMan calls a new instance of DAGMan (instance nr.2) with the submit files $Su(A)$. This is reflected in the DAGMan $(Su(A))$ node in Fig. 5; it is a nested call to DAGMan within DAGMan. Once the second instance of DAGMan concludes successfully, implying that the concrete workflow corresponding to the partial abstract workflow A has successfully executed, the first instance of DAGMan calls Pegasus with the abstract workflow B, and the process repeats until all the partitions of the workflow are refined to their concrete form and executed.

Initial results of using this approach for gravitational-wave applications proved that the approach is viable. Although we have not yet performed a formal study, it is clear that there are benefits of deferred planning. For example, assume that a resource fails during the execution of the workflow. If the workflow was fully scheduled ahead of time to use this resource, the execution will fail. However, if the failure occurs at the partition boundary, the new partition will not be scheduled onto the failed resource. An interesting area of future research is to evaluate various workflow partitioning algorithms and their performance based on the characteristics of the workflows and the characteristics of the target execution systems.

5 Related Work

There have been a number of efforts within the Grid community to develop general-purpose workflow management solutions. WebFlow [3] is a multileveled system for high performance distributed computing. It consists of a visual interface and a java-based enactment engine. GridFlow [8] has a two-tiered architecture with global Grid workflow management and local Grid sub workflow scheduling. GridAnt [20] uses the Ant [1] workflow processing engine. GridAnt

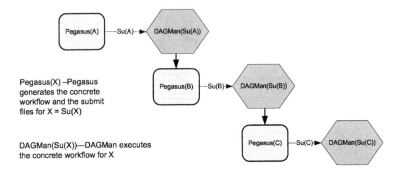

Fig. 5. Deferred Workflow Mapping

has predefined tasks for authentication, file transfer and job execution. Nimrod-G [7] is a cost and deadline based resource management and scheduling system.

The main difference between Pegasus and the above systems is that while most of the above system focus on resource brokerage and scheduling strategies Pegasus uses the concept of virtual data and provenance to generate and reduce the workflow based on data products which have already been computed earlier. Pegasus also automates the job of replica selection so that the user does not have to specify the location of the input data files. Pegasus can also map and schedule only portions of the workflow at a time, using deferred planning techniques.

6   Conclusions and Future Directions

Pegasus, a Grid workflow mapping system presented here, has been successfully used in a variety of applications, from astronomy, biology and physics. Although Pegasus provides a feasible solution, it is not necessarily a low cost one in terms of performance. Deferred planning is a step toward performance optimization and reliability. An aspect of the work we plan to focus on in the near future is the investigation of various partitioning methods that can be applied to dividing workflows into smaller components. In the future work, we also plan to investigate scheduling techniques that would schedule partial workflows onto the Grid.

Acknowledgments. Many GriPhyN members need to be thanked for their contributions and discussions regarding Pegasus. Many scientists have also contributed to the successful use of Pegasus in their application domain. For the Galaxy Morphology: G. Greene, B. Hanisch, R. Plante, and others; for Montage: B. Berriman, J. Good, J.C. Jacob, D.S. Katz, and A. Laity; for BLAST: N. Matlsev, M. Milligan, V. Nefedova, A. Rodriguez, D. Sulakhe, J. Voeckler,and M. Wilde; for LIGO: B. Allen, K. Blackburn, A. Lazzarini, S. Koranda, and M. A. Papa; for Tomography: M. Ellisman, S. Peltier, A. Lin, T. Molina; and for CMS: A. Arbree and R. Cavanaugh.

References

1. Ant: http://ant.apache.org
2. A. Abramovici et al. *LIGO: The Laser Interferometer Gravitational-Wave Observatory (in Large Scale Measurements).* Science, 256(5055), 1992.
3. E. Akarsu et al. Webflow - high-level programming environment and visual authoring toolkit for high performance distributed computing. In *Sc'98*, 1998.
4. B. Allcock et al. *Data management and transfer in high performance computational grid environments,* Parallel Computing Journal, 28, 5, 2002a, 749-771, 2002.
5. J. Annis and others. *Applying Chimera Virtual Data Concepts to Cluster Finding in the Sloan Sky Survey.* in Supercomputing. 2002. Baltimore, MD, 2002.
6. B. Berriman et al. Montage: A grid-enabled image mosaic service for the nvo. In *Astronomical Data Analysis Software & Systems (ADASS) XIII*, October 2003.
7. R. Buyya et al. *Nimrod/G: An Architecture for a Resource Management and Scheduling System in a Global Computational Grid,.* HPC Asia, 2000.
8. J. Cao et al. Gridflow: Workflow management for grid computing. In *3rd Int. Symposium on Cluster Computing and the Grid*, pages 198–205, 2003.
9. A. Chervenak et al. *Giggle: A framework for constructing scalable replica location services,* Proceedings of Supercomputing 2002 (SC2002), November 2002.
10. K. Czajkowski et al. *A resource management architecture for metacom-puting systems.* Workshop on Job Scheduling Strategies for Parallel Processing, 1998.
11. K. Czajkowski et al. *Grid information services for distributed resource sharing.* HPDC, 2001.
12. E. Deelman et al. Transformation catalog design for griphyn, prototype of transformation catalog schema. Technical Report 2001-17, GRIPHYN, 2001.
13. E. Deelman et al. Grid-based galaxy morphology analysis for the national virtual observatory. In *SC 2003*, 2003.
14. E. Deelman et al. *The Grid Resource Management,* chapter Workflow Management in GriPhyN. Kluwer, J. Jabrzyski and J. Schopf and J. Weglarz (eds.), 2003.
15. E. Deelman et al. Mapping abstract complex workflows onto grid environments. *Journal of Grid Computing*, 1, 2003.
16. I. Foster et al. *Chimera: A Virtual Data System for Representing, Querying, and Automating Data Derivation.* SSDBM, 2002.
17. I. Foster, C. Kesselman, and S. Tuecke. *The Anatomy of the Grid: Enabling Scalable Virtual Organizations.* Intl. Journal of High Performance Computing Applications, 15(3):200-222, 2001. http://www.globus.org/-research/papers/anatomy.pdf, 2001.
18. J. Frey et al. *Condor-G: A Computation Managament Agent for Multi-Institutional Grids.* In Proceedings of the Tenth IEEE Symposium on High Performance Distributed Computing (HPDC10), 2001.
19. Condor Team. The directed acyclic graph manager, http://www.cs.wisc.edu/condor/dagman, 2002.
20. G. von Laszewski et al. Gridant-client-side management with ant. Whitepaper, 2002.

A Low-Cost Rescheduling Policy for Dependent Tasks on Grid Computing Systems

Henan Zhao and Rizos Sakellariou

Department of Computer Science, University of Manchester
Oxford Road, Manchester M13 9PL, UK
{hzhao,rizos}@cs.man.ac.uk

Abstract. A simple model that can be used for the representation of certain workflows is a directed acyclic graph. Although many heuristics have been proposed to schedule such graphs on heterogeneous environments, most of them assume accurate prediction of computation and communication costs; this limits their direct applicability to a dynamically changing environment, such as the Grid. To deal with this, run-time rescheduling may be needed to improve application performance. This paper presents a low-cost rescheduling policy, which considers rescheduling at a few, carefully selected points in the execution. Yet, this policy achieves performance results, which are comparable with those achieved by a policy that dynamically attempts to reschedule before the execution of every task.

1 Introduction

Many use cases of Grid computing relate to applications that require complex *workflows* to be mapped onto a range of distributed resources. Although the characteristics of workflows may vary, a simple approach to model a workflow is by means of a *directed acyclic graph* (DAG) [8]. This model provides an easy way of addressing the mapping problem; a schedule is built by assigning the nodes (the term task is used interchangeably with the term node throughout the paper) of the graph onto resources in a way that respects task dependences and minimizes the overall execution time. In the general context of heterogeneous distributed computing, a number of scheduling heuristics have been proposed (see [13, 15, 17] for an extensive list of references). Typically, these heuristics assume that accurate prediction is available for both the computation and the communication costs. However, in a real environment and even more in the Grid, it is difficult to estimate accurately those values due to the dynamic characteristics of the environment. Consequently, an initial schedule may be built using inaccurate predictions; even though the schedule may be optimized with respect to these predictions, real-time variations may affect the schedule's performance significantly.

An obvious response to changes that may occur at run-time is to reschedule, or readjust the schedule dynamically, using additional information that becomes available at run-time. In the context of the Grid, rescheduling of one kind or

M. Dikaiakos (Ed.): AxGrids 2004, LNCS 3165, pp. 21–31, 2004.

the other has been considered by a number of projects, such as AppLeS [2, 6], Condor-G [7], Data Grid [9] and Nimrod-G [4, 5]. However, all these projects consider the dynamic scheduling of sets of independent tasks. For DAG rescheduling, a hybrid remapper based on list scheduling algorithms was proposed in [12]. Taking a static schedule as the input, the hybrid remapper uses the run-time information that obtained from the execution of precedence nodes to make a prediction for subsequent nodes that is used for remapping.

Generally speaking, rescheduling adds an extra overhead to the scheduling and execution process. This may be related to the cost of reevaluating the schedule as well as the cost of transferring tasks across machines (in this paper, we do not consider pre-emptive policies at the task execution level). This cost may be offset by gains in the execution of the schedule; however, what appears to give an indication of a gain at a certain stage in the execution of a schedule (which may trigger a rescheduling), may not be good later in the schedule. In this paper, we attempt to strike a balance between the cost of rescheduling and the performance of the schedule. We propose a novel, *low-cost*, rescheduling policy, which improves the initial static schedule of a DAG, by considering *only* selective tasks for rescheduling based on measurable properties; as a result, we call this policy *Selective Rescheduling* (SR). Based on preliminary simulation experiments, this policy gives equally good performance with policies that consider for rescheduling every task of the DAG, at a much lower cost; in our experiments, SR considers less than 20% of the tasks of the DAG for rescheduling.

The remainder of this paper is organized as follows. Section 2 defines two criteria to represent the robustness of a schedule, spare time and the slack. We use these two criteria to make decisions for the *Selective Rescheduling* policy, presented in Section 3. Section 4 evaluates the performance of the policy and, finally, Section 5 concludes the paper.

2   Preliminaries

The model used in this paper to represent an application is the *directed acyclic graph* (DAG), where nodes (or tasks) represent computation and edges represent communication (data flow) between nodes. The DAG has a single entry node and a single exit node. There is also a set of machines on which nodes can execute (with a different execution cost on each machine) and which need different time to transmit data. A machine can execute only one task at a time, and a task cannot start execution until all data from its parent nodes is available. The scheduling problem is to assign the tasks onto machines so that precedence constraints are respected and the makespan is minimized. For an example, see Figure 1, and parts (a), (b), and (c).

Previous work has attempted to characterize the robustness of a schedule; in other words, how robust the schedule would be if variations in the estimates used to build the schedule were to occur at run-time [1, 3]. Although the robustness metric might be useful in evaluating overall different schedules, it has little direct value for our purposes; here, we wish to use specific criteria to select, at run-

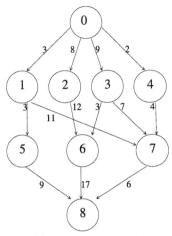

(a) an example graph

task	m0	m1	m2	task	m0	m1	m2
0	13	10	11	5	12	14	10
1	9	11	16	6	10	16	10
2	13	18	10	7	11	10	6
3	7	4	9	8	13	10	10
4	9	12	15				

(b) the computation cost of nodes
on three different machines

machines	time for a data unit
m0 - m1	1.5
m1 - m2	1.0
m0 - m2	2.0

(c) communication cost between the
machines

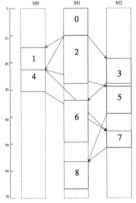

(d) the schedule derived by the
HEFT algorithm

node	start time	finish time
0	0	10
1	14.5	23.5
2	10	28
3	19	28
4	23.5	32.5
5	29.5	39.5
6	34	50
7	45.5	51.5
8	57.5	67.5

(e) the start time and finish time of each
node in (d)

Fig. 1. An example: schedule generated by the HEFT algorithm

time, particular tasks before the execution of which it would be beneficial to reschedule. To achieve this, we build on and extend two fundamental quantities that have been used to measure robustness; the *spare time*, and the *slack* of a node. The spare time, computed between a pair of dependent nodes that are either connected by an edge in the DAG (data dependence), or are to be executed successively on the same machine (machine dependence), shows what is the maximal time that the source of dependence can execute *without* affecting the start time of the sink of the dependence. The slack of a node is defined as the minimum spare time on any path from this node to the exit node of the DAG. This is the maximum delay that can be tolerated in the execution time of the node without affecting the overall schedule length. If the slack of a node is zero, the node is called *critical*; any delay on the execution time of this node will affect the makespan of the application.

A formal definition and an example follow below; we note that the definitions in [3] do not take into account the communication cost between data dependent tasks, thereby limiting their applicability. Our definitions are augmented to take into account communication.

2.1 Spare Time

Consider a schedule for a given DAG; the spare time between a node i and an immediate successor j is defined as

$$Spare_{DAG}(i, j) = ST(j) - DAT(i, j),$$

where $ST(j)$ is the expected start time of node j (on the machine where it has been scheduled to), and $DAT(i, j)$ is the time that all the data required by node j from node i will arrive on the machine where node j executes. To illustrate this with an example, consider Figure 1 and the schedule in Figure 1(d) (derived using the HEFT heuristic [17]). In this example, the finish time of task 4 is 32.5 and the data transfer time from task 4 (on machine 0) to task 7 (on machine 2) is 8 (4 * 2 = 8) time units, hence the arrival time of the data from task 4 to task 7 is 40.5. The start time of task 7 is 45.5, therefore, the spare time between task 4 and task 7 is 5. This is the maximal value that the finish time of task 4 can be delayed at machine 0 without changing the start time of task 7.

In addition, for tasks i and j, which are adjacent in the execution order of a particular machine (and task i executes first), the spare time is defined as

$$Spare_{SameMach}(i, j) = ST(j) - FT(i),$$

where $FT(i)$ is the finish time of node i in the given schedule. In Figure 1, for example, task 3 finishes at time 28, and task 5 starts at time 29.5; both on machine 2. The spare time between them is 1.5. In this case, if the execution time of task 3 delays for no more than 1.5 , the start time of task 5 will not be affected. However, one may notice that even a delay of less than 1.5 may cause some delay in the start time of task 6; to take this into account, we introduce one more parameter.

To represent the minimal spare time for each node, i.e., the maximal delay in the execution of the node that will not affect the start time of any of its dependent nodes (both on the DAG or on the machine), we introduce $MinSpare$, which is defined as

$$MinSpare(i) = \min_{\forall j \in D_i} Spare(i, j)$$

where D_i is the set of the tasks that includes the immediate successors of task i in the DAG and the next task in the execution order of the machine where task i is executed, and $Spare(i, j)$ is the minimum of $Spare_{DAG}(i, j)$ and $Spare_{SameMach}(i, j)$.

2.2   The Slack of a Node

In a similar way to the definition in [3], the slack of a node i is computed as the minimum spare time on any path from this node to the exit node. This is recursively computed, in an upwards fashion (i.e., starting from the exit node) as follows:

$$Slack(i) = \min_{\forall j \in D_i} (Slack(j) + Spare(i,j)).$$

The slack for the exit node is set equal to

$$Slack(i_{exit}) = 0.$$

The slack of each task indicates the maximal value that can be added to the execution time of this task without affecting the overall makespan of the schedule. Considering again the example in Figure 1, the slack of node 8 is 0; the slack of node 7 is also zero (computed as the slack of node 8 plus the spare time between 7 and 8, which is zero). Node 5 has a spare time of 6 with node 7 and 9 with node 8 (its two immediate successors in the DAG and the machine where it is executing); since the slack of both nodes 7 and 8 is 0, then the slack of node 5 is 6. Indeed, this is the maximal time that the finish time of node 5 can be delayed without affecting the schedule's makespan.

Clearly, if the execution of a task will start at a time which is greater than the statically estimated starting time plus the slack, the overall makespan (assuming the execution time of all other tasks that follow remains the same) will change. Our rescheduling policy is based on this observation and will selectively apply rescheduling based on the values of slack (and the spare time). This is presented in the next section.

3   A Selective Rescheduling Policy

The key idea of the selective rescheduling policy is to evaluate, at run-time, before each task starts execution, the starting time of each node against its estimated starting time in the static schedule and the slack (or the minimal spare time), in order to make a decision for rescheduling. The input of this rescheduler is a DAG, with its associated values, and a static schedule computed by *any* scheduling algorithm. The objective of the policy is to optimize the makespan of the schedule while minimizing the frequency of rescheduling attempts.

As the tasks of the DAG are executed, the rescheduler maintains two schedules, S_1 and S_2. S_1 is based on the static construction of the schedule using estimated values; S_2 keeps track of what the schedule looked like for the tasks that have been executed (i.e., it contains information about only the tasks that have finished execution). Before each task (except the entry node) can start execution, its (real) start time can be considered as known. Comparing the start time that was statically estimated in the construction of S_1 and the slack (or the minimal spare time), a decision for rescheduling is taken. The algorithm will

Input: an application graph G and a schedule S_1 produced by an algorithm A
    (any algorithm for DAG scheduling onto heterogeneous systems may be used)

Selective rescheduling policy:
(1) Mark all tasks in S_1 as unexecuted, *Unexecuted[]*
    $S_2 \leftarrow$ the real, post-execution schedule (initially empty)
(2) Compute for each task i from S_1, *Slack(i)* // (or *MinSpare(i)*)
(3) While (*Unexecuted[]* is not empty)
    $t \leftarrow$ first task in S_1, which is in *Unexecuted[]*
    $m \leftarrow$ the allocated machine for t in schedule S_1
    if (t is not the entry task in G)
        $EST \leftarrow$ the expected start time of t in schedule S_1
        $RST \leftarrow$ the real start time of t on m in S_2
        delay $\leftarrow RST$ - EST
        if (*delay* > *Slack(t)*) // or (*delay* > *MinSpare(t)*)
            $S_1 \leftarrow A(Unexecuted[], S_2)$ // reschedule
            compute *MinSpare* for all tasks in S_1, also in *Unexecuted[]* // or *Slack*
            $t \leftarrow$ first task in S_1, which is in *Unexecuted[]*
            $m \leftarrow$ the allocated machine for t in schedule S_1
        endif
    endif
    execute task t on machine m
    $S_2 \leftarrow S_2 \cup \{(t, m)\}$
    Unexecuted[] $\leftarrow$ *Unexecuted[]* \ t
    endwhile

Fig. 2. The Selective Rescheduler

proceed to a rescheduling action *if* any delay between the real and the expected start time (in S_1) of the task is greater than the value of the *Slack* (or, in a variant of the policy, the *MinSpare*). This indicates that, in the first variant (*Slack*), the makespan is expected to be affected, whereas, in the second variant, the start time of the successors of the current task will be affected (but not necessarily the overall makespan). Once a rescheduling is decided, the set of unexecuted tasks (and their associated information) and the already known information about the tasks whose execution has been completed (stored in S_2) are fed to the scheduling algorithm used to build a new schedule, which is stored in S_1. The values of *Slack* (or *MinSpare*), for each task, are subsequently recomputed from S_1.

The policy is illustrated in Figure 2.

4   Simulation Results

4.1   The Setting

To evaluate the performance of our rescheduling policy, we simulated both variants of our rescheduling policy (i.e., based on spare time and the slack) using four different DAG scheduling algorithms: Fastest Critical Path (FCP) [14], Dynamic

Level Scheduling (DLS) [16], Heterogeneous Earliest Finish Time (HEFT) [17] and Levelized-Min Time (LMT) [10]. Each algorithm provides the initial static schedule and is called again when the rescheduler decides to remap tasks.

We have evaluated, separately, the behaviour of our rescheduling policy with each of the four different algorithms, both in terms of the performance of the final schedule and in terms of the running time. We used randomly generated DAGs, each consisting of 50 to 100 tasks, following the approach described in [18], and we tried to schedule them on 3 to 8 machines (randomly chosen with equal probability for each machine). The estimated execution of each task on each different machine is randomly generated from a uniform distribution in the interval [50,100], while the communication-to-computation ratio (CCR) is randomly chosen from the interval [0.1,1]. For the actual execution time of each task we adopt the approach in [6], and we use the notion of *Quality of Information* (QoI). This represents an upper bound on the percentage of error that the static estimate may have with respect to the actual execution time. So, for example, a percentage error of 10% would indicate that the (simulated) run-time execution time of a task will be within 10% (plus or minus) of the static estimate for the task. In our experiments we consider an error of up to 50%.

4.2   Scheduling Performance

In order to evaluate the performance of our rescheduling policy, in terms of optimising the length of the schedule produced, we implemented both the spare time and the slack variants, and compared the schedule length they generate with three other approaches; these are denoted by *static*, *ideal*, and *always*. *Static* refers to the actual run-time performance of the original schedule (which was constructed using the static performance estimates); that is, no change in the original static schedule takes place at run-time. *Ideal* refers to a schedule, which is built *post mortem*; that is, the schedule is built *after* the run-time execution of each task is known. This serves as a reasonable lower bound to the performance that rescheduling can achieve. Finally, *always* refers to a scheme that re-schedules all remaining non-executed tasks each time a task is about to start execution.

The results, for each of the four different algorithms considered, are shown in Figure 3. We considered a QoI error percentage from 10% to 50 %. As expected, larger values of the QoI error result in larger differences between the *static* and the *ideal*. The values of the three different rescheduling approaches (i.e., *always*, and the two variants of the policy proposed in this paper, *slack*, *spare*) are roughly comparable. However, this is achieved at a significant benefit, since our policy attempts to reschedule only in a relatively small number of cases rather than always.

Another interesting remark from the figures is that rescheduling falls short of what can be assumed to be the ideal time; this is in line with the results in [12]. The results also indicate that even for relatively high percentage errors, it is still the behaviour of the scheduling algorithm chosen that has the highest impact on the makespan.

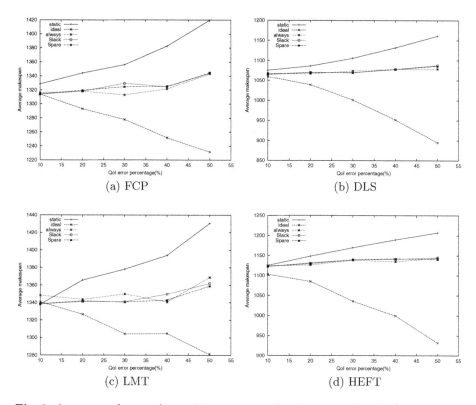

Fig. 3. Average makespan (over 100 runs on randomly generated DAGs) for various levels of QoI with four scheduling algorithms

Table 1. Average running time and number of times rescheduling is attempted for each of three rescheduling approaches using four algorithms. The average is over 50 runs using randomly generated DAGs each with 50 tasks, QoI 20% and scheduling on 5 machines

	Always		Slack		Spare	
	R.T.	#R	R.T.	#R	R.T.	#R
FCP	345.77	49	66.87	6.82	74.28	7.83
DLS	699.33	49	122.18	7.35	126.23	7.95
LMT	528.23	49	77.93	6.51	97.15	8.41
HEFT	357.40	49	73.01	7.51	86.20	8.86

4.3   Running Time

Although the three rescheduling approaches that were compared in the previous section perform similarly, the approaches based on the policy proposed in this paper (i.e., *slack* and *spare*) achieve the same result (with *always*) at a significantly reduced cost. Table 1 shows the running time of each of the 3 approaches averaged over 50 runs on DAGs of 50 tasks each, using QoI 20%, and scheduling

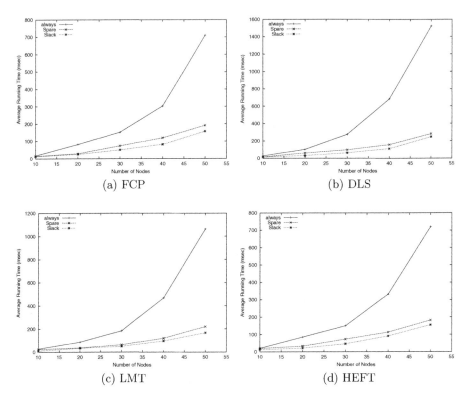

Fig. 4. Average running time (over 100 runs on randomly generated DAGs with fixed 5 machines) of four scheduling algorithms with dynamic scheduling and our rescheduling policy

on 5 machines. It can be seen also that the two variants of our policy run at no more than 25% of the time that is needed and attempt to reschedule tasks at no more than 20% of the total number of tasks (note that *always* would attempt to reschedule all the tasks except the entry node, hence the value 49). Figure 4 shows how the running time varies if DAGs having 10 to 50 nodes are used. It can be seen that attempting to rescheduling always leads to faster increases in the running time than our policy. It is worth noting that the slack variant is slightly faster than the spare variant; this is because the slack is cumulative and refers to the makespan of the schedule (as opposed to the spare time) and, as a result, it will lead to fewer rescheduling attempts.

5   Conclusion

This paper presented a novel rescheduling policy for DAGs, which attempts to reschedule selectively (hence, without incurring a high overhead), yet achieving results comparable with those obtained when rescheduling is attempted for every task of the DAG. The approach is based on evaluating two metrics, the minimal spare time and the slack, and is general, in that it can be applied to any scheduling algorithm.

Although there has been significant work in static scheduling heuristics, limited work exists in trying to understand how dynamic, run-time changes can affect a statically predetermined schedule. The emergence of important use cases in Grid computing, such as workflows, as well as new ideas and approaches related to scheduling [11] are expected to motivate further and more elaborate research into different aspects related to the management of run-time information.

References

1. S. Ali, A. A. Maciejewski, H. J. Siegel and J-K. Kim. Definition of a Robustness Metric for Resource Allocation. In *Proceedings of IPDPS 2003*, 2003.
2. F. Berman, and R. Wolski. The AppLeS project: a status report. Proceedings of *8th NEC Research Symposium*, Berlin, Germany, 1997.
3. L. Boloni, and D. C. Marinescu. Robust scheduling of metaprograms. In *Journal of Scheduling*, 5:395-412, 2002.
4. R. Buyya, D. Abramson and J. Giddy. Nimrod-G: an architecture for a resource management and scheduling system in a global Computational Grid. In *International Conference on High Performance Computing in Asia-Pacific Region (HPC Asia 2000)*, Beijing, China.
5. R. Buyya, J. Giddy and D. Abramson. An evaluation of economy-based resource trading and scheduling on computational power Grids for parameter sweep applications. In *2nd International Workshop on Active Middleware Service (AMS 2000)*, USA, 2000.
6. H. Casanova, A. Legrand, D. Zagorodnov and F. Berman. Heuristics for scheduling parameter sweep applications in Grid environments. In *9th Heterogeneous Computing Workshop (HCW'00)*, 2000.
7. J. Frey, T. Tannenbaum, I. Foster, M. Livny and S. Tuecke. Condor-G: a computation management agent for multi-institutional Grids. *Journal of Cluster Computing*, 5:237-246, 2002.
8. A. Hoheisel and U. Der. An XML-Based Framework for Loosely Coupled Applications on Grid Environments. In *Proceedings of ICCS 2003*, Springer-Verlag, LNCS 2657, 2003.
9. H. Hoschek, J. J. Martinez, A. Samar, H. Stockinger and K. Stockinger. Data management in an international Data Grid project. Proceedings of *the First IEEE/ACM International Workshop on Grid Computing*, India, 2000.
10. M. Iverson, F. Ozguner, and G. Follen. Parallelizing existing applications in a distributed heterogeneous environment. In *4th Heterogeneous Computing Workshop (HCW'95)*, pp. 93-100, 1995.
11. J. MacLaren, R. Sakellariou, J. Garibaldi and D. Ouelhadj. Towards Service Level Agreement Based Scheduling on the Grid. Proceedings of the *2nd Across Grids Conference*, Cyprus, 2004.
12. M. Maheswaran and H. J. Siegel. A dynamic matching and scheduling algorithm for heterogeneous computing systems. In *7th Heterogeneous Computing Workshop(HCW'98)*, March 1998.

13. A. Radulescu and A.J.C. van Gemund. Low-Cost Task Scheduling for Distributed-Memory Machines. *IEEE Transactions on Parallel and Distributed Systems*, 13(6), pp. 648-658, June 2002.
14. A. Radulescu and A. J. C. van Gemund. On the complexity of list scheduling algorithms for distributed memory systems. In *ACM International Conference on Supercomputing*, 1999.
15. R. Sakellariou and H. Zhao. A Hybrid Heuristic for DAG Scheduling on Heterogeneous Systems. In *13th International Heterogeneous Computing Workshop (HCW'04)*, 2004 (to appear).
16. G. C. Sih and E. A. Lee. A compile-time scheduling heuristic for interconnection-constrained heterogeneous processor architecture. *IEEE Transactions on Parallel and Distributed Systems*, 4(2):175–187, February 1993.
17. H. Topcuoglu, S. Hariri, and M. Wu. Performance-effective and low-complexity task scheduling for heterogeneous computing. *IEEE Transactions on Parallel and Distributed Systems*, 13(3):260–274, March 2002.
18. H. Zhao and R. Sakellariou. An experimental investigation into the rank function of the heterogeneous earliest finish time scheduling algorithm. In *Euro-Par 2003*. Springer-Verlag, LNCS 2790, 2003.

An Advanced Architecture
for a Commercial Grid Infrastructure

Antonios Litke[1], Athanasios Panagakis[1], Anastasios Doulamis[1],
Nikolaos Doulamis[1], Theodora Varvarigou[1], and Emmanuel Varvarigos[2]

[1] Electrical and Computer Engineering Dept.
National Technical University of Athens
ali@telecom.ntua.gr
[2] Computer Engineering and Informatics Dept., University of Patras

Abstract. Grid Infrastructures have been used to solve large scale scientific problems that do not have special requirements on QoS. However, the introduction and success of the Grids in commercial applications as well, entails the provision of QoS mechanisms which will allow for meeting the special requirements of the users-customers. In this paper we present an advanced Grid Architecture which incorporates appropriate mechanisms so as to allow guarantees of the diverse and contradictory users' QoS requirements. We present a runtime estimation model, which is the heart of any scheduling and resource allocation algorithm, and we propose a scheme able to predict the runtime of submitted jobs for any given application on any computer by introducing a general prediction model. Experimental results are presented which indicate the robustness and reliability of the proposed architecture. The scheme has been implemented in the framework of GRIA IST project (Grid Resources for Industrial Applications).

1 Introduction

Grid computing is distinguished from conventional distributed computing by its focus on large-scale resource sharing, innovative applications, and, in some cases, high-performance orientation. It supports the sharing, interconnection and use of diverse resources in dynamic computing systems that can be sufficiently integrated to deliver computational power to applications that need it in a transparent way [1], [2].

However, until now grid infrastructure has been used to solve *large-scale scientific* problems that are of known or open source code and *do not* have specific *Quality of Service* (QoS) requirements [1], [3]. For example, in the current Grid architecture, there is no guarantee that particular users' demands, such as the deadlines of the submitted tasks, are always satisfied. This means that the current Grid architecture can not provide an agreed upon QoS, which is important for the success of the Grid, especially in commercial applications. Users of the Grid are not willing to pay for Grid services or contribute resources to Grids, if there are not appropriate mechanisms able to guarantee the negotiated QoS

M. Dikaiakos (Ed.): AxGrids 2004, LNCS 3165, pp. 32–41, 2004.

users' requirements. This need has been confirmed by the Global Grid Forum (GGF) in the special working group dealing with "scheduling and resource management" for Grid computing [4].

Scheduling and resource allocation is of vital important in the commercialization of Grid, since it allows management of the contradictory and diverse QoS requirements. Furthermore, scheduling and resource allocation is strongly related with the adopted charging policy. More resources of the Grid should be given to users that are willing to pay more. However, efficient scheduling and resource allocation requires estimation of the *runtime of each task requesting* for service in the Grid, which in the sequel requires *prediction of the task workload as well as task modeling*. Different applications are characterized by different properties and thus require different modeling and prediction schemes.

In this paper, we enhance the current Grid architecture by incorporating all the aforementioned described mechanisms so as to allow guarantees of the diverse and contradictory users' QoS requirements. Our focus is oriented on developing a proper runtime estimation model, which is the heart of any scheduling and resource allocation algorithm. In particular, we propose a scheme able to predict the runtime of submitted jobs for any given application on any given computer by introducing a general prediction model. The model is applied to any application using features derived from the task modeling module. To achieve this goal, a set of *common parameters* is defined, which affect the runtime and are the same for any application.

The proposed runtime estimation model is separated in two parts. The part of the consumer's (client's) side, which is responsible for *workload estimation* and the supplier's part, which evaluates the *resource performance*. The resource performance parameters are designed so that they can be applied to heterogeneous platforms, while the workload performance parameters are designed to be the same for every application.

The workload parameters are classified into a) computation, b) communication and c) availability parameters. Computation parameters are associated with the task execution. These are: the *number of float point operations per task, the number of exchanged memory I/O messages per task* and *the number of exchanged disk I/O messages per task*. The communication parameters are separated in the two parts; the *send* and the *receive* part. In this analysis we assume that the amount of bytes which is *sent and received* are used as communication parameters. Finally, the availability parameters are *the minimum free memory* (i.e., the sum of available minimum free memory, which is allocated by the system during processing), *the minimum disk space* (i.e., the sum of storage space, which is allocated by the resource during processing), and *the queue time interval* (i.e., the total waiting time in the queue for a newly arrived job).

As far as the resource performance parameters are concerned, *the CPU speed* (expressed as the MFLOPs rate), *the average memory I/O bandwidth* (in Mbytes/sec) and *the average disk I/O bandwidth* (in Kbytes/sec) are selected. The choice of these parameters is due to the fact that they are measurable in any heterogeneous platform and characterize the performance of a system [5].

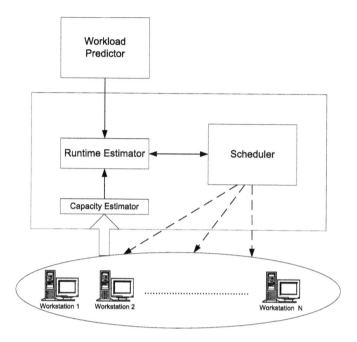

Fig. 1. The proposed architecture adopted for the commercialization of the Grid

The MFLOPs rate is a performance measure independent of the CPU architecture, thus allowing comparing different CPUs. Moreover, most of the MFLOPs benchmarks take into account the bottleneck due to L1 and L2 cache, eliminating the need of benchmarking L1 and L2 cache performance. Besides L2 cache, the main bottleneck in I/O communication is the RAM bandwidth. Since every application accesses RAM in a different way, in order to cover any option we take an average measure of memory I/O. For applications that need a huge amount of disk I/O we consider the disk performance bottleneck, defined as the average I/O bandwidth in Kbytes/sec [5].

2   The Proposed Commercial Grid Architecture

In this section we present the proposed architecture for a commercial Grid infrastructure, which extends the Globus architecture [3] by contributing QoS aspects in the resource management model. Even that the Globus layered architecture can be enhanced with such mechanisms, QoS in Grid computing has not been addressed currently. In the sequel, we present the necessary architectural components that implement the QoS mechanism proposed. The architecture has been implemented in the framework of GRIA project [6]. Figure 1 presents the proposed adopted architecture.

a. Workload Predictor. It is the part that evaluates the application specific input parameters that affect the runtime. These parameters are then used to predict the workload performance parameters that are needed for the runtime estimation. It estimates a set of workload parameters for a given set of application specific input parameters. These are passed to the Runtime Estimator in order to be used for further processing so as to estimate the execution time of the job. The Workload Predictors are each one dedicated for each different application that is incorporated on the system.

b. Capacity Estimator. It calculates the resource performance parameters for each different resource of the supplier. The Capacity Estimator should calculate the resource performance parameters of the runtime estimation model, through a benchmarking process that is the same for every heterogeneous resource platform, thus providing a way to compare heterogeneous resource performance. By using the same parameters for every heterogeneous resource platform we can incorporate different platforms on the system and we can define a cost of use per performance unit.

c. Runtime Estimator. It uses a mathematical model to combine the workload parameter set from the Workload Predictor, with the resource parameter set from the Capacity Estimator to give estimation about the execution time of the specific job on the specific resource.

d. Scheduler. It is the main module that applies the scheduling policy and procedure based on the Runtime Estimator, and according to the deadlines of the jobs as they are given by the customer.

3   Runtime Estimation Model

3.1   Resource Performance Parameters for Heterogeneous Platforms

A generic PC architecture consists of a CPU, L1, L2 cache and RAM (memory hierarchy) and the hard disk. There are several different architectures for each of the above components and different operating systems. For the CPU performance the most suitable generic measurement is the MFLOPS benchmark [5]. Since the majority of the MFLOPS benchmarks take into account the L1 and L2 cache rates, we can assume that the only suitable measurement for the memory performance is the average RAM I/O bandwidth. Also for the hard disk performance we consider as suitable performance measurement the average read/write disk I/O bandwidth.

We now see that the achieved application performance can be expressed in conjunction with these three values. Therefore, we denote as $\mathbf{r}$, the *resource parameter vector*, the elements of which r_i, i=1,2,3 correspond to the CPU speed (in MFLOPS/sec), average memory I/O (in MB/sec) and average disk I/O (in KB/sec).

$$\mathbf{r} = [r_1, r_2, r_3]^T \tag{1}$$

The resource parameter vector can be calculated for each resource through a benchmarking process. In this study we assume that the resources that are taken into consideration are limited to standalone PC platforms and not clusters or batch systems. Thus we consider a Grid infrastructure with single node tasks on single PCs. The important thing about the runtime estimation model is that on every resource that we want to have runtime estimation we have to use the same benchmarks. Since the benchmarks can be compiled for different operating systems and platforms, we can use the same **r** vector for any heterogeneous platform, thus having the capability of incorporating any heterogeneous resource on the Grid infrastructure using the same resource performance description.

Equation (1) refers to the computational resource parameters. Concerning the communication parameters, we use the *Send Communication Bandwidth* and the *Receive Communication Bandwidth* both measured in Kbytes/sec. For the availability resource parameters we use the *Minimum Free Memory* (in MB) and *Minimum Free Disk Space* (in KB) of the resource where the task will be allocated. However these additional parameters are not being taken into consideration within the scope of this paper, since the work presented in this paper is focused on the Runtime Estimation model. The overall system that has been designed and implemented within the framework of GRIA project [6] uses the aforementioned parameters to calculate a Remote Runtime that consists additionally of the communication time (send and receive time intervals of the application data) and the queue time interval that is the waiting time for the application to start execution on the selected resource. However the scope of this paper is to propose and validate a new model of Grid architecture incorporating QoS aspects, and thus it is focused on proving the validity of the proposed Runtime Estimation model, which is used to calculate the execution time only.

The proposed scheme is not used for application tasks that run in parallel. Thus the latency factor has not been taken into consideration because there are no continuous transaction between the individual resources during the execution phase of a job.

3.2   Definition of Application Workload Parameters

The workload parameters must be defined in conjunction with the resource parameters, in order to use the same runtime estimation model for every application. In this paper we have used for the resource parameters the MFLOPS/sec, the average memory I/O and the average disk I/O (see section 3.1), and thus the workload parameters are defined only by the *computational parameters*. Extension of our study for including the affect of the other workload parameters can be performed in a similar way.

To estimate the workload of a task we need a) to extract features which describe the specific application from which the task derive and b) to define a set of parameters which are in conjunction with the three resource performance values [see equation (1)].

Let us first denote as **x** a vector which describes the "computational load" of a task derived from an application. We call vector **x** *workload parameter vector*. In our paper and without loss of generality we assume that vector **x** consists of three elements

$$\mathbf{x} = [x_1, x_2, x_3]^T , \tag{2}$$

where the elements x_i, i=1,2,3 correspond to the CPU instructions per task (in MFLO), the average memory I/O amount per task (in MB) and the average disk I/O amount (in KB).

To estimate vector $\mathbf{x}$, we need to extract for each specific application those features which affect the respective workload. Let us denote as $\mathbf{s}$ the *descriptor parameters vector*

$$\mathbf{s} = [s_1, s_2, ..., s_n]^T,\qquad(3)$$

the elements of which s_i, i=1,..,n correspond to the individual application *descriptors*. The descriptors s_i are independent of the execution environment. For example, in case we refer to 3D rendering applications the descriptors s_i are the image resolution, number of polygons, number of light sources and so on. It is clear that for different applications different descriptors are required [7], [8], [9]. So, for each application incorporated to the system we must construct a different predictor for estimating vector $\mathbf{x}$.

3.3   Workload Prediction

Vector $\mathbf{s}$ is used as input to the Workload Predictor module, which is responsible for estimating vector $\mathbf{x}$ from $\mathbf{s}$, through a non-linear model $\mathbf{x} = g(\mathbf{s})$. Generally, the function $g(\mathbf{s})$ is unknown and thus it can not be estimated in a straightforward way. For this reason, modeling of function $g(\cdot)$ is required for predicting vector $\mathbf{x}$ from vector $\mathbf{s}$. Usually, linear models cannot effectively estimate the application workload. This is caused since usually there does not exist a simple linear relation, which maps the specific input parameters (e.g., vector $\mathbf{s}$) with the corresponding workload parameters (e.g. vector $\mathbf{x}$). Alternatively, modeling can be performed using simplified non-linear mathematical models (such as exponential and/or logarithmic functions) and applying estimation techniques [10] for predicting the vector $\mathbf{x}$. However, these approaches present satisfactory results only in case of data that follow the adopted pre-determined function type, which is not be extended to any type of application.

In order to have a *generic* workload prediction module, which can be applied to any type of application, modeling of the unknown function $g(\cdot)$ is performed through a neural network architecture. This is due to the fact that neural networks are capable of estimating any continuous non-linear function with any degree of accuracy [11]. In particular, neural networks provide an approximation of function $g(\cdot)$, say $\hat{g}(\cdot)$, through a training set of samples consisting of appropriate selected vectors $\mathbf{x}_i$ and the respective vectors $\mathbf{s}_i$. Training is performed based on a Least Squares algorithms, such as the Marquardt-Levenberg algorithm [11].

3.4   The Runtime Estimation Model

As already mentioned, the amount of workload that is served per second is given by the resource capability. We recall that x_i is the workload of the i-th task being executed on a resource characterized by a resource parameter r_i. We denote as

t_i the time interval needed to accomplish the execution of x_i on a resource with related resource parameter r_i. The t_i is related with x_i and r_i as follows

$$t_i = \frac{x_i}{r_i}. \tag{4}$$

To estimate the total run time of a task, we assume that total execution time equals the sum of individual execution times. Therefore, we have that

$$t_{run} = \sum_{i=1}^{n} t_i, \quad or \quad t_{run} = \sum_{i=1}^{n} x_i \cdot r_i^{-1} \tag{5}$$

However, estimation of the total run time based on the previous equation does not result in reliable results since only one measure is taken into consideration. To have a more reliable estimate of the total run time, several measurements are taken into account and a linear system is constructed for estimating t_{run}. In particular, the total run time t_{run} is provided by minimizing the following equation

$$\hat{t}_{run} = \arg\min E, \tag{6}$$

where

$$E = \sum_{j=1}^{N} \{\hat{t}_{run} - \sum_{i=1}^{n} x_{i,j} \cdot r_{i,j}^{-1}\}^2 \tag{7}$$

In previous equation $x_{i,j}$, $r_{i,j}$ is the j-th sample of the x_i and r_i respectively. Minimization of (7) is accomplished through the Least Square method.

4   Scheduling

The purpose of a scheduling algorithm is to determine the "queuing order" and the "processor assignment" for a given task so that the demanded QoS parameters, i.e., the task deadlines, are satisfied as much as possible. The "queuing order" refers to the order in which tasks are considered for assignment to the processors. The "processor assignment" refers to the selection of the particular processor on which the task should be scheduled.

In the proposed Grid architecture, two approaches for queuing order selection have been adopted, which are described shortly in the following. The first algorithm exploits the urgency of the task deadlines, while the second is based on a fair policy. The most widely used urgency-based scheduling scheme is the Earliest Deadline First (EDF) method, also known as the deadline driven rule [12],[13]. This method dictates that at any point the system must assign the highest priority to the task with the most imminent deadline. The concept behind the EDF scheme is that it is preferable to serve first the most urgent tasks (i.e., the task with the earliest deadline) and then serve the remaining tasks according to their urgency. The above mentioned queuing order selection algorithm does not make any attempt to handle the tasks requesting for service in a fair way.

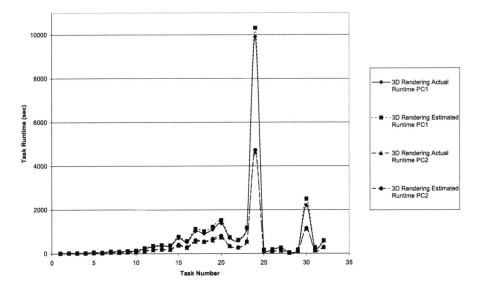

Fig. 2. The *actual* and the *estimated* total run time for the two *PCs* that have been used for the 32 different 3D image rendering tasks

The second algorithm uses a Max-Min fair sharing approach for providing fair access to Grid resources to all users. When there is no shortage of resources, the algorithm assigns to each task enough computational power for it to finish within its deadline. In case of congestion the CPU rates assigned to the tasks are reduced fairly, so that the share of the resources that each user gets is proportional to the users' contribution to the Grid infrastructure or alternatively to the price he is willing to pay. As an example, we can assume three tasks whose fair completion times are 8, 6 and 12 respectively. As a result, the second, first and finally the third task is assigned for execution.

5   Experimental Results

The Grid architecture of the GRIA Project has been tested for two different applications, 3D image rendering with BMRT2.6 and the Finite Element Method (FEM) with INDIA, used in construction engineering. The results indicate the validity of the Runtime Estimation model that has been described in this paper. Ten computers of the Grid infrastructure have been used in this study as resources and they were benchmarked with SiSoftware Sandra Standard Unicode (32-bit x-86) 2003.1.9.31 under Microsoft Windows 2000.

For the 3D rendering application the runtime of 32 different tasks has been measured over the 10 different computers. For each one of the 8 PCs out of the 10 we formed the equation (5). We solved this over-determined system of the 8 equations ($N=8$), so as to calculate the **x** vector in (2). The actual values of the execution on the remaining 2 PCs are compared against the estimated

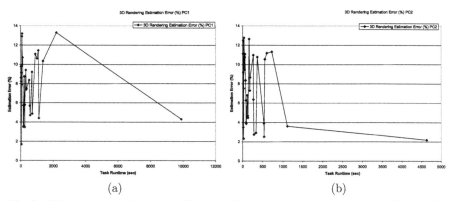

Fig. 3. 3D image rendering case - The error for the runtime estimation is calculated as the *relative absolute error* (in percentage) for a) the first of the 2 PCs and b) for the second PC

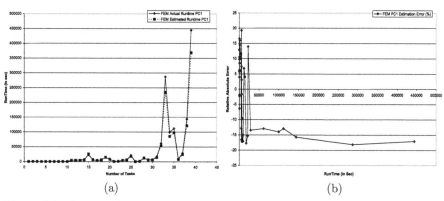

Fig. 4. (a) The *actual* and *estimated* total *runtime* for the FEM case; (b) The *error* for the run time estimation (in percentage) for the FEM case

time which is calculated using this **x** vector. Figure 2 presents the actual and predicted runtime of the 3D rendering application for the two PCs used for testing the results, while Fig. 3 presents the error for the two PCs. We can see that the error of the runtime estimation model is less than 13%.

For the FEM application we measure the runtime of 39 different tasks over 6 different computers. The over-determined system of 5 equations ($N=5$) has been solved to estimate the run time model, while the remaining 1 PC has been used to compare the estimated time with the actual one. Again, we can see that the error does not exceed 19%. Figure 4(a) presents the actual and the predicted run time, while Fig. 4(b) the error for the 1PC.

6   Conclusions

In order to commercialize the Grid infrastructure, we need to satisfy the QoS requirements imposed by the users who are willing to use the Grid infrastructure for fulfilling their commercial needs. To accomplish such Grid commercialization we need a modification of the existing architectures, so that the QoS requirements are satisfied as much as possible. This is proposed in this paper by introducing a Workload Predictor, a Capacity Estimator, a Runtime Estimator and a Scheduler. We also propose an accurate Runtime Estimation model. This model has been implemented and evaluated in the framework of the GRIA EU funded project. The experimental results illustrate accurate runtime prediction of the model in all the examined cases. The results have been obtained using 2 different commercial applications, the 3D image rendering and the Finite Element Method used in construction engineering.

References

1. Foster, I., Kesselman, C., Tuecke, S.: The Anatomy of the Grid: Enabling Scalable Virtual Organizations. Inter. Journal Supercomputer Applications. **15** (2001).
2. Leinberger, W., Kumar, V.: Information Power Grid: The new frontier in parallel computing? IEEE Concur., **7** (1999), 75-84.
3. Foster, I., Kesselman, C., Nick, J., Tuecke, S.: The Physiology of the Grid, An Open Grid Services Architecture for Distributed Systems Integration. www.globus.org (The Globus Project), 6/22/2002.
4. Scheduling Working Group of the Grid Forum, Document: 10.5, September 2001.
5. Vraalsen, F., Aydt, R., Mendes, C., Reed, D.: Performance Contracts: Predicting and Monitoring Grid Application Behavior. Proceedings of the 2nd International Workshop on Grid Computing/LNCS, **2242** (2001), 154-165.
6. IST-2001-33240: Grid Resources for Industrial Applications (GRIA). European Union program of Information Societies Technology.
7. Doulamis, N., Doulamis, A., Panagakis, A., Dolkas, K., Varvarigou, T., Varvarigos, E.: A Combined Fuzzy-Neural Network Model for Non-Linear Prediction of 3D Rendering Workload in Grid Computing. IEEE Trans. on Systems, Man and Cybernetics -Part B (to be published in 2004).
8. Doulamis, N., Doulamis, A., Panagakis, A., Dolkas, K., Varvarigou T., Varvarigos, E.: Workload Prediction of Rendering Algorithms in GRID Computing. European Multigrid Conference, (2002), 7-12.
9. Doulamis, N., Doulamis, A., Dolkas, K., Panagakis, A., Varvarigou T., Varvarigos, E.: Non-linear Prediction of Rendering Workload for Grid Infrastructure. International Conference on Computer Vision and Graphics, Poland Oct. 25-28, 2002.
10. Kobayashi, H.: Modeling and Analysis. Addison-Wesley 1981.
11. Haykin, S.: Neural Networks: A Comprehensive Foundation. New York: Macmillan.
12. Peha, J.M., Tobagi, F.A.: Evaluating scheduling algorithms for traffic with heterogeneous performance objectives. IEEE Global Telecom. Conf., **1**, (1990) 21-27.
13. Ku, T.W., Yang, W.R., Lin, K.J.: A class of rate-based real-time scheduling algorithms. IEEE Trans. on Computers, **51** (2002),708-720.

Managing MPI Applications
in Grid Environments[*]

Elisa Heymann[1], Miquel A. Senar[1], Enol Fernández[1],
Alvaro Fernández[2], and José Salt[2]

[1] Universitat Autónoma de Barcelona, Barcelona, Spain
{elisa.heymann,miquelangel.senar,enol.fernandez}@uab.es
[2] Instituto de Física Corpuscular, Valencia, Spain
{alferca,salt}@ific.uv.es

Abstract. One of the goals of the EU CrossGrid project is to provide a basis for supporting the efficient execution of parallel and interactive applications on Grid environments. CrossGrid jobs typically consist of computationally intensive simulations that are often programmed using a parallel programming model and a parallel programming library (MPI). This paper describes the key components that we have included in our resource management system in order to provide effective and reliable execution of parallel applications on a Grid environment. The general architecture of our resource management system is briefly introduced first and we focus afterwards on the description of the main components of our system. We provide support for executing parallel applications written in MPI either in a single cluster or over multiple clusters.

1 Introduction

Grid technologies started to appear in the mid-1990s. Much progress has been made on the construction of such an infrastructure since then, although some key challenge problems remain to be solved. There are many Grid initiatives that are still working in the prototype arena. And only a few attempts have been made to demonstrate production-level environments up to now. The Compact Muon Solenoid (CMS) Collaboration [1], which is part of several large-scale Grid projects, including GriPhyN [2], PPDG [3] and EU DataGrid [4], is a significant example that has demonstrated the potential value of a Grid-enabled system for Monte Carlo analysis by running a number of large production experiments but not in a continuous way.

Fundamental to any Grid environment is the ability to discover, allocate, monitor and manage the use of resources (which traditionally refer to computers, networks, or storage). The term *resource management* is commonly used to describe all aspects of the process of locating various types of resources, arranging these for use, utilizing them and monitoring their state. In traditional

---

[*] This work has been supported by the European Union through the IST-2001-32243 project "CrossGrid" and partially supported by the Comisión Interministerial de Ciencia y Tecnología (CICYT) under contract TIC2001-2592.

M. Dikaiakos (Ed.): AxGrids 2004, LNCS 3165, pp. 42–50, 2004.

computing systems, resource management is a well-studied problem and there is a significant number of resource managers such as batch schedulers or workflow engines. These resource management systems are designed and operate under the assumption that they have complete control of a resource and thus can implement mechanisms and policies for the effective use of that resource in isolation. Unfortunately, this assumption does not apply to Grid environments, in which resources belong to separately administered domains.

Resource management in a Grid therefore has to deal with a heterogeneous multi-site computing environment that, in general, exhibits different hardware architectures, loss of centralized control, and as a result, inevitable differences in policies. Additionally, due to the distributed nature of the Grid environment, computers, networks and storage devices can fail in various ways.

Most systems described in the literature follow a similar pattern of execution when scheduling a job over a Grid. There are typically three main phases, as described in [5]:

- Resource discovery, which generates a list of potential resources that can be used by a given application. This phase requires the user to have access to a set of resources (i.e. he/she is authorized to use them) and has some mechanism to specify a minimal set of application requirements. These requirements will be used to filter out the resources that do not meet the minimal job requirements.
- Information gathering on those resources and the selection of a best set. In this phase, given a group of possible resources, all of which meet the minimum requirement for the job, a single resource must be selected on which to schedule the job. The resource selection may be carried out by some form of heuristic mechanism that may use additional information about the dynamic state of the resources discovered in the first phase.
- Job execution, which includes file staging and cleanup. Once resources are chosen, the application can be submitted to them. However, due to the lack of standards for job submission, this phase can be made very complicated because it may involve setup of the remote site, staging of files needed by the job, monitoring progress of the application and, once the job is completed, retrieving of output files from the remote site, and removing temporary settings.

The resource management system that we are developing in the CrossGrid project follows the same approach to schedule jobs as described above. However, our system is targeted to a kind of applications that have received very little attention up to now. Most existing systems have focussed on the execution of sequential jobs, the Grid being a large multi-site environment where the jobs run in a batch-like way. The CMS Collaboration constitutes a remarkable example, in which research on job scheduling has also taken into account the location and movement of data, and the coordinated execution of multiple jobs with dependencies between them (when a job X depends on job Y, this means that X can start only when Y has completed).

CrossGrid jobs are computationally intensive applications that are mostly written with the MPI library. Moreover, once the job has been submitted to the

Grid and has started its execution on remote resources, the user may want to steer its execution in an interactive way. This is required to analyze intermediate results produced by the application and to react according to them. For instance, in the case where a simulation is not converging, the user may kill the current job and submit a new simulation with a different set of input parameters. From the scheduling point of view, support for parallel and interactive applications introduces the need for some mechanisms that are not needed when jobs are sequential or are submitted in a batch form. Basically, jobs need more than one resource (machine) and they must start *immediately*, i.e. in a period of time very close to the time of submission. Therefore, the scheduler has to search for sets of resources that are all already and wholly available at the time of the job submission. On the other hand, if there are no available resources, some priority and preemption mechanisms might be used to guarantee, for instance, that interactive jobs (which will have the highest priority) will preempt low priority jobs and run in their place.

In this paper, we focus on the description of the basic mechanisms used in our resource management system that are related to the execution of parallel applications on a Grid environment, assuming that free resources are available and no preemption is required. Preemption on grid environments is a complex problem and, to the best of our knowledge, no attempts have been made to address this problem. We are also investigating this issue and have designed certain preliminary mechanisms, which we plan to complete and test them in the near future.

The rest of this paper is organized as follows: Section 2 briefly describes the overall architecture of our resource management services, Section 3 describes the particular services that support submission of MPI applications on a cluster of a single site or on several clusters of multiple sites, and Section 4 summarizes the main conclusions to this work.

2   Overall Architecture of CrossGrid Resource Management

This section briefly describes the global architecture of our scheduling approach. A more detailed explanation can be found in [6]. The scenario that we are targeting consists of a user who has a parallel application and wishes to execute it on grid resources. When users submit their application, our scheduling services are responsible for optimizing scheduling and node allocation decisions on a user basis. Specifically, they carry out three main functions:

1. Select the "best" resources that a submitted application can use. This selection will take into account the application requirements needed for its execution, as well as certain ranking criteria used to sort the available resources in order of preference.
2. Perform a reliable submission of the application onto the selected resources.
3. Monitor the application execution and report on job termination.

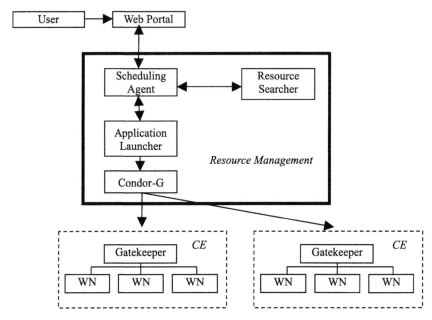

Fig. 1. Resource-Management Architecture

Figure 1 presents the main components that constitute the CrossGrid resource-management services. A user submits a job to a Scheduling Agent (SA) through a web portal. The job is described by a *JobAd* (Job Advertisement) using the EU-Datagrid *Job Description Language (JDL)* [7], which has been conveniently extended with additional attributes to reflect the requirements of interactive and parallel applications.

The SA asks the Resource Searcher (RS) for resources to run the application. The main duty of the RS is to perform the matchmaking between job needs and available resources. The RS receives a job description as input, and returns as output a list of possible resources within which to execute the job. The matchmaking process is based on the Condor ClassAd library [8], which has been extended with a set matchmaking capability, as described in [6]. Currently, set matchmaking is used for MPI applications that require a certain number of free CPUs and there is no single cluster that can provide such a number of free CPUs. Set matchmaking generates sets (groups) of clusters so that the overall number of free CPUs in each set fulfils application requirements.

The SA passes the job and the first-selected cluster (or group of CEs), also referred to as Computing Element (CE) in CrossGrid terminology, to the Application Launcher, who is responsible for the actual submission of the job on the specified CE or groups of CEs.

The Application Launcher is responsible for providing a reliable submission service of parallel applications on the Grid. Currently, two different launchers are used for MPI applications, namely MPICH ch-p4 [9] and MPICH-G2 [10]. In the following section both launchers are described.

3   MPI Management

An MPI application to be executed on a grid can be compiled either with MPICH-p4 (ch-p4 device) or with MPICH-G2, depending both on the resources available on the grid and on user-execution needs.

On the one hand, MPICH-p4 allows use of machines in a single cluster. In this case, part of the MPICH library must be installed on the executing machines. On the other hand, with MPICH-G2 applications can be submitted to multiple clusters, thus using the set matchmaking capability of the Resource Searcher. However, this approach is limited to clusters where all their machines have public IP addresses. MPICH-G2 applications, unlike MPICH-p4 do not require that the MPICH library is installed on the execution machines.

Taking into account the limitations on IP addresses, the Resource Searcher matches MPICH-p4 applications with single clusters independently of whether they have public or private addresses. The MPICH-G2 application, however, should be matched only with clusters with public IPs. Unfortunately, this information is not announced by the clusters and, therefore, the match generated by the Resource Searcher may include machines with private IPs. As a consequence, the part of the application that is submitted to one of those machines with a private IP will not be started successfully, blocking the whole application. As we explain below, detection of this kind of problem is left to the Application Launcher, who will be in charge of detecting the problem and reacting accordingly.

3.1   MPICH-p4 Management

MPICH-p4 applications will be executed on a single site, as shown in figure 2. Once the Scheduling Agent (SA) is notified that an MPICH-p4 application needs to be executed, the Matchmaking process is performed in order to determine the site for executing the application. When this is complete, the SA launches the application on the selected site following 2 steps:

- Using Condor-G [11] a launcher script is submitted to the selected site (arrow A in fig. 2). This script is given to the site job scheduler (for example PBS), which reserves as many machines (worker nodes) as specified in the Condor submission file.
- The script is executed on one such machine, for example in WN1. This script is in charge of obtaining the executable code (arrow B in fig. 2), as well as the files specified in the *InputSandbox* parameter of the *jdl* file. After obtaining such files, the script performs an *mpirun* call for executing the MPICH-p4 code on the required number of workers.

In this approach, it is assumed that all the worker nodes share the part of the file system where the users are located (traditionally */home*); therefore by transferring the executable file to one worker node, it is accessible to the rest of worker nodes. Additionally it is worth mentioning that *ssh* had been configured to not ask for any password, therefore the MPICH-p4 subjobs can start their execution automatically on the worker nodes.

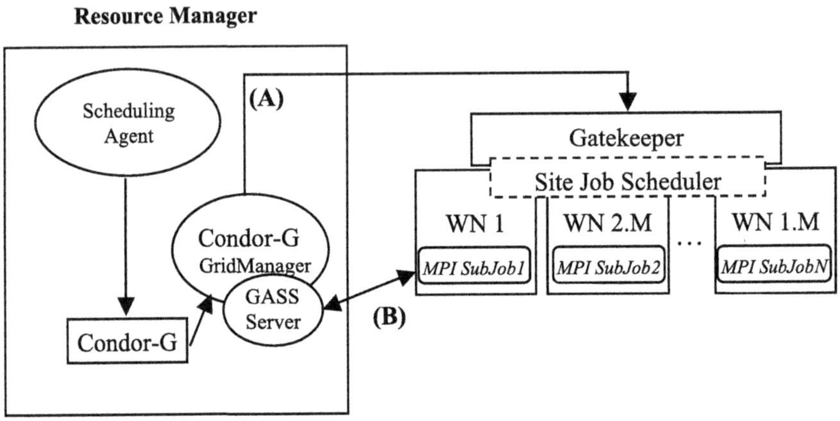

Resource Manager

Fig. 2. MPI execution on a single site

Currently the Crossgrid testbed contains both single CPU and SMP machines. It is worth to mention that applications are executed on both types of machines in a transparent way.

3.2 MPICH-G2 Management

When the parallel application needs more machines than the machines provided by any single site, multi-site submission is required. By using MPICH-G2, a parallel application can be executed on machines belonging to different sites.

An MPICH-G2 application can be executed on multiple sites using the globus-run command in the following way: `globusrun -s -w -f app.rsl`, the various gatekeepers where the different subjobs of the MPICH-G2 application are expected to be executed being specified in the app.rsl file. The *globusrun* call invokes DUROC [12] for subjob synchronization through a barrier mechanism. But when executing jobs with *globusrun*, the user should be aware of the need of asking for the status of his/her application, resubmitting the application again if something has gone wrong, and so on. In order to free the user of such responsibilities, we propose using Condor-G for a reliable job execution on multiple sites. Our MIPCH-G2 application launcher handles subjob synchronization using the same services provided by DUROC, but also obtains the advantages of using Condor-G. The main benefits offered by the MPICH-G2 Application Launcher are the following:

- An once-only execution of the application.
- A coordinated execution of the application subjobs, which means that the subjobs will be executed when all of them have resources to run on.
- A reliable use of the resources: if a subjob cannot be executed, the whole application will fail, therefore the machines will not be blocked and will be ready to be used by other applications.

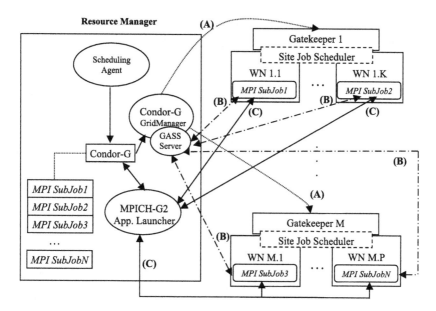

Fig. 3. MPI execution on multiple sites

Once the Scheduler Agent (SA) detects that an MPI application is submitted, it launches an MPICH-G2 application launcher (MPI-AL), through Condor-G. Figure 3 depicts how the execution over multiple sites is performed. In this example scenario, we have N subjobs that constitute an MPICH-G2 application. These subjobs will be executed on different sites. For the sake of simplicity, figure 3 only shows 2 sites. This MPI-AL coallocates the different subjobs belonging to the parallel application, following a two-step commit protocol:

- In the first step, all the subjobs are submitted through Condor-G. The A arrows show the subjobs submission to the remote machines. It is important to note that the GASS server is contacted to stage executable files to the remote worker nodes, and to bring the output files back to the submitting machine. This is shown by the B arrows.
- A second step guarantees that all the subjobs have a machine to be executed on, and that they have executed the *MPI_Init* call. This MPICH-G2 call invokes DUROC, and synchronization is achieved by a barrier released by the MPI-AL. After such synchronization, the subjobs will be allowed to run. Once the subjobs are executing on the worker node machines, the MPI-AL monitors their execution and writes an application global log file, providing complete information of the jobs' execution. This monitoring is shown by the C arrows in figure 3, and constitutes the key point for providing reliable execution of the applications and robustness.

Either if the application ends correctly or if there is any problem in the execution of any subjob, the MPI-AL records this in a log file that will be checked by the SA. Table 1 shows the problems that can appear and the corresponding actions taken. By handling adequately all these problems a reliable MPI execution is guaranteed.

Table 1. Problems reported by the MPI-AL and handled by the Scheduling Agent

Problem detected	Action
A subjob was not executed because a Globus resource was down.	Mark such Globus resource as "unavailable" so it will not be eligible for executing jobs for a certain amount of time. Repeat the Matchmaking process.
The two-step commit protocol cannot be completed within a limited amount of time.	All the subjobs will be killed, and then the same submission will be retried. If the submission continues failing on the same set of machines, the Matchmaking process will be repeated.
The MPI-AL crashes.	The SA will submit another MPI-AL that will take over the identification of the crashed item and will control the subjobs of the application. If the subjobs are after the two-steps commit protocol, they will continue their execution without noticing the MPI-AL replacement, otherwise they will be killed and the whole submission will be repeated.
Abnormal subjob termination.	The SA will notify the user.

4   Conclusions

We have described the main components of the resource management system that we are developing at the EU-CrossGrid in order to provide automatic and reliable support for MPI jobs over grid environments. The system consists of three main components: a Scheduling Agent, a Resource Searcher and an Application Launcher.

The Scheduling Agent is the central element that keeps the queue of jobs submitted by the user and carries out subsequent actions to effectively run the application on the suitable resources. The Resource Searcher has the responsibility of providing groups of machines for any MPI job with both of the following qualities: (1) desirable individual machine characteristics, and (2) desirable characteristics as an aggregate. Finally, the Application Launcher is the module that, in the final stage, is responsible for ensuring a reliable execution of the application on the selected resources. Two different Application Launchers have been implemented to manage the MPICH parallel applications that use the ch-p4 device or the G2 device, respectively.

Both launchers take advantage of the basic services provided by Condor-G for sequential applications submitted to a Grid. The launchers also extend these services in order to provide a reliable submission service for MPI applications. As a consequence, our resource management service handles resubmission of failed parallel jobs (due to crashes or failures in the network connecting, the resource manager or the remote resources), reliable co-allocation of resources (in the case of MPICH-G2), and exactly-once execution (even in the case of a machine crash where the resource manager is running).

Our first prototype has been based on the EU-Datagrid Resource Broker (release 1.4.8). However, this prototype has been mainly used for testing purposes. Our subsequent prototype is compatible with the next CrossGrid testbed deployment, which is based on EU-Datagrid release 2.0, and is integrated with two middleware services (namely, a Web Portal and a Migrating Desktop) providing a user-friendly interface to interact with the Grid.

References

1. K. Holtman. CMS requirements for the Grid. In Proceedings of International Conference on Computing in High Energy and Nuclear Physics (CHEP 2001), 2001.
2. GriPhyN: The Grid Physics Network. http://www.griphyn.org.
3. PPDG: Particle Physics Data Grid. http://www.ppdg.net.
4. European DataGrid Project. http://www.eu-datagrid.org
5. Jennifer M. Schopf, "Ten Actions When Grid Scheduling", in Grid Resource Management - State of the Art and Future Trends (Jarek Nabryzki, Jennifer Schopf and Jan Weglarz editors), Kluwer Academic Publishers, 2003.
6. E. Heymann, M.A.Senar, A. Fernandez, J. Salt, "The Eu-Crossgrid approach for Grid Application Scheduling", to appear in the post-proceedings of the 1st European Across Grids Conference February, LNCS series, 2003.
7. Fabricio Pazini, JDL Attributes - DataGrid-01-NOT-0101-0_4.pdf, http://www.infn.it/workload-grid/docs/DataGrid-01-NOT-0101-0_4-Note.pdf, December 17, 2001.
8. Rajesh Raman, Miron Livny and Marvin Solomon, "Matchmaking: Distributed resource management for high throughput computing", in Proc. Of the seventh IEEE Int. Symp. On High Perfromance Distributed Computing (HPDC7), Chicago, IL, July, 1998.
9. W. Gropp and E. Lusk and N. Doss and A. Skjellum, "A high-performance, portable implementation of the MPI message passing interface standard", Parallel Computing, 22(6), pages 789-828, 1996.
10. N. Karonis, B. Toonen, and I. Foster. MPICH-G2: A Grid-enabled implementation of the message passing interface. Journal of Parallel and Distributed Computing, 62, pp. 551-563, 2003.
11. James Frey, Todd Tannenbaum, Ian Foster, Miron Livny, and Steven Tuecke, "Condor-G: A Computation Management Agent for Multi-Institutional Grids", Journal of Cluster Computing, vol. 5, pages 237-246, 2002.
12. K. Czajkowsi, I. Foster, C. Kessekman. "Co-allocation services for computational Grids". Proceedings of the Eighth IEEE Symposium on High Performance Distributed Computing, IEEE Computer Society Press, Silver Spring MD, 1999.

Flood Forecasting in CrossGrid Project

L. Hluchy, V.D. Tran, O. Habala, B. Simo,
E. Gatial, J. Astalos, and M. Dobrucky

Institute of Informatics – SAS, Dubravska cesta 9, 845 07 Bratislava, Slovakia

Abstract. This paper presents a prototype of flood forecasting system based on Grid technologies. The system consists of workflow system for executing simulation cascade of meteorological, hydrological and hydraulic models, data management system for storing and accessing different computed and measured data, and web portals as user interfaces. The whole system is tied together by Grid technology and is used to support a virtual organization of experts, developers and users.

1 Introduction

Due to situation over the past few years in the world, modeling and simulation of floods in order to forecast and to make necessary prevention is very important. Simulating river floods is an extremely computation-intensive undertaking. Several days of CPU-time may be needed to simulate floods along large sections of rivers. For critical situations, e.g. when an advancing flood is simulated in order to predict which areas will be threatened so that necessary prevention measures can be implemented in time, long computation times are unacceptable. Therefore, using high performance computing platforms to reduce the computational time of flood simulation is imperative.

In ANFAS project [11], several flood models have been parallelized. Remote processing tools have been also created for running simulations on remote high performance systems automatically from client system. The simulation results can be imported to GIS system for visualization and analysis.

In CrossGrid project [12], meteorological and hydrological simulations are integrated into the system in order to forecast flood accurately. That requires cooperation between scientists in different areas, efficient data management system and a workflow system that can connect meteorological, hydrological and hydraulic simulations in a cascade. Therefore, Grid technologies are employed for implementing the system.

This paper will describe the Grid-based flood forecasting system (Flood Virtual Organization - FloodVO) that is developed in CrossGrid project, its current status and future work. Section 2 briefly describes the architecture of FloodVO and its components. Details about each component are provided in Sections 3-5. In Section 6, the future work on knowledge system is described and Section 7 concludes the paper.

M. Dikaiakos (Ed.): AxGrids 2004, LNCS 3165, pp. 51–60, 2004.

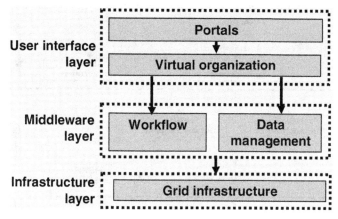

Fig. 1. FloodVO architecture

2   Flood Forecasting System Architecture

The architecture of FloodVO can be divided into three layers (Fig. 1). The testbeds of CrossGrid project provide the infrastructures for running Grid jobs. The executions of meteorological, hydrological and hydraulic simulations are managed by workflow system. Measured meteorological and hydrological data and simulation results are stored in storage elements and accessible via data management system. Users can access the data and models via web-based portals or Java-based migrating desktop.

3   Workflow in FloodVO

A workflow system that we designed for our flood prediction system enables the user to define whole cascade execution in advance as a workflow and run it with the possibility to inspect every step.

The whole flood simulation uses three main steps - meteorology, hydrology and hydraulics - to produce the final result - the prediction of the parts of the target area that are going to be flooded. When the expert wants to use already computed results or does not need to compute the last step of the cascade, just parts of the cascade are required. The run of a single simulation model represents the simplest case. So we have several possible workflow templates that may be executed. We have decided to constrain the workflow selection to several predefined workflows in the first version. Workflow is defined for each target area based on the computation dependencies for that particular area. The changing part of the workflow is mainly hydrology because the run-off in the target catchment is computed from several subcatchments.

3.1   Use Case

An expert who wants to perform a simulation chooses a target area and time for which to make the prediction. The choice is made by clicking on the map

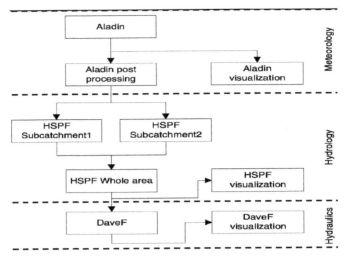

Fig. 2. Workflow in FloodVO

or choosing the name of the area from the list and entering the desired time span. Then the user chooses the workflow template from the list of templates available for the area of interest and selects the model to be used in each step. The possibility to select more models for the same step or even to enter user defined values instead of running a particular simulation step makes it possible to have several parallel instances of a workflow giving several results for the same time and area (Fig. 2).

3.2 Workflow Monitoring

Outside of monitoring single job execution, it is possible to monitor the execution of whole workflows. List of workflows is similar to list of jobs, it presents workflow name, description, start time, current state and so on. Moreover, it is possible to look inside at the workflow structure to see the progress in detail. Results produced by a single step of the workflow can be inspected once that particular step has finished. There is a possibility to change the output of each step and run the rest of the workflow from that point with modified results.

3.3 Workflow Information Storage

The simulation model parameters for each model are stored in a corresponding configuration file. This file is stored in a temporary directory belonging to the workflow instance that the model is part of. As there is a static set of predefined workflow templates, workflow composition definition file does not have to be generated. Only the workflow instance file is created specifying concrete jobs representing each node of the workflow.

4   Data Management in FloodVO

This section will describe the current status of data management in FloodVO, as well as envisioned future development. It starts with the description of collected data and its path to FloodVO storage. Then the prototype implementation of data management system and metadata schema are briefly presented. The section is concluded with a general outline of our future plans for the final data management system of FloodVO.

4.1   Data Sources Implemented in Prototype

The general schema of possible data sources for FloodVO operation was described in previous articles [6] and also included in the virtual organization (VO) figure. From these sources, only some were realised in the prototype stage of FloodVO.

The most important data in FloodVO storage are the boundary condition for the operation of our meteorological prediction model ALADIN. The ALADIN boundary conditions, as well as the rest of all currently available data, is provided by our partner in the CROSSGRID project (a subcontractor), the Slovak Hydrometeorological Institute (SHMI).

The second type of data implemented in the prototype stage of FloodVO are radar images of current weather conditions in the pilot operation area. These are created by postprocessing of larger images at SHMI every 30 minutes and made immediatelly available for download by our software. The download occurs as well, twice each hour and the images are stored in the FloodVO SE

The third type of currently available data are the ground-based water level, precipitation and temperature measurements provided by SHMI network of measurement stations. These measurements are periodically (the period depends on the type of data and the used measurement device) integrated into SHMI database. Only some of the available measurement points are extracted from the database (shown as bright red dots in Fig. 3). The data is then written to a text file, which is downloaded to FloodVO SE, integrated into a relational database and archived. The last type of data currently under development are satellite images of the pilot operation site. The negotiations with SHMI are not finished yet and the images will be available later for use in the FloodVO operation.

4.2   Prototype Implementation of Data Management Software

Data management in the prototype of FloodVO was implemented mainly using software tools, provided by the European DataGrid (EDG) IST project [7]:

- EDG Replica Manager (EDG RM)
- EDG Local Replica Catalog (EDG LRC)
- EDG Replication Metadata Catalogue (EDG RMC)
- EDG Replica Optimization Service (EDG ROS)
- EDG Spitfire [9]

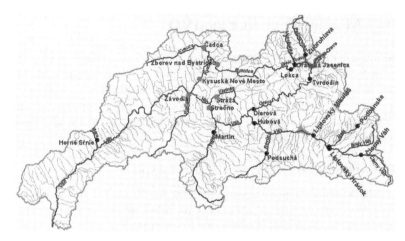

Fig. 3. Measurement points of the regional centre Zilina

The prototype implementation defined only one storage element, located at flood vo.ui.sav.sk. This SE concentrates all existing files needed in FloodVO operation. It is probable that this will change in the later development of FloodVO infrastructure.

The metadata database was implemented using the MySQL [8] RDBMS and the EDG Spitfire Grid interface to this RDBMS. The client enables to add, modify, locate and delete metadata for given file in the FloodVO SE (identified by its GUID). The client can be also accessed from flood-vo.ui.sav.sk or (after installation) from any FloodVO member's workstation.

5   User Interfaces

There are three different user interfaces in various stages of development that provide access to the grid for the flood application. We have developed GridPort [1] based application portal, we are developing flood application specific portlets for the Jetspeed portal framework based application portal and we are being integrated with Java based client called Migrating Desktop. All of them are described in more detail below.

5.1   Application Portal Based on GridPort Toolkit

We have started development of this version of application portal in the early stage of the CrossGrid project in order to provide basic demonstration and testing interface for our flood application (Fig. 4). The new grid and user interface technologies and support planned to be developed in the CrossGrid project were not available at that time so we decided to use already existing GridPort toolkit.

This toolkit enabled the Perl CGI scripts to use grid services of underlying Globus [2] toolkit by wrapping Globus command line tools. It provided no

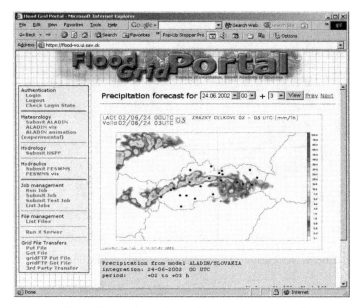

Fig. 4. Screenshot of our GridPort based portal

additional support for building portals nor did it provide any support for new services being developed in the CrossGrid project.

The portal provided access to basic grid services such as authentication of the users, job submission and management, file management and also enabled the user to run simulation models forming the flood application and view their results.

We have dropped its further development when CrossGrid user interfaces became available.

5.2   Application Portal Based on the Jetspeed Portal Framework

The Jetspeed [3] portal framework has been chosen in the CrossGrid project as a modern powerful platform for creating grid application portal for the applications in the project (Fig. 5). This framework is also being used by other grid projects such as Alliance portal [4] and the new version of the GridPort toolkit - GridPort 3.0 [5].

Jetspeed is implemented as a server-side Java based engine (application server). Client services are plugged in using software components called portlets. Each portlet has a dedicated space on the screen, which it uses for communication with users. Portlets are independent from each other and user can arrange their position, size and visibility.

Jetspeed, in contrast to GridPort, provides framework for building information portals (pluggable portlets mechanism, user interface management, security model based on permissions, groups and roles, persistence of information etc.)

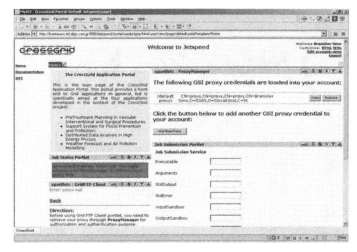

Fig. 5. Screenshot of the Jetspeed based application portal

but does not provide any support for grid services and applications. Common grid portlets that can be used in Jetspeed are being developed in CrossGrid and other projects.

Portlet for submission of specific simulation models of flood application has been developed and now we are focusing on automatization of a computation of the flood simulation cascade by employing workflows.

We are also investigating the possibility of using groupware portlets from the CHEF [5] project.

5.3 Migrating Desktop

Migrating Desktop is a Java client being developed in the CrossGrid project (Fig. 6). The idea was to create user interface with greater interactivity than could be possible to achieve by using web technology.

Current version provides access to basic grid services such as authentication, job management, file management. Support for specific application features is addressed by application and tool plugin interfaces that enable to plug in code handling application specific parameter definition and visualization. We have implemented both plugins for the flood application.

Application plugin enables a user to specify input parameters for specific simulation model and submit it to the grid. Interface for parameter input is dynamically generated from the XML configuration files and default values are suggested.

Examination of visualized results of the simulations is done via the tool plugin. Output of the visualization of meteorological and hydraulics simulations is a sequence of pictures so the tool plugin is a picture browser with simple animation feature.

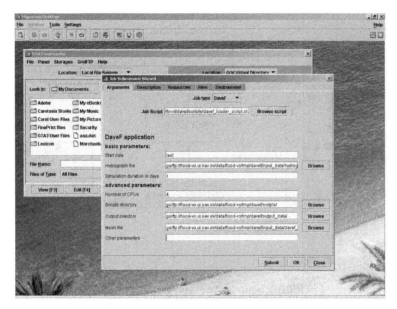

Fig. 6. Screenshot of the Migrating Desktop

6   Future Work

Many simulation models, in some cases, are not very reliable and are also dependent on many other factors (physical phenomena), which are not included in evaluation process of the models. Knowledge based treatment of historical data could provide enhanced functionality for the simulation models which strictly relies on the recent data sets. It also allows to construct several predicates of states according to knowledge evaluation with simulation run. Knowledge repository will store information for the particular simulation and also for the reasoning process (Fig. 7). The information sets stored in the repository will depend on post-processing of simulation output, evaluation of relevance (relevance ranking) and user assessment (expert point of view). This enables to compare consequent data sets which are going to be processed and data sets which have already occurred in previous simulation processing. For example in meteorological simulation, similar cases of weather conditions can be found in the same season, but in different years. The statistical analysis methods can be used to search for similar cases. So, the reasoning process will have available information about the simulations, which had the most similar input data sets, also its outcomes and relevant information about condition of simulated environment.

It is up to reasoning process implementation, whether it allows user to run next simulation job automatically with or without any changes or provides options to change simulation properties according to given information about previous simulation runs. The reasoning could be also able to obtain/store the information from/to external resources (e.g. utilize web service) and as well as experts.

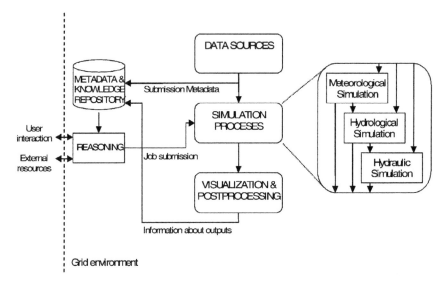

Fig. 7. Knowledge system in FloodVO

Reasoning system will cover ontological description of terms and its inter-relations (e.g. relations between inputs and outputs of simulations), moreover, it will define possible inputs and outputs form/to external resources. Generally, ontology could be recorded in the DAML+OIL description language and accessed with reasoning application. According to this ontology, the information will be evaluated for every particular type of simulation. The user could be able to adjust behavior of reasoning by choosing different templates. The evaluation process includes relevant knowledge acquisition (to restrict irrelevant information), processing of data sets to prepare information (to reduce the detail level in information) and make available information for user and for inference algorithm. The algorithm of inference must also be able to process incomplete information about possible states.

However, the reasoning procedure is in the phase of research, it will utilize methods from [13] propositional calculus and reasoning with uncertain information (probabilistic reasoning). It will be designed and tested as the last issue according to requests from users and developers of the simulation methods.

7 Conclusion

In this paper, the Grid-based flood forecasting system is presented. The system consists of different user interfaces, workflow system for executing cascade of meteorological, hydrological and hydraulic simulations and data management system for storing and accessing different types of data

References

1. GridPort toolkit. https://gridport.npaci.edu
2. Globus toolkit. http://www.globus.org
3. Jetspeed. http://jakarta.apache.org/jetspeed/site/index.html
4. Alliance portal. http://www.extreme.indiana.edu/alliance/
5. Grid Port 3.0 Plans presentation. http://www.nesc.ac.uk/talks/261/Tuesday/GP3
6. Hluchý L., Habala O., Simo B., Astalos J., Tran V.D., Dobruck M.: Problem Solving Environment for Flood Forecasting. Proc. of The 7th World Multiconference on Systemics, Cybernetics and Informatics (SCI 2003), July 2003, Orlando, Florida, USA, pp. 350-355.
7. Hoschek, W., et. al.: Data Management in the European DataGrid Project. The 2001 Globus Retreat, San Francisco, August 9-10 2001.
8. Widenius, M., Axmark, D.: MySQL Reference Manual. O'Reilly and Associates, June 2002, 814 pages.
9. Bell, W., et. al.: Project Spitfire - Towards Grid Web Service Databases. Technical report, Global Grid Forum Informational Document, GGF5, Edinburgh, Scotland, July 2002
10. WMO Core Metadata Standard - XML representation. World Weather Watch. http://www.wmo.ch/web/www/metadata/WMO-metadata-XML.html
11. ANFAS: Data Fusion for Flood Analysis and Decision Support. IST-1999-11676. http://www.ercim.org/anfas/
12. Development of Grid Environment for Interactive Applications. IST-2001-32243. http://www.eu-crossgrid.org/
13. Nilsson J. Nils, Artificial intelligence: A New Synthesis, Morgan Kaufmann Publishers, Inc., San Francisco, California.

MPICH-G2 Implementation of an Interactive Artificial Neural Network Training

D. Rodríguez[1], J. Gomes[2], J. Marco[1], R. Marco[1], and C. Martínez-Rivero[1]

[1] Instituto de Física de Cantabria (CSIC-UC),
Avda. de los Castros s/n, 39005 Santander, Spain
[2] Laboratório de Instrumentação e Física de Partículas, Lisbon, Portugal

Abstract. Distributed Training of an Artificial Neural Network (ANN) has been implemented using MPICH-G2, and deployed on the testbed of the european CrossGrid project. Load balancing, including adaptative techniques, has been used to cope with the heterogeneous setup of computing resources. First results show the feasibility of this approach, and the opportunity for a Quality of Service framework. To give an example, a reduction in the training time from 20 minutes using a single local node downto less than 3 minutes using 10 nodes distributed across Spain, Poland, and Portugal, has been obtained.

1 Introduction

The Grid [1] provides access to large shared computing resources distributed across many local facilities.

MPICH-G2 [2] is a Grid enabled implementation of MPICH [3]; it uses the Globus Toolkit 2 [4] to access Grid resources and perform tasks such as authentication, authorization, process creation and communications.

Training of Artificial Neural Networks (ANN) algorithms, depending on the size of the samples used, and the ANN architecture, may require large computation time in a single workstation, preventing an interactive use of this technique for data-mining.

As an example, the ANN used in the search for the Higgs boson using the data collected by the DELPHI detector [5] at the LEP accelerator at CERN, required from several hours to days to complete the training process using about one million simulated events for a simple two hidden layer architecture with about 250 internode weights. This prevents the final user from working in a real interactive mode while looking for an optimal analysis.

A previous work [6] has shown that a usual ANN training algorithm, BFGS [7], can be adapted using MPI to run in distributed mode in local clusters. A reduction in the training time from 5 hours to 5 minutes was observed when using 64 machines on a cluster [8] built using linux nodes connected by fast ethernet.

In this paper a first experience in a Grid framework is reported. The adaptation is based on the use of MPICH-G2, and has been deployed in the testbed of the european project CrossGrid [9].

M. Dikaiakos (Ed.): AxGrids 2004, LNCS 3165, pp. 61–68, 2004.

The scheme of the paper is as follows: first the computing problem is described, including a reference example, and the adaptation using MPICH-G2 in a local cluster (section 2). First results in the Grid environment are given in section 3, where the load balancing mechanism is discussed. Section 4 presents the conclusions and a description of the future work.

2   Distributed Training of an Artificial Neural Network Using MPICH-G2 in a Local Cluster

Parallel ANN training is a topic that has been studied for a long time. A good review can be found in [10]. The program used in this work is based on the one already cited before [6].

The objective of the training is the minimization of the total error, given by the sum of errors for all events, each one defined as the quadratic difference between the ANN output computed corresponding to each event and the 1 or 0 value corresponding to a signal or background event. The minimization procedure is iterative, each iteration being called an epoch. The BFGS [7] gradient descent method has been used in the ANN training. In this method, errors and gradients are additive in each epoch. The results obtained in each slave can be added and transmitted to the master. This is a very good characteristic for a parallelization in data strategy.

The parallel training algorithm goes as follows:

1. The master node starts the work reading the input parameters for the ANN architecture, and setting the initial weights to random values.
2. The training data is split into several datasets of similar size (taking into account the computing power of each node to assure load balancing by data partitioning) and distributed to each slave node.
3. At each step, the master sends the weight values to the slaves, which compute the error and the gradient on the partial dataset and return them to the master; as both are additive, total errors are calculated by the master that prepares the new weights along the corresponding direction in the multidimensional space and updates the weights. The error computed in a separated test dataset is used to monitor the convergence.
4. The previous step (an epoch) is repeated until a convergence criterion is fulfilled or a predetermined number of epochs is reached. The master returns as output the ANN weights, to prepare the corresponding multidimensional function.
5. The whole training can be repeated with different initial random weights to prevent bad results due to local minima. The final error can be used to select the best final ANN function if different minima are found.

A first step was to move from MPICH with the ch_p4 device to MPICH-G2, i.e. MPICH with the globus2 device. This implies the use of the Globus Toolkit. The Globus Toolkit is a collection of software components for enabling Grid computing: security, resource allocation, etc.

Table 1. Performance comparison with the previous version of the program (using ch_p4)

Number of Slaves	ch-p4 (s)	mpich-g2 (s)
1	11290	11242
8	1435	1448
16	720	736

Table 2. Results in local cluster up to 32 slaves

Number of Slaves	Total time (s)
1	11242
2	5652
4	2827
8	1448
12	966
16	736
20	609
24	527
28	455
32	401

The comparison of the new program results, using the globus2 device, with those obtained with the previous version (the ch_p4 one) is done on a smeared simulated sample with a total of 412980 events, comparing the program execution time for a 1000 epoch training of an ANN with the 16-10-10-1 architecture. In table 1 one can see that performances are very similar.

The tests in a cluster environment were done at the IFCA's cluster at Santander [8]. It has 80 dual Pentium III IBM x220 servers (1.26 GHz, 512 Kb cache, 640 MB RAM with 36 GB SCSI and 60 GB IDE disks) running RedHat Linux 7.2. For these tests we used a maximum of 32 slaves.

To be able to change the number of participating slaves, all the data was distributed amongst the nodes. In this way each slave can access the data it needs independently of their number.

The tests using a single processor in each node show a time reduction from about three hours in a single node to near seven minutes with 32 nodes, considering the same 16-10-10-1 architecture trained over 1000 epochs (see table 2). The speedup in the local cluster is plotted in figure 1.

3   From Cluster to Grid Computing

The testbed used in the tests, described in detail in [11], includes 16 sites distributed across 9 different european countries, interconnected through the academic network Géant [12] and the corresponding national networks. Access to the testbed is granted through the use of certificates to users and its inclusion in a Virtual Organization. For this first study, only few nodes distributed at several sites in Spain, Portugal and Poland have been used, in order to reduce the complexity of understanding the results obtained, while preserving the distributed nature of the experiment.

Topology-aware collective operations as discussed in [13] can provide significant performance improvements over a non topology-aware approach in the case of MPI applications in the Grid. In our case the MPI_Reduce operation used for the addition of errors and gradients in each epoch could be the critical one.

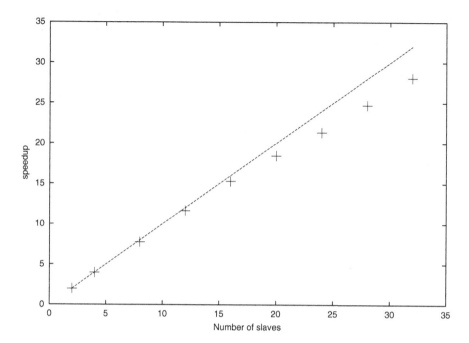

Fig. 1. Speedup in a local cluster for a 16-10-10-1 architecture using a single processor in each node

3.1 Security

Security issues are extremally challenging when moving to a Grid environment. In this transition one has to move from a locally administered environment to a heterogeneous WAN with multiple administrators. Mutual trust between the users and the sites is essential. The authentication of users and systems is done through a public key infrastructure (PKI) based on X.509 certificates that must be recognized and accepted by all intervening parties. The authorization is performed through a *Virtual Organizations* (VO) mechanism thus allowing users to access resources across sites with the same authentication credentials. The CrossGrid virtual organization was used to perform the Grid tests. A VO as defined in [14], is a set of individuals and/or institutions defined by several rules for sharing computing resources: machines, software, data, etc. In out tests all the security uses this grid certificates mechanism. The security infrastructure thus relays in the testbed (see [11]).

3.2 Data Stripping and Transfer

An important issue is the availability of distributed replica for the training data, as its proximity in access time to the computing resources is a key point to reduce the waiting time. The Grid framework provides several interesting possibilities on

Table 3. Load balanced gain in the CrossGrid testbed for an ANN train epoch. The times are the mean of the times consumed in each epoch in the corresponding slave, not the total application time divided by the number of epochs

Node	Not balanced		Balanced	
	Num. events	Time per epoch (s)	Num. events	Time per epoch (s)
Node 1	82651	0.757	87677	0.808
Node 2	82576	0.757	87736	0.816
Node 3	82576	0.758	87760	0.825
Node 4	82576	0.759	87764	0.813
Node 5	82061	1.07	62061	0.848

data replication and distributed data access (see for example [15], [16] and [17]). For this first deployment the data has been directly transferred to the different nodes and the corresponding computing elements. In this note we have placed our data inside the computing elements, in order to minimize its exchange.

3.3 Load Balancing

Taking into account that the speed of a training step is the speed of the slowest slave, the need for a good load balance is essential.

The used dataset contains a total of 412980 events and has the following components: 4815 signal (Higgs bosons) events and two different kinds of background events: 326037 WW events, and 82128 QCD events. For our tests we further divided each of the subsets in 80 slices, and replicated them across the participating nodes.

In a configuration using a 1.26 GHz PIII master, and 5 slaves (4 dual 2.4 GHz P4 Xeon in a cluster in Poland and one 1.7 GHz P4 in Portugal), we observed that an equal distribution of events between them resulted in a heavy performance penalization due to the slowest slave. This one spends – and thus increases the total time – near a 40% more time than the fastest one per training epoch.

Introducing an automatic data distribution amongst the slaves based on a weighting factor that, in a first approach, was chosen to be the CPU speed, the 1.7 GHz node continues to be the slowest slave, but the delay per epoch is reduced to only a 5% time increase with respect to the fastest slave. One can compare the results obtained with and without load balance in table 3. These results show how a balanced training reduces the time spent per epoch in the slowest node, increasing thus the overall speed of the program.

A further improvement would be to benchmark the nodes in order to refine the weighting factor. Preliminary results running a version of our program with only one slave and the full data sample show sizeable improvements.

It is worth noticing that both methods imply an a priori knowledge of the nodes where the application will be run that will not be available in a Grid production environment. This knowledge should be substituted by the information provided by Grid utilities.

Table 4. Performance comparison with different testbed nodes

Master	slaves@krakow	slaves@lisbon	Total time (s)
IFCA	9	1	218.4
IFCA	7	1	230.8
IFCA	5	1	258.9
IFCA	6	0	254.0
IFCA	4	0	312.0
IFCA	2	0	525.8
INP	2	0	452.3

One can compare the results obtained using different testbed configurations in table 4. In all cases a node placed at IFCA in Spain acted as a master except in the last case where everything was done inside the same cluster (INP at Krakow in Poland); one can see then how the computation time decreases with respect to the previous line in the table due to the absence of network delay. To compare with, the same program needs 1197 seconds to run on a dual PIII 1.26 GHz. So, even in the Grid environment, you can get a clear time improvement when parallelizing the ANN training. The training time is reduced from 20 minutes in the local node, to a bit more than 3 minutes with 10 slaves.

A first attempt to use an adaptative technique to cope with changing testbed conditions has been performed. As the program is meant to be part of an inter-active training process we consider that the loss of some events is not critical. Thus, when a node is slowing significantly the training process we can reduce the number of events it uses in the training. Anyhow, the total amount of events lost should not exceed a certain percentage of the total events, and the error display (figure 2) is a good monitoring tool. This can result in a useful feature as changing conditions in the network traffic or in the machines load would severely damage performance even having a good a–priori load balancing. This feature can be disabled if desired by the user, and was only used for the last test referred in this note.

4   Conclusions and Future Work

The results of this paper show the feasibility of running a distributed neural network in a local cluster reducing the wait time for a physicist using this tool from hours to minutes. They also indicate that this approach can be extended to a Grid environment, with nodes distributed across a WAN, if the latency is low enough. The time reduction obtained shows that the resources made available by the Grid can be used to perform an interactive ANN training. The nature of the ANN training problem let us implement an especially dynamic load balancing approach, based on the reduction of the number of events, that might not be applied for many other problems. A more general solution should be researched in the future.

Along these tests we noticed a strong need for a quality of service approach in Grid applications, especially for interactive ones. The reservation of resources

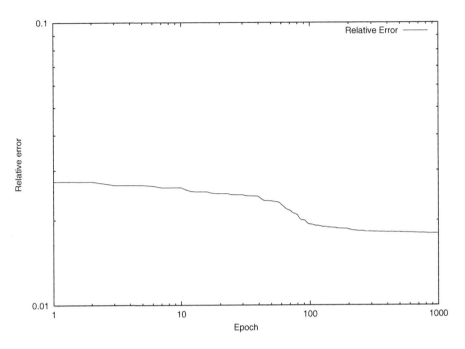

Fig. 2. Error display of the ANN program. Both axes are in logarithmic scale

(network bandwith, processing and memory capacity) is critical for a satisfactory execution of this sort of applications (of which our parallel ANN training is a good example). Although we have the possibility to query the resources availability when starting execution, not having a guarantee on the availability of resources during execution can severely damage the performance.

Parallel (MP) applications can be a very challenging case for Quality of Service frameworks. In our case, the master cannot compute the weights for the new epoch until it receives the errors and gradients from all the slaves. So computation is stopped (and time is lost) while waiting for communications to complete. On the other hand, while the master or the slaves are computing, there are no communications; so we have a very irregular communication pattern. There are peaks of communications at the beginning and at the end of each training epoch, and no communications at all during the new epoch error computation.

Furthermore, communications can involve many processes making the problem even more complex. Not only the fact that more computing nodes increase the number of sites sending packets, but also the waiting time between epochs is reduced as the number of computing nodes increases, reducing the time between communication peaks, and potentially increasing the contention problem in shared networks.

A prototype implementation of a Quality of Service architecture for MPI programs can be found in [18]. We think this is a very interesting topic that can be critical for the success of interactive applications on the Grid. We are working for a Quality of Service for the network in the CrossGrid testbed.

Some further improvements that are being considered are:

- Improving the event reduction mechanism.
- Usage of Grid information utilities.
- Integration in a portal.

Acknowledgements. This work has been mainly supported by the European project CrossGrid (IST-2001-32243). We would like to thank in particular all the testbed sites for offering the possibility to run our tests.

References

1. I. Foster and C. Kesselman, editors. *The Grid: Blueprint for a Future Computing Infrastucture*. Morgan Kaufmann Publishers, 1999.
2. N. Karonis, B. Toonen, and I. Foster, *MPICH-G2: A Grid-Enabled Implementation of the Message Passing Interface*, Journal of Parallel and Distributed Computing (JPDC), to appear, 2003.
3. MPICH. http://www-unix.mcs.anl.gov/mpi/mpich
4. The Globus Project. http://www.globus.org
5. DELPHI collaboration. http://delphiwww.cern.ch/
6. O. Ponce et al. *Training of Neural Networks: Interactive Possibilities in a Distributed Framework*. In D. Kranzlmüller et al. (Eds.) 9th European PVM/MPI, Springer-Verlag, LNCS Vol. 2474, pp. 33-40, Linz, Austria, September 29-October 2, 2002.
7. Broyden, Fletcher, Goldfarb, Shanno (BFGS) method. For example in *Practical Methods of Optimization* R.Fletcher. Wiley (1987)
8. Santander Grid Wall. http://grid.ifca.unican.es/sgw
9. CrossGrid European Project (IST-2001-32243). http://www.eu-crossgrid.org
10. Manavendra Misra. *Parallel Environments for Implementing Neural Networks*. Neural Computing Survey, vol. 1., 48-60, 1997.
11. J. Gomez et al. *First Prototype of the CrossGrid Testbed*. Presented at the 1st Across Grids Conference. Santiago de Compostela Feb. 2003.
12. Géant. http://www.dante.net/geant/
13. N. Karonis et al. *Exploiting hierarchy in parallel computer networks to optimize collective operation performance*. In Proceedings of the 14th International Parallel and Distributed Processing Symposium, 2000.
14. I. Foster,C. Kesselman, S. Tuecke. *The Anatomy of the Grid: Enabling Scalable Virtual Organizations*. International J. Supercomputer Applications, 15(3), 2001.
15. H. Stockinger et al. File and Object Replication in Data Grids. Journal of Cluster Computing, 5(3)305-314,2002.
16. A. Chervenak et al. *Giggle: A Framework for Constructing Scalable Replica Location Services*. In Proceedings of SC2002, Nov. 2002.
17. OGSA-DAI. Open Grid Services Architecture Data Access and Integration http://www.ogsadai.org.uk/
18. A. Roy et al. *MPICH-GQ: Quality-of-Service for Message Passing Programs*. Proceedings of SC2000. Dallas, Nov. 2000.

OpenMolGRID, a GRID Based System
for Solving Large-Scale Drug Design Problems

Ferenc Darvas[1], Ákos Papp[1], István Bágyi[1], Géza Ambrus[2], and László Ürge[1]

[1] ComGenex, Inc., Bem rkp. 33-34, H-1027 Budapest, Hungary
www.comgenex.hu
[2] RecomGenex Ltd., Bem rkp. 33-34, H-1027 Budapest, Hungary

Abstract. Pharmaceutical companies are screening millions of molecules *in silico*. These processes require fast and accurate predictive QSAR models. Unfortunately, nowadays these models do not include information-rich quantum-chemical descriptors, because of their time-consuming calculation procedure. Collection of experimental data is also difficult, because the sources are usually located in disparate resources. These challenges make indispensable the usage of GRID systems. OpenMolGRID (Open Computing GRID for Molecular Science and Engineering) is one of the first realizations of the GRID technology in drug design. The system is designed to build QSAR models based on thousands of different type of descriptors, and apply these models to find novel structures with targeted properties. An implemented data warehouse technology makes possible to collect data from geographically distributed, heterogeneous resources. The system will be tested in real-life situations: Predictive models will be built on *in vitro* human toxicity values determined for 30,000 novel and diverse chemical structures.

1 Introduction

Molecular engineering can be applied for designing compounds with predefined target properties. The challenge for the industrial applications of molecular engineering is to develop novel compounds that have not yet been discovered for the intended purpose and can be patented. This development is a multistep procedure starting with the design of drug discovery compound libraries that are collecting the candidate structures into specific biological clusters. The so-called library design refers to this dynamic procedure that also includes several steps from the discovery of the library core idea through the generation (enumeration) of compound structures to the evaluation in the paper chemistry and medicinal chemistry/ADMETox points of view. The ADMETox (Absorption, Distribution, Metabolism, Excretion, and Toxicity) characterization of compounds has an extreme importance in library design, because almost 60% of drug candidates surviving the traditional drug development process fail in the clinical trials due to inappropriate ADMETox properties [1], [2]. This characterization can be made by calculation of physicochemical properties [3], [4], [5], [6], [7], [8], such as acidity/basicity (pK_a) [9], octanol-water partition coefficients ($\log P$ and $\log D$ values) [10], [11], hydrogen-bond donor and acceptor counts (HBDC and HBAC), CHI values [12], etc, and by prediction of metabolism and toxicity [13].

M. Dikaiakos (Ed.): AxGrids 2004, LNCS 3165, pp. 69–76, 2004.
© Springer-Verlag Berlin Heidelberg 2004

The selection of the appropriate compounds to be synthesised is a complex decision that has to be done in a relatively short time. For a single discovery library hundred thousands of structures are considered, and recently pharmaceutical companies deal with millions of candidate compound structures. To be able to deal with such a large number of structures, the medicinal chemistry and the ADMETox evaluation require the implementation of in silico tools for the prediction of physicochemical properties applying fast predictive QSAR/QSPR (Quantitative Structure-Activity/ Property Relationship) models. Unfortunately, at the moment fast models are usually not accurate enough, because they do not include information-rich quantum-chemical descriptors due to their time-consuming calculation procedure. An accurate model regularly contains more than 100 descriptors, so altogether well over 1,000,000 data should be calculated for each library. These challenges make indispensable the usage of large-scale molecular design techniques, especially high-performance QSAR calculations.

Most companies involved in the drug design field participate in collaborative R&D projects consisting of multinational organizations sometimes from several continents. The communication and decision processes require the use of e-R&D tools. A common task in library design procedure is to organize a meeting over the Internet with the participation of highly specialized experts. In such a meeting, only a short discussion time (30-60 minutes) is available, and in many cases the next meeting can be organized only 1-2 weeks later. The participants have to make high value decisions, which are based on the selection of structures according to their properties. The related information has to be available at the time of the meeting for all experts irespectively of their location, and even if some structures are modified or added just during the meeting.

The above considerations lead to the application of GRID systems. These "high-throughput" informatics systems provide the facility to develop fast and accurate predictive QSAR models on a huge number of model compounds in a short time and apply this novel method on an unprecedently high number of molecules.

2 Overview

OpenMolGRID [14] (Open Computing GRID for Molecular Science and Engineering) is going to be one of the first realizations of the GRID technology in drug design.

The system is developed in an international project (Estonia, Northern Ireland, Germany, Italy, and Hungary) partly funded by the European Commission under the 5th Framework Project (IST-2001-37238).

The project goals are as follows:

- Smooth integration of resources
- Large-scale molecular calculations
- Real life testing
- On-site toxicity prediction for large libraries
- Identification of potential anticancer drug candidates

The OpenMolGRID system is designed to create QSPR/QSAR models and use them to predict biological activities or ADME related properties. Most of the modern data mining techniques (MLR, PCA, PLS, ANN, etc) and thousands of different type of descriptors are available for model building purposes. Many of the descriptors require computation intensive 3D structure optimization and quantum chemical calculations, but still can be estimated in a relatively short time.

Using its implemented data warehouse technology, the system is suitable to collect data from geographically distributed, heterogeneous resources. For additional details on the OpenMolGRID warehouse technology, please see the contribution of Damian McCourt et al., titled 'The OpenMolGRID Data Warehouse, MOLDW'. For storage of local data the system contains a Custom Data Repository, as well.

OpenMolGRID is based on the adaptation and integration of existing, widely accepted, relevant computing tools and data sources, using the UNICORE [15] infrastructure, to make a solid foundation for the next step molecular engineering tools. For detailed description please refer to the contribution of Mathilde Romberg et al., titled 'Support for Classes of Applications on the Grid'.

The system is capable to build and apply reverse-QSAR models, to find novel structures with favourable properties. The structural ideas are generated by a molecular engineering tool that is based on the application of a unique structure enumeration technique. It creates the structures by considering all possible connection of building blocks selected from the implemented fragment library using specified chemical connectivity rules. The candidates are selected based on additive fragment descriptors, and only the reliable structures are created. The properties of these structures are predicted, and the final hit list is prepared by the predefined property filters.

The process flowchart of the system can be seen on the following figure:

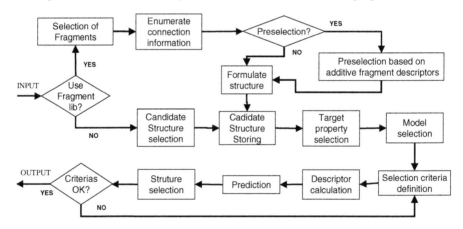

Fig. 1.

The system can also be used for forward-QSAR purposes: in this case candidate structures are imported to the system from an external data source.

One of the key tasks of the development of the OpenMolGRID system is its accurate evaluation. The task includes functional and *in silico* testing steps, however, the most important issue is proving the system capabilities when facing real life problems. It has to contain real compounds and real properties and a discovery scenario that is commonly present in the pharmaceutical industry. For the real-life testing, new compounds have to be synthesised and an interesting biological activity have to be measured. A QSAR model have to be built using the experimental data, then the predictive power of the system has to be proven by validating the accuracy of the model.

Finally, the most important function of the system has to be proved, the generation of structures with predefined properties.

In the real-life testing of OpenMolGRID the number of tested compounds is adjusted to a typical discovery problem and a biological property with general importance is selected. At ComGenex sometimes the fate of more than 100,000 compounds should be decided during a short meeting or net meeting that involves a number of highly specialized experts, sometimes from several continents. The predicted parameters requested for the decision are preliminary calculated, and available at the time of the meeting. However, in case of any modification in the building block lists, the corresponding new structures have to be enumerated, and the necessary drug design calculations cannot be finished during the meeting without the help of a GRID system. Presently, the cluster of more than 40 computers operating at ComGenex needs an overnight calculation time to finish the minimum necessary calculations for an average series of 50,000 compounds. The highly specialized discovery experts are not available on daily basis and the creative process that is needed to invent the new drug candidates is effectively broken by the fact that the next meeting cannot be organized earlier than one or more weeks.

Since the innovative creation of new molecules is an iterative procedure composed of several man/machine/man cycles, the present long response time from the computers effectively impedes to utilize a number of design software for large compounds sets. The practical compromise today in the industry is to use the computers for evaluation of large compound sets via batch operations, very similar to the way as computers were utilized twenty years ago.

Based on the above considerations, the real-life test set was decided to contain compound collection of 30,000 novel and diverse structures having experimental human fibroblast toxicity data. Since activity values were not available for such a large number of compounds in this property type, the compound libraries have been designed, the molecules have been synthesized, and IC_{50} values for *in vitro* human fibroblast cytotoxicity are being determined. The real-life testing require a novel and diverse compound set to avoid congeneric structures (including redundant information), and to cover a wide range of the chemical space. On the other hand, to prove the predictive power of the system a critical mass for the test set is needed, which fulfils the diversity density criteria, i.e. a sufficient representation of the chemical clusters. Therefore the size of the test set was set to 10,000 compounds and – for proving the predictive power of the model in extreme situations – one complete cluster independent from the training set was included in it. The fact, that the size of the training set has to be at least double of the test set for model building purposes, also underlined that minimum 30,000 compounds have to be included in the real-life testing. The library design procedure is detailed in Section 4.

Using the experimental data, linear and non-linear QSAR models are being developed and the predictive capability of these models is going to be validated. The best model will be used to generate compounds with lowest and highest cytotoxicity, which provides the possibility to identify leads for potential anticancer agents.

3 Conclusions and Future Directions

The system will analyze millions of structures in a considerable time using the obtained QSAR/QSPR equations with traditional and grid based computation procedures, and select the most promising hits from this huge virtual chemical domain. OpenMolGRID enables highly specialized experts from several continents to make immediate decisions in the library design phase during a net meeting.

A further development possibility is to extend the knowledge managing tools and facilities, incorporating large discovery related knowledge management systems, like Emil (Example-Mediated Innovation for Lead Evolution [16]).

4   Methods

4.1   Library Design Procedure

The design started with the selection of structures based on Lipinski filtering followed by a diverse selection procedure (using the Optisim diverse selection method implemented in the Sybyl software [17]). The normal distribution of predicted ADME properties was validated, and a heterogeneous target library size (300-3,000) was set. The resulted 19 synthetic libraries have novel, drug-like and diverse Markush (core) structures. The libraries were synthesized using well-defined building block pools in multiple synthesis steps, and they represent a wide variety of chemistry. All of the 30,000 compounds have high purity (>85%). The structure collection, therefore, is suitable for *in vitro* experiments and finally for model building purposes.

4.2   Determination of *in vitro* Human Fibroblast Cytotoxicity

The cytotoxicity of the compounds is expressed as IC_{50} values, the concentration of the compound that kills half of the cells within a specific time (in our case in one day). The particular compound is added to the cell samples in 4 different concentrations, in duplicates. The samples are incubated for 24 hours, and then alamarBlue^{TM} is added in the concentration specified by the manufacturer. Subsequently, the samples are incubated for additional 4 hours prior to fluorimetric detection. Percentage cell death is determined for each sample, and the IC_{50} value is calculated using an automatic algorithm.

5   Case Studies for Earlier Solutions

Under the frame of a multiyear project at ComGenex 5 to 10,000 compounds had to be synthesized per month. For this purposes every month 11 new combinatorial libraries in average had to be developed. The key step of the design procedure is the selection of the building blocks with favourable ADME properties. There are altogether 14 predicted properties taken into account, which are divided into 4 groups, as follows:

- 1st group: pK_a, logP, logD
- 2nd group: metabolites, first pass effect, toxicity
- 3rd group: MW, rotatable bonds, HBDC (Hydrogen Bond Donor Count), HBAC (Hydrogen Bond Acceptor Count), HBD groups, HBA groups
- 4th group: solubility, CHI index

In the present case study 70,000 compounds were generated for selection of 7,000 to 15,000 synthesis candidates (taking into account that the effectivity of the synthesis is ca 70%).

Actually, the building block selection is a multistep procedure, where the druggability and the ADME properties have to be considered besides many other aspects (like synthesizability, potential activity, diversity, etc.). The final selection step requires involving experts from the different partners participating in the development. Biweekly internet-based discussion sessions are organized for this purpose, normally scheduled for 40 Minutes. In case of any changes in the building block lists, the corresponding new structures have to be generated, and their properties have to be calculated to be able to make the decision. If the results are not ready during the meeting, it postpones the decision, and consequently the start of the production with at least 2 weeks. There have been much effort done to develop solutions that are quick enough to respond to this challenge; now we outline 2 of them:

5.1 Parallel Solution, 1999–2001

We used 4 high-speed computers, and each group of properties was calculated in a separate computer. The rate limiting calculation is metabolism prediction, because in average 10 metabolites/parent compound is generated, so in the present case approximately 700,000 metabolites were generated.

The time needed for the calculation was 4 days.

5.2 Cluster Solution, 2001–2003

In the ComGenex PC cluster we used 40 computers, and the Enterprise calculator, an inhouse software for distributed calculations. The cluster was scheduled to automatic calculation working only at nights.

The capacity of the system is 50,000 compounds/night, so the time needed for the calculation was 2 nights.

5.3 Conclusions of Case Studies

Before the decision making Web meeting a preliminary calculation were made on the CGX cluster. 7 experts attended the decision session from Europe and US West Coast. They selected the appropriate building blocks, but the final collection were not enough to realize the targeted number compounds, therefore they suggested additional building blocks. Using the new building blocks a new set of structures had to be generated (enumerated). 1 additional night was needed for the property prediction. As a consequence, the meeting had to be postponed to the following week due to the lack of ADME properties.

6 Summary

The system will analyze millions of structures in a considerable time using the obtained QSAR/QSPR equations with traditional and grid based computation procedures, and select the most promising hits from this huge virtual chemical domain. OpenMolGRID enables highly specialized experts from several continents to make immediate decisions in the library design phase during a net meeting.

A further development possibility is to extend the knowledge managing tools and facilities, incorporating large discovery related knowledge management systems, like Emil (Example-Mediated Innovation for Lead Evolution [16]).

Acknowledgements

The development of OpenMolGRID is partially supported by the European Commission under the 5th Framework Project (IST-2001-37238).

Thanks for colleagues from the following partners involved in the project:

- University of Tartu, Tartu, Estonia
- University of Ulster, Ulster, Northern Ireland
- Mario Negri Institute, Milano, Italy
- Forschungszentrum Jülich, Jülich, Germany

References

1. Darvas, F.; Keserű, G. M.; Papp, Á.; Dormán, G.; Ürge, L.; Krajcsi, P. In Silico and Ex Silico ADME Approaches for Drug Discovery, Curr. Top. in Med. Chem. **2** (2002) 1269-1277
2. Lipinski, C. A. Drug-like properties and the causes of poor solubility and poor permeability. J Pharmacol. Toxicol. Methods. **44(1)** (2000) 235-49
3. Kramer, S. D. Absorption prediction from physicochemical parameters. Pharm. Sci. Technol. Today **2** (1999) 373-380
4. Matter, H.; Baringhaus, K.-H.; Naumann, T.; Klaubunde, T.; Pirard B. Computational Approaches towards the Rational Design of Drug-like Compound Libraries. Comb. Chem & HTS **4** (2001) 453-475
5. Ghose, A. K.; Vishwanadhan, V. N.; Wendoloshki, J. J. A Knowledge-Based Approach in Designing Combinatorial or Medicinal Chemistry Libraries for Drug Discovery. 1. A Qualitative and Quantitative Characterization of Known Drug Databases. J. Comb. Chem. **1** (1999) 55-68
6. van de Waterbeemd, H.; Kansy, M. Hydrogen-Bonding Capacity and Brain Penetration, Chimia **46** (1992) 299-303
7. Palm, K.; Luthmann, K.; Ungell, A. L.; Strandlund, G.; Artursson, P. Correlation of Drug Absorption with Molecular Surface Properties. J. Pharm. Sci. **85** (1996) 32-39
8. Clark, D. E. Prediction of Intestinal Absorption and Blood-Brain Barrier Penetration by Computational Methods. Comb. Chem. & HT. Scr. **4** (2001) 477-496
9. Csizmadia, F.; Szegezdi, J.; Darvas, F. Expert system approaches for predicting pKa. Trends in QSAR and Molecular Modeling 92, Escom, Leiden (1993) pp. 507-510
10. Martin, Y. C.; Duban, M. E.; Bures, M. G.; DeLazzer, J. Virtual Screening of Molecular Properties: A Comparison of LogP Calculators. In Pharmacokinetic Optimization in Drug Research, Official publication of the logP2000 Symposium, VHCA – VCH, Zürich (2000), pp 485
11. Csizmadia, F.; Tsantili-Kakoulidou, A.; Panderi, I.; Darvas, F, Prediction of Distribution Coefficient from Structure 1. Estimation Method. J. Pharm. Sci., 1997, 86(7), 865-871

12. Valko, K.; Bevan C.; Reynolds. Chromatographic Hydrophobicity Index by Fast-Gradient RP-HPLC: A High-Throughput Alternative to logP/logD. Anal. Chem. **69** (1997) 2022-2029

13. Darvas, F.; Marokházy, S.; Kormos, P.; Kulkarni, G.; Kalász, H.; Papp, Á. MetabolExpert: Its Use in Metabolism Research and in Combinatorial Chemistry. In: Drug Metabolism: Databases and High-Throughput Screening Testing During Drug Design and Development, (Ed. Erhardt PW), Backwell Publisher (1999) pp. 237-270

14. The project homepage can be found at www.openmolgrid.org

15. Details can be found at www.unicore.org

16. Fujita T., Concept and Features of EMIL, a System for Lead Evolution of Bioactive Compounds, in "Trends in QSAR and Molecular Modelling 92" (Ed. C. G. Wermuth) Escom, Leiden (1993) pp.143-159

17. Sybyl software is a trademark of Tripos, Inc.

Integration of Blood Flow Visualization on the Grid: The FlowFish/GVK Approach*

Alfredo Tirado-Ramos[1], Hans Ragas[1], Denis Shamonin[1], Herbert Rosmanith[2], and Dieter Kranzmueller[2]

[1] Faculty of Sciences, Section Computational Science
University of Amsterdam
Kruislaan 403, 1098 SJ Amsterdam, The Netherlands
{alfredo,jmragas,dshamoni}@science.uva.nl
[2] GUP, Joh. Kepler University Linz
Altenbergerstr. 69, A-4040 Linz, Austria/Europe
{rosmanith,kranzlmueller}@gup.jku.at

Abstract. We have developed the FlowFish package for blood flow visualization of vascular disorder simulations, such as aneurysms and stenosis. We use a Lattice-Boltzmann solver for flow process simulation to test the efficiency of the visualization classes, and experiment with the combination of grid applications and corresponding visualization clients on the European Crossgrid testbed, to assess grid accessability and visualization data transfer performance.

Keywords: computational grids, blood flow visualization, grid-based visualization, blood flow simulation, problem solving environment, grid portal

1 Introduction

Experience shows that even during simple simulations of real life problems in an environment of reduced complexity, large amounts of computed data must be analysed. Nevertheless, numerical or analytical analysis is not always possible. Computers can help to handle these large amounts of data by using automatic feature extraction, but it is often hard to define exact parameters, and it is difficult to describe an algorithm which extracts useful information from classifications of any kind [1]. A good example is offered by Trotts et al, who have shown a hybrid form of critical point classification and visualization applied to the investigation of flowfields [2].

This extended abstract briefly describes our FlowFish/Grid Visualization Kernel (GVK) approach to blood flow visualization, and then focuses on the initial integration of this work in a PSE running on a computational Grid. GVK is a middleware developed at GUP Linz within the European CrossGrid project [3], which aims to enable the use of visualization services within computational

---

* This research is partly funded by the European Commission IST-2001-32243 Project CrossGrid.

M. Dikaiakos (Ed.): AxGrids 2004, LNCS 3165, pp. 77–79, 2004.

grids [4]. Furthermore, we have extended the FlowFish/GVK functionality by integrating it with a Grid portal provided by the CrossGrid project. We have found during our initial integration efforts that integration of our testbed and visualization libraries are not a trivial task, but the added functionality and security infrastructure offered by grid technologies come at a minimal performance payoff. For further information beyond the scope of this abstract, please contact the authors.

2 FlowFish and the Grid Visualization Kernel

The FlowFish libraries for Flow visualization are developed as part of the simulated Virtual Radiology Explorer PSE project of the University of Amsterdam. The aim of this project is to provide a surgeon with an intuitive environment to visualize and explore a patient's vascular condition prior to intervention. By placing her in an interactive virtual simulation environment, a surgeon or radiologist can examine the patient's bloodflow in a non-invasive mode. FlowFish enables the employment of investigation methods which cannot be used in the original environment of the flow. To test a hypothesis, different surgical procedures can be applied while surgeons can monitor direction, speed and pressure of the bloodflow through the human vascular system.

Furthermore, the Grid Visualization Kernel (GVK) [5], a grid aware application built on top of the FlowFish libraries, addresses the combination of grid applications and corresponding visualization clients on the grid. While grids offer a means to process large amounts of data across different, possibly distant resources, visualization aids in understanding the meaning of data. For this reason, the visualization capabilities of GVK are implemented using Globus [6] services, thereby providing flexible grid visualization services via dedicated interfaces and protocols while at the same time exploiting the performance of the grid for visualization purposes.

3 Integration with the CrossGrid Computational Grid Portal

We have experimented with extending our work on medical data simulation and visualization to the Grid via the Migrating Desktop (MD) [7] grid portal. MD is an application that offers a seamless Grid portal which is independent of software and hardware environments, on which applications and resources may be highly distributed. It allows users to handle Grid and local resources, run applications, manage data files, and store personal settings. The MD provides a front-end framework for embedding some of the application mechanisms and interfaces, and allows the user virtual access to Grid resources from other computational nodes.

4 Results and Discussion

In order to integrate our visualization libraries to the computational grid testbed, we dynamically linked application XML schema for job submission to the MD grid portal. We created links within the MD to initialization of both the GVK client and server startup applications, and experimented with rendering the flow both remotely and locally in the access storage element. This way, GVK remote visualization and local rendering are fully linked via the MD. We integrated our local desktop visualization and mesh creation application with GVK, configuring VTK and other relevant libraries, and registered Amsterdam and Leiden sites for testing secure grid data transfer. We experimented with the transfer of a few segmented medical datasets, ranging from 24252 Byte to 5555613 Byte loads. When comparing the transfer times of the data, at time steps of 20 seconds, we found that average transfer times to both Linux and Windows roaming storage elements running nodes, once taking into account the Globus caching mechanism, did not vary much above 200 milliseconds for the smaller size files and no more than 350 miliseconds for the larger size files. We considered these initial figures encouraging, though we plan more extensive testing with streaming flow data.

For our next integration steps, we will work on full integration with CrossGrid replication services, as well as experiment with the advanced MPI support and monitoring functionalities that will allow us to fine-tune, monitor on the fly, and predict better performance results for our solver, on-line.

Acknowledgments. We would like to thank Peter Sloot, Abdel Artoli, Jens Volkert, Paul Heinzlreiter, Alfons Hoekstra, Elena Zudilova, Marcin Plociennik, and Pawel Wolniewicz for their meaningful contributions to this work.

References

1. A. Schoneveld. *Parallel Complex Systems Simulation*. PhD thesis, University of Amsterdam, Amsterdam, The Netherlands, 1999. Promotor: Prof. Dr. P.M.A. Sloot.
2. I. Trotts, D. Kenwright, and R. Haimes. Critical points at infinity: a missing link in vector field topology.
3. CrossGrid - Development of Grid Environment for interactive Applications, EU Project, IST-2001-32243, http://www.eu-crossgrid.org
4. I. Foster, C. Kesselman, S. Tuecke. The Anatomy of the Grid: Enabling Scalable Virtual Organizations International J. Supercomputer Applications, 15(3), 2001.
5. Sloot P.M.A., van Albada G.D., Zudilova E.V., Heinzlreiter P., Kranzlmüller D., Rosmanith H., Volkert J. Grid-based Interactive Visualisation of Medical Images S. Norager, editor, Proceedings of the First European HealthGrid Conference, January 2003, pp. 57 - 66. Commissi on of the European Communities, Information Society Directorate-General, Brussels, Belgium.
6. I. Foster, C. Kesselman. Globus: A Metacomputing Infrastructure Toolkit Intl J. Supercomputer Applications, 11(2):115-128, 1997.
7. http://ras.man.poznan.pl/crossgrid/

A Migration Framework
for Executing Parallel Programs in the Grid*

József Kovács and Péter Kacsuk

MTA SZTAKI, Parallel and Distributed Systems Laboratory,
1518 Budapest, P.O. Box 63, Hungary
{smith,kacsuk}@sztaki.hu

Abstract. The paper describes a parallel program checkpointing mechanism and its potential application in Grid systems in order to migrate applications among Grid sites. The checkpointing mechanism can automatically (without user interaction) support generic PVM programs created by the PGRADE Grid programming environment. The developed checkpointing mechanism is general enough to be used by any Grid job manager but the current implementation is connected to Condor. As a result, the integrated Condor/PGRADE system can guarantee the execution of any PVM program in the Grid. Notice that the Condor system can only guarantee the execution of sequential jobs. Integration of the Grid migration framework and the Mercury Grid monitor results in an observable Grid execution environment where the performance monitoring and visualization of PVM applications are supported even when the PVM application migrates in the Grid.

1   Introduction

An important aspect of executing a parallel program in the Grid [5] is job migration. The Grid is an inherently dynamic and error prone execution environment. The optimal selection of a Grid resource for a particular job does not mean that the selected resource remains optimal for the whole execution of the job. The selected resource could be overloaded by newly submitted higher priority jobs or even worse, it can go down partially or completely due to some hardware or software errors. These are situations that should be solved by the Grid middleware transparently to the user. Process migration in distributed systems is a special event when a process running on a resource is redeployed on another one in a way that the migration does not cause any change in the process execution. It means the process is not restarted; its execution is temporarily suspended and later resumed on a new resource. In order to provide this capability special techniques are necessary to save the total memory image of the target process and to reconstruct it. This technique is called checkpointing. During checkpointing a tool suspends the execution of the process, collects all those internal status information necessary for resumption and terminates the process. Later it creates a new process and all the collected information is restored for the process to continue its execution without any modification.

* The work presented in this paper has been supported by the Hungarian Chemistrygrid OMFB-00580/2003 project, the Hungarian Supergrid OMFB-00728/2002 project, the Hungarian IHM 4671/1/2003 project and the Hungarian Research Fund No. T042459.

M. Dikaiakos (Ed.): AxGrids 2004, LNCS 3165, pp. 80–89, 2004.

Migration mechanism can be advantageously used in several scenarios. First, in supercomputing applications load-balancing is a crucial issue. Migration can solve the problem of unbalanced parallel sites of the Grid. Processes on overloaded machines can be migrated to underloaded machines without terminating the entire application. Similarly, load-balancing can be ensured among different sites of the Grid, i.e., when a site becomes overloaded complete applications can migrate to other sites. The second situation is related to high-throughput computing where free cycles of underloaded machines are collected. In such a scenario the owner of the Grid site has got always priority over the guest applications and hence all the guest applications should be removed from the site when the owner increases the usage of the site. Third, the migration module can be used for the sake of providing fault-tolerance capability. During the execution of a long-running application, one machine may be corrupted or needs system maintenance. Fourth, migration can be driven by resource needs, i.e. processes can be moved in order to access special unmovable or local resources. For example, processes may need the usage of special equipments or huge databases existing on a dedicated machine of the Grid.

A migration tool typically consists of a checkpoint server, checkpoint information store and a checkpoint library. To provide fault-tolerance, application-wide checkpoint saving is performed, i.e., checkpoint information are stored into files for roll-back if necessary. These files are maintained by a checkpoint server and written/read by the checkpoint library attached to the process to be migrated. There are several existing libraries performing sequential program checkpointing like esky [4] libckpt [11] condor [9] or the one integrated in our system, Zandy's ckpt library [14]. To start checkpointing the checkpoint libraries should be notified and checkpointed/resumed processes need to be managed. In our proposed solution it is done by a migration co-ordination module built into the application. It checkpoints, terminates and restarts processes belonging to the application. Since this co-ordination module is responsible for keeping the application alive at all time by reconstructing terminated processes using available nodes of the cluster, this structure provides a fault-tolerant application that adopts itself to the dynamically changing execution environment.

Beyond the execution of a parallel program another important aspect of a Grid end-user - among others - is the creation of a Grid program. Unfortunately, there are no widely accepted graphical tools for high-level development to create parallel applications. This is exactly the aim of the PGRADE (Parallel Grid Run-time and Application Development Environment) Grid programming environment that has been developed by MTA SZTAKI. PGRADE currently generates either PVM or MPI code from the same graphical notation according to the users' needs. It may also support any kind of middleware layer which is going to be released in the future, like the GAT (Grid Application Toolkit) that is under design in the EU Gridlab project.

In order to prove the concept presented in this paper it has been integrated with PGRADE. Recently, the solution has been presented in a live demonstration on the EuroPar 2003 conference.

2 Structure of the Parallel Application

In order to understand the realisation of the checkpoint and migration mechanism [7], a short summary of the execution mechanism (shown in Fig. 1) is required. PGRADE

compiler generates [3] executables which contain the code of the client processes defined by the user and an extra process, called as grapnel server which is coordinating the
run-time set-up of the application. The client processes at run-time logically contain the
user code, the message passing primitives and the Grapnel library that manages logical
connections among them. To set-up the application first the Grapnel Server comes to
live and then it creates the client processes containing the user computation.

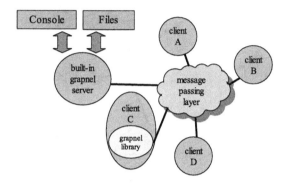

Fig. 1. Structure of the Grapnel Application Generated by PGRADE

As a result of the co-operation between the Grapnel Server and Grapnel library the
message passing communication topology is built up. To access all necessary input-
output files and the console, the Client processes ask the server to act on behalf of
them. The Client processes send requests to the server for reading and writing files and
console, and the necessary data are transferred when the action is finished by the server
on its executor host.

3   The Flow of Checkpoint Mechanism

The checkpointing procedure is maintained by the Grapnel library, so no modification
of the user code or the underlying message passing library is required to support process
and application migration. The Grapnel Server performs a consistent checkpoint of the
whole application where checkpoint files contain the state of the individual processes
including in-transit messages so the whole application can be rebuilt at any time and
on the appropriate site. The checkpoint system of a Grapnel application contains the
following elements (see Fig. 2):

1. Grapnel Server (GS): an extra co-ordination process that is part of the application
   and generated by PGRADE. It sets up the application by spawning the processes
   and defining the logical communication topology for them.
2. Grapnel library: a layer between the message passing library and the user code,
   automatically compiled with the application, co-operates with the server, performs
   preparation for the client process environment and provides a bridge between the
   server process and the user code.

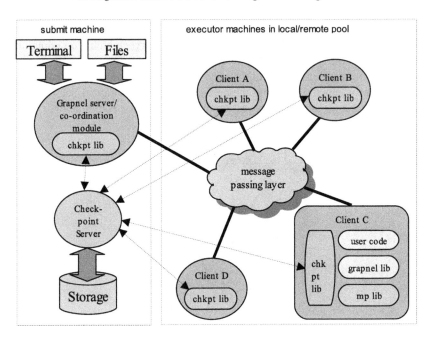

Fig. 2. Structure of Application in Checkpoint Mode

3. Checkpoint module in Grapnel library: in client processes it prepares for check-point, performs synchronisation of messages and re-establishes connection to the application after a process is rebuilt from checkpoint; in GS it coordinates the checkpointing activities of the client processes.
4. Dynamic checkpoint library: loaded at process start-up and activated by receiving a predefined chkpt signal, reads the process memory image and passes this infor-mation to the Checkpoint Server
5. Checkpoint Server: a component that receives data via socket and puts it into the chkpt file of the chkpt storage and vice versa.

Before starting the execution of the application, an instance of the Checkpoint Server (CS) is running in order to transfer checkpoint files to/from the dynamic check-point libraries linked to the application. Each process of the application at start-up loads automatically the checkpoint library that checks the existence of a previous checkpoint file of the process by connecting to the Checkpoint Server. If it finds a checkpoint file for the process, the resumption of the process is automatically initiated by restoring the process image from the checkpoint file otherwise, it starts from the beginning.

When the application launched, the first process that starts is the Grapnel Server (GS) performing the coordination of the Client processes. It starts spawning the Client processes. Whenever a process comes to alive, it first checks the checkpoint file and gets contacted to GS in order to download parameters, settings, etc. When each process has performed the initialisation, GS instructs them to start execution.

While the application is running and the processes are doing their tasks the migration mechanism is inactive. Migration is activated when a Client process detects that it is about to be killed (TERM signal). The Client process immediately informs GS which in turn initiates the checkpointing of all the Client processes of the application. For a Client process checkpointing is initialised either by a signal or by a checkpoint message sent by GS in order to make sure that all processes is notified regardless of performing calculation or communication. Notified processes initiate synchronisation of messages aiming at receiving all the in-transit messages and store them in the memory. Finally, Client processes send their memory image to the Checkpoint Server.

All checkpointed processes then wait for further instruction from GS whether to terminate or continue the execution. For terminated processes GS initiates new node allocations. When host allocations are performed, migrating processes are resumed on the allocated nodes.

Each migrated process automatically loads the checkpoint library that checks for the existence of a previous checkpoint file of the process by connecting to the Checkpoint Server. This time the migrated processes will find their checkpoint file and hence their resumption is automatically initiated by restoring the process image from the checkpoint file. The migrated processes first execute post-checkpoint instructions before resuming the real user code. The post-checkpoint instructions serve for initialising the message-passing layer and for registering at GS. When all the checkpointed and migrated processes are ready to run, GS allows them to continue their execution.

4   Process Migration Under Condor

The checkpoint system has been originally integrated with PVM in order to migrate PVM processes inside a cluster. However, in order to provide migration among clusters we have to integrate the checkpoint system with a Grid-level job manager that takes care of finding new nodes in other clusters of the Grid. Condor flocking [13] mechanism provides exactly this function among friendly Condor pools and hence the next step was to integrate the checkpoint system with Condor.

The basic principles of the fault-tolerant Condor MW type execution are that the Master process spawns workers to perform the calculation and it continuously watches whether the workers successfully finish their calculation. In case of failure the Master process simply spawns new workers passing the unfinished work to them.

The situation when a worker fails to finish its calculation usually comes from the fact that Condor removes the worker because the executor node is no longer available. This action is called vacation of the PVM process. In this case the master node receives a notification message indicating that a particular node has been removed from the PVM machine. As an answer the Master process tries to add new PVM host(s) to the virtual machine with the help of Condor, and gets notified when host inclusion is done successfully. At this time it spawns new worker(s).

For running a Grapnel application, the application continuously requires the minimum amount of nodes to execute the processes. Whenever the number of the nodes decreases below the minimum (which is exactly the number of the Grapnel client processes, since Condor-PVM executes only one process per PVM daemon), the Grapnel

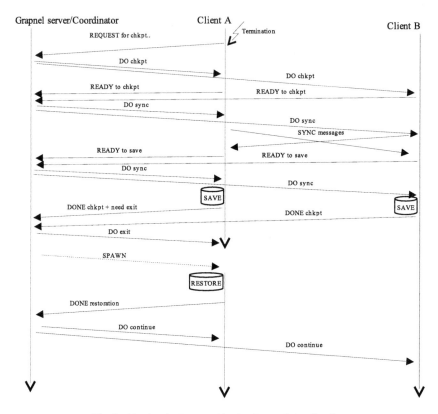

Fig. 3. Checkpoint Protocol in the Grapnel Application

Server (GS) tries to extend the number of PVM machines above the critical level. It means that the GS process works exactly the same way as the Master process does in the Condor MW system.

Under Condor the Master PVM process is always started on the submit machine and is running until the application is finished. It is not shut down by Condor, even if the submit machine becomes overloaded. Condor assumes that the Master process of the submitted PVM application is designed as a work distributor. The functionality of the Grapnel Server process fully meets this requirement, so Grapnel applications can be executed under Condor without any structural modification and the server can act as the coordinator of the checkpointing and migration mechanism just like it was described in the previous section.

Whenever a process is to be killed (see Fig. 3) (e.g. because its node is being vacated), an application-wide checkpoint must be performed and the exited process should be resumed on another node. The application-wide checkpointing is driven by GS, but it can be initiated by any client process which detects that Condor tries to kill it. In this case the client process notifies GS to perform a checkpoint. After this notification GS sends the DO_chkpt signal or message to every client process. After checkpointing all the client processes wait for further instruction from the server whether to terminate

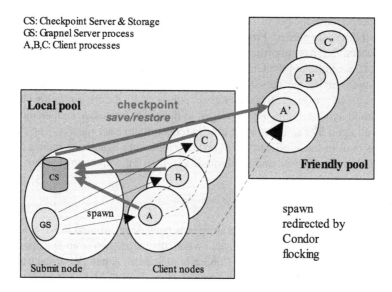

CS: Checkpoint Server & Storage
GS: Grapnel Server process
A,B,C: Client processes

Fig. 4. Checkpoint and Migration Under Condor

or continue the execution. GS sends a terminate signal to those processes that should migrate.

At this point GS waits for the decision of Condor that tries to find underloaded nodes either in the home Condor pool of the submit machine or in a friendly Condor pool. The resume phase is performed only when the PVM master process (GS) receives notification from Condor about new host(s) connected to the PVM virtual machine. When every terminated process is migrated to a new node allocated by Condor, the application can continue its execution according to the protocol shown in Figure 4. This working mode enables the PVM application to continuously adapt itself to the changing PVM virtual machine by migrating processes from the machines being vacated to some new ones that have just been added. Figure 4. shows the main steps of the migration between friendly Condor pools. Notice that the Grapnel Server and Checkpoint Server processes remain in the submit machine of the home pool even if every client process of the application migrate to another pool.

5   Application Level Migration by a Global Application Manager

Condor flocking cannot be applied in generic Grid systems where the pools (clusters) are separated by firewalls and hence global Grid job managers should be used. In such systems if the cluster is overloaded, i.e., the local job manager cannot allocate nodes to replace the vacated nodes; the whole application should migrate to another less loaded cluster of the Grid. It means that not only the client process but even the Grapnel Server should leave the overloaded cluster. We call this kind of migration as total migration opposing the partial migration where the Grapnel Server does not migrate.

In order to leave the pool - i.e. migrate the whole application to another pool - two extra capabilities are needed. First of all, an upper layer, called a Grid Application Manager is needed that has submitted the application and is able to recognise the situation when a total migration of the Grapnel application to another pool is required. Secondly, the checkpoint saving mechanism should include the server itself, i.e., after checkpointing all the client processes, the server checkpoints itself. Before server checkpoint, the server should avoid sending any messages to the client processes and should store the status of all open files in order to be able to reopen them after resume. The checkpoint support is built in the application; the rest e.g. removing from local queue, file movements, resource reselection and resubmission is task of the upper grid layers.

6   Demonstration Scenario

The migration mechanism described above has been demonstrated in Klagenfurt at the EuroPar'2003 conference. Three clusters were connected (two from Budapest and one from London) to provide a friendly Condor pool system. A parallel urban traffic simulation application was launched from Klagenfurt on the SZTAKI cluster.

Then the cluster was artificially overloaded and Condor recognising the situation vacated the nodes of the cluster. The Grapnel Server of PGRADE controlled the checkpointing of the application and then asked Condor to allocate new resources for the application processes. Condor has found the Westminster cluster and PGRADE migrated all the processes except the Grapnel Server to Westminster University. After resuming the application at Westminster we artificially overloaded the Westminster cluster and as a result the application was migrated to the last underloaded cluster of the system at the Technical University of Budapest. The Grid migration framework, the Mercury Grid monitor and the PROVE visualization tool were integrated inside the PGRADE Grid run-time environment. As a result the migration of the PVM application was on-line monitored and visualized.

Regarding the performance of checkpointing overall time spent for migration are checkpoint writing, reading, allocation of new resources and some coordination overhead. The time spent for writing or reading the checkpoint information through a TCP/IP connection definitely depends on the size of the process to be checkpointed and the bandwidth of the connection between the nodes where the process including the checkpoint library and the checkpoint server are running. The overall time a complete migration of a process takes also includes the responding time of the resource scheduling system e.g. while Condor vacates a machine, the matchmaking mechanism finds a new resource, allocates it, initialises pvmd and notifies the application. Finally, cost of synchronisation of messages and some cost used for coordination processing are negligible, less than one percent of the overall migration time.

7   Conclusions

The main contributions of the paper can be summarised as follows:

1. We developed a parallel program checkpointing mechanism that can be applied to generic PVM programs.

2. We showed how such checkpointing mechanism can be connected with Condor in order to realize migration of PVM jobs among Condor pools.
3. We also showed that by integrating our Grid migration framework and the Mercury Grid monitor PVM applications can be performance monitored and visualized even during their migration.

As a consequence, the integrated Condor/PGRADE system can guarantee the execution of any PVM job in Condor-based Grid systems and the user can observe the execution of the PVM job no matter where it is executed and how many times it was migrating in the Grid. Notice that the Condor system can only guarantee the execution of sequential jobs and special Master/Worker PVM jobs and provides only the observability of status changes of those jobs. In case of generic PVM jobs Condor cannot guarantee anything. Therefore, the developed checkpointing mechanism and its integration with the Mercury monitor significantly extend the robustness and observability of Condor-based Grid systems.

More than that, the developed checkpoint mechanism can be applied for other Grid job managers like SGE, etc., hence providing a generic migration framework for any possible Grid system where PVM programs should migrate among different multiprocessor based Grid sites like clusters and supercomputers.

Though there are many existing parallel PVM programs, undoubtedly MPI is more popular than PVM. Hence, supporting the migration of MPI programs would also be very important. In 2004, we will start a new project in which we are going to adopt the developed checkpointing mechanism even for MPI programs.

Condor [9], MPVM [1], DPVM [2], Fail-Safe PVM [8], CoCheck [12] are further software systems supporting adaptive parallel application execution including checkpointing and migration facility. The main drawbacks of these systems are that they are modifying PVM, build complex executing system, require special support, need root privileges, require predefined topology, need operating system support, etc. Contrary to these systems our solution makes parallel applications be capable of being checkpointed, migrated or executed in a fault tolerant way on specific level and we do not require any support from execution environment or PVM.

The migration facility presented in this paper does not even need any modification either in the message-passing layer or in the scheduling and execution system. In the current solution the checkpointing mechanism is an integrated part of PGRADE, so the current system only supports parallel applications created by the PGRADE environment. However, the described checkpoint and migration framework is generic enough to separate it from PGRADE and provide it as a generic solution for the Grid. In the future we are going to create this standalone solution, too.

References

1. J. Casas, D. Clark, R. Konuru, S. Otto, R. Prouty, and J. Walpole, "MPVM: A Migration Transparent Version of PVM", Technical Report CSE-95-002, 1, 1995.
2. L. Dikken, F. van der Linden, J.J.J. Vesseur, and P.M.A. Sloot, "DynamicPVM: Dynamic Load Balancing on Parallel Systems", In W.Gentzsch and U. Harms, editors, Lecture notes in computer sciences 797, High Performance Computing and Networking, volume Proceedings Volume II, Networking and Tools, pages 273-277, Munich, Germany, April 1994. Springer Verlag.

3. D. Drótos, G. Dózsa, and P. Kacsuk, "GRAPNEL to C Translation in the GRADE Environment",Parallel Program Development for Cluster Comp.Methodology,Tools and Integrated Environments, Nova Science Publishers, Inc. pp. 249-263, 2001.
4. esky: A user-space checkp. system, http://ozlabs.org/people/dgibson/esky/esky.html
5. I. Foster, C. Kesselman, S. Tuecke, "The Anatomy of the Grid." Enabling Scalable Virtual Organizations, Intern. Journal of Supercomputer Applications, 15(3), 2001.
6. P. Kacsuk, "Visual Parallel Programming on SGI Machines", Invited paper, Proc. of the SGI Users Conference, Krakow, Poland, pp. 37-56, 2000.
7. J. Kovács and P. Kacsuk, "Server Based Migration of Parallel Applications", Proc. of DAPSYS'2002, Linz, pp. 30-37, 2002.
8. J. Leon, A. L. Fisher, and P. Steenkiste, "Fail-safe PVM: a portable package for distributed programming with transparent recovery". CMU-CS-93-124. February, 1993.
9. M. Litzkow, T. Tannenbaum, J. Basney, and M. Livny, "Checkpoint and Migration of UNIX Processes in the Condor Distributed Processing System", Technical Report #1346, Computer Sciences Department, University of Wisconsin, April 1997.
10. PGRADE Parallel Grid Run-time and Application Development Environment: http://www.lpds.sztaki.hu/pgrade
11. J.S. Plank, M.Beck, G. Kingsley, and K.Li, "Libckpt: Transparent checkpointind under Unix", In Proc. of Usenix Technical Conference 1995, New Orleans, LA, Jan. 1995.
12. G. Stellner, "Consistent Checkpoints of PVM Applications", In Proc. 1st Euro. PVM Users Group Meeting, 1994.
13. D. Thain, T. Tannenbaum, and M. Livny, "Condor and the Grid", in Fran Berman, Anthony J.G. Hey, Geoffrey Fox, editors, Grid Computing: Making The Global Infrastructure a Reality, John Wiley, 2003.
14. http://www.cs.wisc.edu/~zandy/ckpt

Implementations of a Service-Oriented Architecture on Top of Jini, JXTA and OGSI

Nathalie Furmento, Jeffrey Hau, William Lee,
Steven Newhouse, and John Darlington

London e-Science Centre, Imperial College London, London SW7 2AZ, UK
lesc-staff@doc.ic.ac.uk

Abstract. This paper presents the design of an implementation-independent, Service-Oriented Architecture (SOA), which is the main basis of the ICENI Grid middleware. Three implementations of this architecture have been provided on top of Jini, JXTA and the Open Grid Services Infrastructure (OGSI). The main goal of this paper is to discuss these different implementations and provide an analysis of their advantages and disadvantages.

Keywords: Service-Oriented Architecture, Grid Middleware, Jini, JXTA, OGSI

1 Introduction

Service-oriented architectures are widely used in the Grid Community. These architectures provide the ability to register, discover, and use services, where the architecture is dynamic in nature. From all the initiatives to define standards for the Grid, a consensus seems to emerge towards the utilisation of such an architecture, as we can for example see with the OGSI initiative of the Global Grid Forum [4].

The ICENI Grid Middleware [5] is based on a service-oriented architecture (SOA) as well as on an augmented component programming model [6]. The goal of this paper is to show how the SOA has been designed to be implementation-independent. This gives us an open model where different low-level libraries can be plugged in.

The following of the paper is organised as follows. §2 shows in details the design of the Service-Oriented Architecture, the different implementations are explained in §3. A discussion on the current implementations is presented in §4, before concluding in §5.

2 Design of the ICENI's SOA

A typical Service-Oriented Architecture is presented in Figure 1. One can see three fundamental aspects of such an architecture:

1. *Advertising*. The Service Provider makes the service available to the Service Broker.

M. Dikaiakos (Ed.): AxGrids 2004, LNCS 3165, pp. 90–99, 2004.

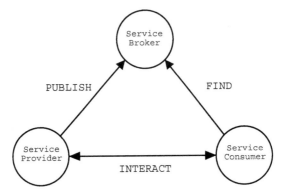

Fig. 1. The Service-Oriented Architecture

2. *Discovery.* The Service Consumer finds a specific Service using the Service Broker.
3. *Interaction.* The Service Consumer and the Service Provider interact.

In the context of ICENI, a Service Broker is represented by a public Computational Community or *Virtual Organisation*, where authorised end-users – the Service Consumers – can connect by using their X.509 certificates to query and access services. Once a service is advertised and discovered, any interaction with it is controlled by the service level agreement (SLA) that is going to define the entities that are allowed or denied access to the service, as well as the interval time the access is allowed or denied.

The lifetime of an ICENI service can be described by the three following steps: creation, advertising and discovery. Each of these steps is represented in ICENI by a set of interfaces. We are now going to explain these different steps and demonstrate them through a basic Counter Service.

2.1 Creation

A service is defined by its interface, i.e. the list of methods it provides. For example, the interface and the implementation of a counter service providing basic functionalities to add and subtract a value can be defined as shown in § A.

It is important at this level to notice there is no information on how the service is going to be implemented. We will see in the following sections how this abstract ICENI service is going to be implemented by using for example the Jini library.

The instantiation of the service is done through a call to the `IceniService-MetaFactory`, which first instantiates a `IceniServiceFactory` for the used implementation, and asks this factory to return a new instance of the service. At that point, all the necessary classes to implement the abstract ICENI service are automatically generated. Calling for example the following line of code results in the creation of an ICENI service of the type `Counter`.

```
IceniService xServ = IceniServiceMetaFactory.newInstance("Counter");
```

2.2   Advertising

Once created, a service can be advertised on a specific domain or virtual organisation through the `IceniServiceAdvertizingManager` service. The service is advertised with a SLA that defines the access policy that will be used to enforce interaction with the service. The same service can be advertised in different organisations with different SLA's. This gives a flexible mechanism to control how different organisations may access the service, by allowing advertising the service capabilities as required.

The advertising of a service is done through a XML document that defines the SLA's of the service for all the virtual organisations where the service is to be made available. Appendix A shows a SLA XML document that gives access from Monday to Friday noon to all the persons connecting from the virtual organisation *public1* and belonging to the organisation *eScience*.

2.3   Discovery

By connecting to a virtual organisation, a service consumer can query a service and interact with it once discovered. ICENI provides different types of query such as interface matching that allow to listen to all services of a specific interface, or service data matching that allow to query services based on the value of their service data elements. The different steps to discover services are shown in Figure 2.

---

1. Instantiate a discovery manager.

   ```
   IceniServiceDiscoveryManager xDiscovery =
                   IceniServiceDiscoveryManagerFactory.newInstance();
   xDiscovery.setLocation("<address of virtual organisation>");
   ```

2. Instantiate a discovery query. Here we use the instantiation mechanism based on the interface of the service to listen to.

   ```
   IceniServiceDiscoveryQuery xQueryCounter =
                   IceniServiceDiscoveryQueryFactory.newInstance(CounterService.class);
   ```

3. Register a listener. For every new service matching the query, the **service-Published()** method will be called with the service as a parameter. Similarly, the **serviceUnpublished()** method will be called for each service disappearing from the virtual organisation.

   ```
   xDiscovery.registerListener(xQueryCounter, new IceniServiceDiscoveryListener() {
     public void servicePublished(IceniService pService) {
       // code to execute when a new service is available
     } // end servicePublished
     public void serviceUnpublished(IceniServiceId pServiceId) {
       // code to execute when a service is no longer available
     } // end serviceUnpublished
   });
   ```

Fig. 2. Discovery and Interaction with ICENI Services

2.4   Invocation

Any interaction with the service is controlled by an external entity, it first authenticates the service consumer through its X.509 certificate and authorises it against the policy of the service it wishes to access.

2.5   Other Requirements

On top of defining an interface, ICENI services also define a set of service data elements. A service data element is defined through a name and a value, the value being either a simple string or a well-formed XML document. These elements also define a liability time interval by specifying from when to when the service data is expected to be valid. Service Data elements are for example used by the JXTA implementation to perform discovery (See § 3.2), and are similar to the service data notion of OGSI (See § 3.3).

One of the main concerns in grid middleware is that security should be present at any level of the infrastructure. We need to provide basic security for remote calls such as mutual authentication, authorisation and integrity. We also need to know that the code downloaded across a network can be trusted. The SOA of ICENI provides an authentication and authorisation model which allows to check the access to its services, but this model needs to be extended into a full security model in order to be used in any production Grid. Applications such as health care applications dealing with patient records require strong security and encryption mechanisms.

3   Implementation of the ICENI's SOA

This section reviews the three different implementations of the ICENI's SOA by showing for each of them how the different aspects of the SOA have been implemented, as well as its advantages and disadvantages.

3.1   Implementation Using Jini

Jini network technology [11] is an open architecture that enables developers to build adaptive networks that are scalable, evolvable and flexible as typically required in dynamic computing environments. The first version of the ICENI Grid Middleware was directly implemented on top of the Jini API [7].

When using Jini, the following classes are automatically generated for a service named MyService.

- **MyServiceJiniNoAbstract.java** extends the implementation of the service MyService to provide an implementation for all the basic ICENI/Jini mechanisms.
- **MyServiceJiniStub.java** is the main Jini interface extending the interface java.rmi.Remote. It acts as a proxy for MyService service, and defines exactly the same methods.

- **MyServiceJiniStubImpl.java** is the implementation of the interface My-
  ServiceJiniStub. It uses a reference to `MyServiceJiniNoAbstract` to redi-
  rect all the method calls on the service.
- **MyServiceJini.java** implements the interface `MyService` by using a refer-
  ence to `MyServiceJiniStub` toredirect an ICENI service's method call as a
  Jini service's method call.

Figure 3(a) shows an interaction diagram of these different classes and interfaces.

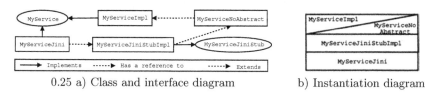

0.25 a) Class and interface diagram   b) Instantiation diagram

Fig. 3. Jini Implementation of an ICENI Service

Creation. This step creates an object of the class `MyServiceJini` and initialises
it with the corresponding stub, i.e. an instance of the class `MyServiceJiniStub-
Impl`. We obtain an object as shown in Figure 3b).

Advertising. The object `MyServiceJiniStubImpl` – hold by the ICENI service
created in the previous step – extends indirectly the interface `java.rmi.Remote`,
it can therefore be made available in a Jini lookup service.

Discovery. The object returned from the Jini lookup service is a
`MyServiceJiniStubImpl`. It is going to be wrapped in an instance of the class
`MyServiceJini` before being returned to the listener. We obtain here a similar
object to the one obtained when creating the service.

Invocation. Any method call is done on an instance of the class `MyServiceJini`
and is finally redirected on an instance of the class `MyServiceImpl` as one can
see in Figure 3.

Advantages/Disadvantages. The functionalities provided by the SOA of
ICENI and the Jini library are basically the same. It was therefore very easy
to implement the SOA on top of Jini without tying up ICENI to Jini and get
an implementation-independent SOA. Moreover, as shown in [8], the Jini implementation is very scalable, these experiments are testing the performance of Jini
when increasing the number of Jini services, they demonstrate a good result in
the performance when discovering and accessing the Jini services. The potential
problems when using Jini lie in security and in the connection of services across
firewalls.

3.2   Implementation Using JXTA

Project JXTA [14] provides a set of XML based protocols for establishing a virtual network overlay on top of current existing Internet and non-IP based networks. This standard set of common protocols defines the minimum network semantics for peers to join and form JXTA peergroups – a virtual network. Project JXTA enables application programmers to design network topology to best match their requirement. This ease of dynamically creating and transforming overlay network topology allows the deployment of virtual organisation.

The fundamental concept of the ICENI JXTA implementation is the ICENI peergroup. The ICENI peergroup provides a virtual ICENI space that all ICENI JXTA services join. The peergroup contains the core ICENI services – `Iceni-ServiceDiscoveryManager` and `IceniServiceAdvertizingManager`. These two services allow any services in the ICENI group to advertise their presence or to discover other services using ICENI ServiceData embodied in JXTA advertisements. Figure 4 presents an overview on how ICENI services behave when implemented on top of JXTA.

Creation. The creation of an ICENI service is just a matter of opening two separate JXTA pipes. Pipes are the standard communication channels in JXTA, they allow peers to receive and send messages. One of the two required pipes is a listening pipe that will listen for the control message broadcast to the whole ICENI peergroup. The other is the service's private ServicePipe. ServicePipes provides the communication channel for invocation messages. Depending on service functionality and requirement, these pipes could have varied properties such as encryption, single/dual-direction, propagation, streaming, . . .

Advertising. Once joined the ICENI peergroup, a service can advertise its presence by publishing its `ServiceData` elements. This is a two step process: (1) Create a new `IceniServiceAdvertisement`. This is a custom advertisement that contains the ICENI service identifier `IceniServiceID` and the service data `ServiceData`. The Service Id can be automatically generated during advertisement creation and `ServiceData` will be converted into XML format and embedded into the advertisement; (2) Publish the advertisement by using the `IceniServiceAdvertizingManager` service from the ICENI peergroup.

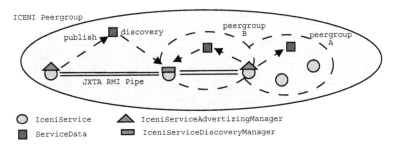

Fig. 4. JXTA Implementation of the SOA

Discovery. Peers in the ICENI peergroup can discover available services by using the `IceniServiceDiscoveryManager` service. Search can be conducted using service ID or service data elements.

Invocation. Invocation behaviour of ICENI JXTA services depends on the specific protocol each service is running. There are currently some projects working on providing different service architecture over JXTA such as JXTA-rmi [15] and JXTA-soap [16]. These projects wrap the original invocation messages (such as SOAP) into JXTA pipe messages and transport them through JXTA pipes to enable peers to invocate services using well-known service invocation API.

Advantages/Disadvantages. JXTA provides an architecture that gives middleware programmers the flexibility and ease of creating virtual organisations. It also provides an easy interface for publishing and discovering data in a peer to peer manner. Different invocation architectures can be overlayed over JXTA pipes. And finally, it is based on lightweight, firewall-proof, interchangeable network protocols. The potential problems with using JXTA as an architecture for building Grid middleware lies in security and performance. JXTA's P2P nature makes it harder to secure than traditional platforms. Also it will be difficult for the requirements of high performance grid application to be met by JXTA's current XML based messaging protocols.

3.3   Implementation Using OGSI

The Open Grid Services Infrastructure is an effort to build on the wide adoption of web services as an inter-operable foundation for distributed computing. The Grid Services Specification [17] describes a set of core port types using WSDL that are essential for the Grid setting. In ICENI, important notions of an `IceniService` are mapped to the relevant constructs in the `GridService` port type, such as meta-data as service data, and lease as termination time. Our implementation is based on the Globus Toolkit 3.0 [1] core distribution. It is the Java reference implementation of the Grid Services Specification. It allows Java objects to be deployed as OGSI services. The hosting environment acts as a SOAP processing engine that can be executed as an embedded HTTP server or operate as a Java Servlet inside a servlet engine. We have enhanced the implementation with an Application Programming Interface (API) for runtime dynamic deployment of service without the use of deployment descriptor. It serves as the kernel for the ICENI OGSI implementation.

Creation. To transparently transform an `IceniService` object into an OGSI-compliant service, the runtime system reflectively interrogate the class information of the service object and generate adapted classes that can be deployed through the deployment API. Adaptation is performed using the ASM byte-code generation library [3]. The adapted class is loaded from the byte stream into the running virtual machine using a specialised `ClassLoader`. The adapted object represents a service object that conforms to the requirement of GT3, such as an extension to the `GridServiceBase` interface. The adapted class acts solely as the delegate hosted by GT3 and directs invocation to the service object.

Advertising and Discovery. OGSI currently does not mandate a particular form of advertising and discovery mechanisms. We have chosen to use an instance of the `ServiceGroup` port type as a representation of a community. A `Service-Group` service is set up at a well-known location. When an `IceniService` is created, the Grid Service Handle of the OGSI-service representing this service object is published to the known `ServiceGroup`. Future implementations can experiment with using UDDI directory for long-lived services, such as Factory or Virtual Organisation Registry. For transient services, the Globus Toolkit 3.0 Index Service [2] can cater for the dynamic of temporal validity of service and its meta-data. Also, it provides a rich query mechanism for locating service instances based on their service data and port types.

Invocation. When a client locates an `IceniService` from the `IceniService-DiscoveryManager`, the OGSI implementation returns a Java Reflection Proxy implementing the interfaces expected by the client. The proxy traps all invocations on the object. The invocation handler uses the JAX-RPC [13] API to marshal the parameters into SOAP message parts based on the WSDL description of the service.

Advantages/Disadvantages. The OGSI-compliant implementation allows ICENI services and clients to communicate through an open transport and messaging layers instead of the proprietary RMI protocol used by Jini. Also, non-ICENI clients can interact with ICENI services as if they are OGSI-compliant services. The extensible nature of OGSI permits different transport and messaging protocols to be interchanged. Our current implementation uses the web service security standards for encrypting message as well as ensuring authenticity of the caller. One disadvantage of the current invocation model is that ICENI clients can only transparently invoke OGSI services that originate from an ICENI Service. This is due to the fact that the Java interface of the OGSI service is pre-established before the conversation. For ICENI client to invoke an external OGSI service, stubs need to be generated at compile-time, or the Dynamic Invocation Interface of the JAX-RPC API could be used instead. Other disadvantages are GT3 is resource hungry, we would need a lightweight OGSI implementation to provide a valid ICENI/OGSI implementation. Moreover, the XML to Java marshaling is expensive, not automatic for complex types, and as for JXTA, XML based messaging protocols cannot meet the requirements of high performance grid application.

4   Discussion

The three implementations we have presented all provide the basic functionalities needed by the ICENI Service-Oriented Architecture at different levels of implementation difficulty. The JINI implementation offers good performances, the two other implementations being based on XML messaging protocols are not as promising, but offer better security models. Working on these three implementations proved to be very beneficial as it showed us that a valid and robust

SOA can only be obtained by good performances and a powerful and extensible security model.

We believe that these concerns can be dealt with by using Jini 2.0 [12]. This new version of the Jini Network Technology provides a comprehensive security model which one of the main goals is to support pluggable invocation layer behaviour and pluggable transport provider. We could therefore use OGSI instead of RMI as a remote communication layer, and benefit of the encryption and authentication features of the web service security standard.

To allow our three implementations to inter-operate and hence be able of getting a virtual organisation composed for example of ICENI/Jini services and ICENI/JXTA services, we have developed a OGSA Gateway that allows ICENI services to be exposed as Grid Services [5]. This allows us for example the following configuration: use Jini inside a local organisation, and use JXTA to cross boundaries between networks potentially configured with firewalls.

In order to improve search capability of ICENI services, an adaptation framework is being developed. The ICENI Service Adaptation Framework [9] builds on top of ICENI middleware to provide ways of annotating services using Resource Description Framework (RDF) and The Web Ontology Language (OWL). Semantic annotated services enable users to search through capability rather than static interface definitions. Once user's requirement is semantically matched with a semantic service, an adaptation proxy conforming to user's interface requirement is automatically generated. The adaptation proxy provides a implementation and architecture independent way for both the client and the server to invoke the required functionality.

5   Conclusion

We have shown in this paper the design of a Service-Oriented Architecture for a Grid Middleware that is implementation-independent. This Service-Oriented Architecture has been successfully implemented on top of Jini. We are currently prototyping the JXTA and the OGSI implementations of the SOA.

These three implementations all provide a useful subset of the functionalities of a Grid Middleware, we are now planning to work on a new implementation which will provide a full security model by using characteristics of our existing implementations.

The ICENI Grid Middleware has been used to develop high level grid services such as scheduler services [18] or visualisation services [10].

References

1. The Globus Toolkit 3.0. http://www-unix.globus.org/toolkit/download.html
2. GT3 Index Service Overview. http://www.globus.org/ogsa/releases/final/docs/infosvcs/indexsvc_overview.html
3. E. Bruneton et al. ASM: A Code Manipulation Tool to Implement Adaptable Systems. In Adaptable and Extensible Component Systems, France, Nov. 2002.

4. Global Grid Forum. http://www.gridforum.org/
5. N. Furmento, W. Lee, A. Mayer, S. Newhouse, and J. Darlington. ICENI: An Open Grid Service Architecture Implemented with Jini. In *SuperComputing 2002*, USA, Nov. 2002.
6. N. Furmento, A. Mayer, S. McGough, S. Newhouse, T. Field, and J. Darlington. ICENI: Optimisation of Component Applications within a Grid Environment. *Parallel Computing*, 28(12):1753–1772, 2002.
7. N. Furmento, S. Newhouse, and J. Darlington. Building Computational Communities from Federated Resources. In *7th International Euro-Par Conference*, volume 2150 of *LNCS*, pages 855–863, UK, Aug. 2001.
8. N. Furmento *et al.* Performance of ICENI/Jini Service Oriented Architecture. Technical report, ICPC, 2002. http://www.lesc.ic.ac.uk/iceni/reports.jsp
9. J. Hau, W. Lee, and Steven Newhouse. Autonomic Service Adaptation using Ontological Annotation. In *4th International Workshop on Grid Computing, Grid 2003*, USA, Nov. 2003.
10. G. Kong, J. Stanton, S. Newhouse, and J. Darlington. Collaborative Visualisation over the Access Grid using the ICENI Grid Middleware. In *UK e-Science All Hands Meeting*, pages 393–396, UK, Sep. 2003. ISBN 1-904425-11-9.
11. Jini Network Technology. http://www.sun.com/software/jini/
12. Jini Network Technology, v2.0. http://developer.java.sun.com/developer/products/jini/arch2_0.html
13. Sun Microsystems. Java API for XML-Based RPC 1.1 Specification. http://java.sun.com/xml/jaxrpc/index.html
14. Project JXTA. http://www.jxta.org/
15. Project JXTA-rmi. http://jxta-rmi.jxta.org/servlets/ProjectHome
16. Project JXTA-soap. http://soap.jxta.org/servlets/ProjectHome
17. S. Tuecke *et al.* Open Grid Service Infrastructure (OGSI) v.1.0 Specification, Feb. 2003.
18. L. Young, S. McGough, S. Newhouse, and J. Darlington. Scheduling Architecture and Algorithms within the ICENI Grid Middleware. In *UK e-Science All Hands Meeting*, pages 5–12, UK, Sep. 2003. ISBN 1-904425-11-9.

A   The Counter Service Example

- **Interface for a Counter Service**

```
public interface CounterService extends ResourceService {
    public int addValue(int pValue) throws IceniServiceException;
    public int subtractValue(int pValue) throws IceniServiceException;
} // end interface CounterService
```

- **Implementation for a Counter Service**

```
public abstract class Counter extends ResourceImpl implements CounterService {
    protected int _counter = 0;
    public int addValue(int pValue) throws IceniServiceException {
    _counter += pValue; return _counter; }
    public int subtractValue(int pValue) throws IceniServiceException {
    return addValue(-pValue); }
} // end class Counter
```

- **Service Level Agreement for a Counter Service**

```
<publicDomain name="public1">
 <policy:accessPolicy>
   <policy:allow startDay="monday" stopDay="friday" stopHour="12" stopMn="00">
    <policy:entity type="organisation" name="eScience"/>
   </policy:allow>
 </policy:accessPolicy>
</publicDomain>
```

Dependable Global Computing with JaWS++

George Kakarontzas and Spyros Lalis

Computer and Communications Engineering Department
University of Thessaly
Volos, Greece
{gkakar,lalis}@inf.uth.gr

Abstract. In this paper we propose a computational grid platform called *JaWS++* that seeks to harvest the power of idle pools of workstations connected through the Internet and integrate them in a grid computing platform for the execution of embarrassingly parallel computations. The computations are developed in the portable Java programming language and an API is provided for application development. JaWS++ is a compromise between scavenging and reservation-based computational grids. Its service layer is composed by pools of workstations that are autonomously administered by different organizations. Each pool participates in JaWS++ under a well defined timetable to reduce unforeseen availability problems, increase dependability and favor batch work allocation and offline execution.

1 Introduction

Until a few years ago, grids were setup almost exclusively by connecting trustworthy, controlled and reliable computing infrastructures with each other, typically under a well-defined resource-sharing scheme and admission policy. Recently there is a lot of activity in trying to "gridify" less reliable computing resources, most notably the idle processors of individual personal computers connected to the Internet or entire networks of workstations located in organizations.

The resulting systems, also referred to as scavenging computational grids [4], fall short on the dependability and consistency characteristics of a "proper" grid. This is primarily due to the intermittent availability/presence of worker processors, which makes efficient scheduling and fault-tolerance hard to achieve. These problems are made even more challenging when the scavenging computational grid spans over wider areas of the Internet. In this case, slow and unreliable network connectivity suggests that large chunks of work should be sent to the workers to favor offline execution and amortize transmission delays. On the other hand volatility of workers suggests that the exact opposite is a better option since sending small chunks of work to workers results in less work lost when worker failures occur.

Dealing with these issues would be easier if the resources were not treated as "an undifferentiated swarm of global scope" [5] but grouped into resource pools of a more "predictable" nature. Moreover, this grouping should take into

M. Dikaiakos (Ed.): AxGrids 2004, LNCS 3165, pp. 100–109, 2004.
© Springer-Verlag Berlin Heidelberg 2004

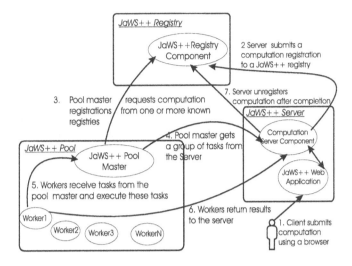

Fig. 1. Components of JaWS++

account not only the physical network structure but also the structure of real-world administrative domains. Work could then be assigned to these pools in batches of tasks in a scalable way and with a given performance expectancy with increased probability.

In this paper we present JaWS++, a scavenging grid system that is designed with these characteristics in mind. JaWS++ employs an open and loosely-coupled architecture with a service layer that consists of pools of worker machines rather than individual workers. These pools are typically commercial-off-the-self (COTS) nodes connected via a LAN, under the same administration domain [2].

The rest of the paper is organized as follows. In Sect. 2 the overall system architecture is described. In Sect. 3 we describe JaWS++ computations, and in Sect. 4 the approach for determining the expected performance of pools is discussed. Section 5 compares our approach with other work. Finally, Sect. 6 gives the status of the system and describes future plans.

2   Overall Architecture of the JaWS++ System

JaWS++ comprises a number of key software components residing on different machines that are connected through the Internet. The system's components and an indicative work flow of a computation process are depicted in Fig. 1.

The JaWS++ Server. This component runs on a dedicated server machine. It comprises two software components: a web application and a computation server component. The web application is used by clients to submit computations to the system, view their progress, get results back or cancel submitted computations. The computation server component has the following responsibilities. First it advertises submitted computations to known registries. As pools discover the computation (this process is explained in detail in the sequel) they contact the server to retrieve all the information and files that are needed to launch the computation. The server also collects and merges the results as they are being produced by the pools, and when a computation finishes, it unregisters the computation from the registries. Finally it monitors the tasks allocated to pools and reallocates unfinished tasks in cases of excessive delays. Clients can choose to setup their own JaWS++ server or use servers already available. It is thus possible -and desirable- to have numerous servers manging different computations.

The JaWS++ Registry. The registry is a database where JaWS++ servers register their computations, and typically runs on a remote dedicated machine. Each server knows one or more registries and is provided with the necessary credentials to be allowed to submit registrations to them. Along the same lines, JaWS++ pools contact the registries to learn about computations and be forwarded to the corresponding server. A registry also applies a global scheduling policy. Although pools proactively contact a registry they know, it is up to the registry to decide which registration (computation part) they will dispatch to the pool. For example, a least recently fetched policy could be applied in an attempt to be fair to all computations. Other options, taking into account priorities of different clients, can also be applied. It is important to note that the scheduling policy is entirely encapsulated into the registry logic (or configuration) thus can be adjusted in a straightforward way.

The JaWS++ Pool Master. The pool master runs inside a JaWS++ pool of worker machines with the primary task of managing them. It has two modes of operation determined by its schedule which is set by the pool administrator. It can operate either in *idle mode* when there is no usual business activity or in *opportunistic mode* when the pool worker machines are likely to be used by their owners. When in idle mode, the pool master queries known registries that it is authorized to access to receive a computation registration, and subsequently contacts the server at the address recorded in the registration. When the server is contacted for the first time, the pool master receives a benchmark that is used to decide how many tasks it can take on (more on this in Sect. 4). The pool master then requests a number of tasks and downloads all the required files for the tasks. Then it starts distributing tasks to the workers. It continually monitors its workers and in cases of failures or worker reclaiming by their owners it reallocates the tasks to other workers. The opportunistic mode is used for the execution of any remaining allocated tasks. As will be shown in Sect. 4 the JaWS++ pool master will allocate only as many tasks as can be completed during the idle mode of operation. Only in cases when this time is not enough, the execution of the remaining tasks will be extended to the opportunistic mode of operation. This is done in an attempt to minimize worker reclaiming and therefore avoid the performance penalty associated with task migrations in global computing systems.

The JaWS++ Workers. These are the machines where the actual computation takes place. A daemon running as a background process on every machine monitors local activity. When the daemon detects idleness it sends a registration message to the pool master, and then keeps sending heartbeat signals at regular intervals. When a worker receives a task from the pool master, this is executed. The results are sent directly to the corresponding server (not the pool master) and the pool master is notified accordingly so that it can update the task list and send the worker a new task. If a network partition occurs and the pool becomes isolated, the worker will send the result to the pool master where it can be stored for transmission at a later point in time, when the server becomes reachable. In this case, the pool master periodically tries to contact the server until all pending results are delivered or a maximum timeout period expires (given that the pool master is expected to run on a dedicated server machine with abundant storage capacity, this timeout can be very generous).

We envision a global system where servers and pools get together through known computation registries. Many instances of these components can coexist at any given time. In Fig. 2 we can see an example where two servers advertise their computation to two registries. Three pools discover these computations and execute tasks returning the results to their servers. The system is easily scalable since several servers and pools can coexist, linked only through registries which maintain a simple registration record for each computation.

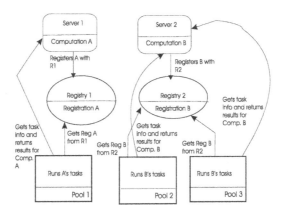

Fig. 2. JaWS++ servers, registries and pools

3   JaWS++ Computations

Computations in JaWS++ are embarrassingly or "pleasantly" parallel [13] composed by a number of independent tasks executable in any order. Tasks may or may not have similar computation requirements. Developers differentiate tasks with different computation requirements by declaring them in different *task group* elements of an XML descriptor file, the so-called *computation descriptor*. Developers also declare within each task group element a *benchmark task* that is a

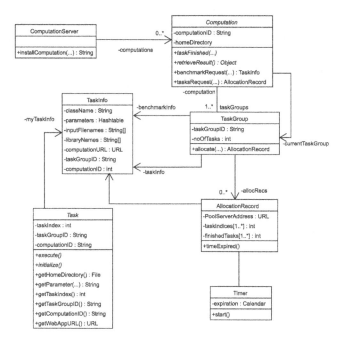

Fig. 3. Computation classes in JaWS++

small but representative task compared to the real tasks of the group. The overhead of the real task compared to the benchmark task is declared with the *Task-
To-Benchmark-Ratio (TTBR)* numeric attribute of the benchmark element. If,
for example, the real tasks require 60 times the processing time of the benchmark
task, TTBR will be 60. In cases when the real tasks complete in a few minutes
developers may skip the creation of a separate benchmark task and declare as
benchmark task one of the real tasks of the group with a TTBR equal to one. In
cases, however, when the real tasks take a long time to complete the provision
of a separate benchmark task is necessary to speedup scheduling (more on this
in Sect. 4).

Computation descriptors must be consistent with the *JaWS++ XML schema*.
The descriptor contains information about the structure of the computation in
terms of task groups as well as references to various input and class files needed.
To launch a computation, the programmer develops the code, prepares the input
files and libraries and the XML descriptor, and packs them in a compressed file.
The file is then uploaded to a JaWS++ server via a web application interface.
In Fig. 3 we can see a UML class diagram with the main classes of a JaWS++
computation.

When a computation is first uploaded the installComputation method of the
ComputationServer checks the computation descriptor against the *JaWS++ XML
schema*. It then checks that all the required files exist and then creates the Computation, TaskGroup and TaskInfo instances and their associations.

The Computation class is an abstract class that programmers subclass to develop a specific computation, by providing implementation of the two abstract methods, taskFinished and retrieveResult. The taskFinished method is responsible for receiving a result of a task. It should be implemented as to integrate the result with the other results received so far in a meaningful way. The retrieveResult method returns a partial or complete result to clients that monitor the computation's progress through the web interface of the server.

The Task class is also an abstract class and programmers provide the initialize method and the execute method to develop their own concrete Task subclasses. The initialize method is called after the creation of a Task instance to initialize the task. Subsequently, the execute method is called which executes the actual task code. Upon completion, the Task object, which encapsulates the result of the completed task, is returned to the server.

When a pool master first contacts a server, it requests a benchmark through the benchmarkRequest method. When the pool master decides how many tasks to allocate, it calls the tasksRequest method and as a result receives an AllocationRecord which holds the information for the tasks and the indexes of the tasks to be created on the pool master. A copy of the allocation record is kept on the server. After receiving the tasks the pool master will estimate the time that the allocated tasks will be completed and will notify this estimation to the server. When the deadline specified by the pool master expires the allocation record is marked as delayed. When all tasks of a computation are delivered and new requests for tasks arrive, unfinished tasks of delayed allocation records will be reallocated.

When all tasks of a computation complete, the computation is marked as finished and all registrations are removed. Also all participating pools for this computation are notified for the computation termination. Finished computations are *passivated* in permanent storage to preserve memory. When later clients request the result of a passivated computation the computation is *activated* back in memory. After clients get the result of a computation, the computation is removed from memory and all storage associated with the computation is released.

4   Calculating the Expected Pool Performance

JaWS++ workers have characteristics, such as CPU speed, memory capacity etc. In the present phase of development we simply request that the pool administrator should group workers according to their hardware configuration, so that workers in the same *worker group* have more or less the same configuration. However, this process could as well be entirely automated.

When a pool master receives a new computation registration, it contacts the server and downloads the benchmark information for the tasks of the current task group of the computation. Lets denote the number of worker groups with N, worker group i with WG_i and the number of registered workers of worker group i with $Workers(WG_i)$. It is expected that $Workers(WG_i)$ will be equal to the total number of workers in group i, since the pool master requests computation registrations only when it operates in idle mode of operation, thus when more or less all workers in the pool are expected to be idle. However the $Workers(WG_i)$ used is the actual number of registered workers of group i at the time that the work allocation process takes place.

When the pool master receives the benchmark information it chooses randomly an idle worker from each worker group and simulates the process of the task execution cycle which includes the downloading of the required files, the benchmark task creation, and the dispatching and receipt of the delivery confirmation by the workers after they have executed the benchmark task and returned the result to its server.

Lets denote with $BS(WG_i)$ the time units required for the randomly chosen worker of WG_i to complete the cycle. This is the *benchmark score* of WG_i. Let $TTBR$ stand for the overhead of the real tasks of the task group compared to the benchmark task, as declared by the developer in the computation descriptor (see Sect. 3). Also let TR stand for the time units remaining until the idle mode of operation expires and the pool enters the opportunistic mode of operation again, measured from the time when the pool master contacts the server to allocate the tasks. We then define $PC(WG_i)$ the *processing capacity* of WG_i, as the number of tasks that WG_i can deliver until the idle mode of operation expires:

$$PC(WG_i) = \left\lfloor \frac{Workers(WG_i) \times TR}{BS(WG_i) \times TTBR} \right\rfloor , \forall i \in 1 \ldots N \tag{1}$$

and the *total processing capacity* of the pool PC as the total number of tasks that the pool is capable of delivering until the idle mode of operation expires:

$$PC = \sum_{i=1}^{N} PC(WG_i) \tag{2}$$

The pool master will calculate PC after all chosen workers have completed and delivered the benchmark tasks, and it will then request PC tasks from the server. The pool master will receive an allocation record for K tasks where $K \leq PC$. It will then estimate the completion time of the allocated tasks based on the number of tasks actually allocated and will notify this estimation to the server.

The pool master can then download the required files for the allocated tasks and proceed with the creation of tasks and their dispatching to the available workers.

5   Related Work

Several Java-based systems have been proposed for global computing[8–11, 1]. Java is an excellent choice for global computing since it provides the ability for customized security with the concept of Security Managers, class downloading and namespace separation through the use of Class Loaders. All these features are essential for multi-application global computing systems, where clients may upload computations unknown to the system, with arbitrary behavior and with the exact same package and class names. There are some projects such as XtremWeb [3] which favor binary code executables over Java code. While native code computations are faster than their Java counterparts (but note that Java on-the-fly compilers are getting better with time), Java provides better security which increases volunteer participation. Also native code in multi-application global computing systems restricts further the execution pool to those workers which have the appropriate machine architecture and are properly configured.

In comparison to JaWS++ Ninflet [11], SuperWeb [1], Popcorn[9] and even the predecessor of JaWS++, JaWS [6,7], have a flat structure in which workers are monitored directly by one single monitor server, usually the one who provided their tasks. In JaWS++ the pool master monitors its pool and the server monitors the pool master. The flat monitoring approach creates the following issues. Firstly connection between the workers and their monitor servers may be lost too often. Since workers and their monitor servers are not required to be on the same network, network partitions become more likely to occur. In such cases monitor servers may loose contact with numerous workers all at once and proceed with sometimes-unnecessary correcting measures such as redistribution of lost tasks. If the network partition heals before the newly distributed tasks complete then time and resources were spent with no benefit. In contrast in JaWS++ the monitoring of workers is assigned to a pool master residing in the same network making network partitions much more unlikely to occur. We assume of course that partitions may occur in the wide area network isolating pools from JaWS++ servers. Given however that pool masters may keep results and forward them later to their server, servers can be much more assured that the results will ultimately arrive and proceed to redistribution of tasks only after a very generous time period has expired giving time to the network partition to heal. Secondly the flat monitoring approach is inherently non-scalable. Since grid and global computing systems are built to integrate thousands or even millions of machines in one virtual community, having all these machines being monitored by a single server is obviously non-scalable. In JaWS++ this limitation can be overcome by having several different servers managing only a modest amount of computations running on a few machine pools.

XtremWeb [3] and Javelin2 [8] require an overlay network to be built on top of the real network, something common in P2P systems. JaWS++ doesn't require nor supports this, since we want the system to be used both for volunteer-based computing and the formation of virtual organizations. JaWS++ pools reach their computations only through known and trusted computation registries.

Most of the systems already mentioned are cycle stealing systems where a machine becomes a worker of the system when its owner does not use it. When the owner claims the machine back for her own use, any computations running there are quickly moved to the dispatcher and from there are migrated to another available worker for further execution until they complete. It is clear that in such a setting the impact of worker reclaiming can be dramatic in performance since migrations can cause the whole computation to slow down, especially if tasks are migrated over the Internet. In JaWS++ workers are also used when they are idle and are evacuated when their owners claim them. Pool masters however undertake work only when their pool operates in idle mode which is set by the administrator of the JaWS++ pool. The idle mode is the period when the network is not normally used by its owners (e.g. during the night, or during the weekends). This reduces substantially the possibility of task migrations and improves performance.

The use of benchmarks to predict worker capabilities is also advocated in SuperWeb [1] and Popcorn [9]. However benchmarks in these systems are unrelated to the computations.They just provide an indication of how powerful or fast a machine is compared to another candidate machine. In JaWS++ the benchmark task is related to the tasks that a worker will execute since benchmark tasks are provided by the computation developers. Benchmarking is essential for multi-application global computing systems. In JaWS++ the execution of the benchmark can be carried out with no significant performance penalty since the dispatching unit is a group of tasks and not a single task, which means that benchmark is executed once for each allocation of a group of tasks.

6   Current Status and Future Research Directions

We have successfully implemented and tested a prototype for JaWS++, and we are now in the process of making the system more robust and administration free so that it becomes suitable for real-world use. We also plan to investigate the system's scheduling performance using simulations as well as real computations.

In the future, we plan to automate the workers grouping process to ease pool administration and allow dynamic reconfiguration of groups. Technologies such as the Windows Management Instrumentation (WMI) and the Network Weather Service (NWS) [14] can be used to provide the necessary information for the automation of the grouping process.

We also intend to look at the Open Grid Services Infrastructure (OGSI)[12], a set of standards for Grid services defined by the Global Grid Forum (GGF), with the intention to express JaWS++ components as Grid services with WSDL (Web Services Description Language) architecture and programming language neutral interfaces.

Another issue to be further researched is the global scheduling policy adopted by JaWS++ registries. We currently apply a least-recently allocated policy returning the computation registration of the computation that was served least recently. However several policies can be applied very easily and we want to determine the circumstances under which a scheduling policy may be favorable to another.

Last but not least, we intend to investigate the support of non-trivial computations, which are notoriously hard to deal with in"flat-scheduled" or P2P-based systems. Given that in JaWS++ the unit of scheduling is a task group rather than a single task, it becomes possible to support non-trivial parallel computations with extensive inter-task communication. Since task groups are co-scheduled on the same pool, such communication can be efficiently carried out using a variety of (even proprietary) mechanisms and without stumbling on the usual problems of NATs and firewalls.

In conclusion JaWS++ targets the utilization of pools of workstations in an effort to provide a more dependable global computing platform. We believe that this approach fills an empty space in the grid computing landscape and is very promising in terms of addressing several important issues that are prevalent in modern open and dynamic computing environments.

References

1. Albert D. Alexandrov et. al.: "SuperWeb: research issues in Java-based global computing". Concurrency: Practice and Experience, vol. 9, no. 6, pp. 535–553, 1997.
2. Mark Baker ed.: "Cluster computing white paper, ver. 2". December 2000.
3. Gilles Fedak et. al.: "XtremWeb: a generic global computing system". CCGRID 2001.
4. Luis Ferreira et. al: "Introduction to grid computing with Globus". IBM Redbooks, September 2003.
5. Ian Foster and Adriana Iamnitchi: "On death, taxes, and the convergence of Peer-to-Peer and Grid computing". IPTPS'03, February 2003.
6. George Kakarontzas and Spyros Lalis: "A market-based protocol with leasing support for globally distributed computing". Workshop on Global Computing on Personal Devices, CCGRID 2001.
7. Spyros Lalis and Alexandros Karypidis: "An open market-based architecture for distributed computing". International Workshop on Personal Computer-Based Networks of Workstations, International Parallel and Distributed Processing Symposium, 2000.
8. Michael O. Neary et. al.: "Javelin 2.0: Java-based parallel computing on the Internet". Euro-Par 2000, August 2000, Germany.
9. Noam Nisan et. al.: "Globally distributed computation over the Internet - The Popcorn project". ICDCS'98, May 1998, Amsterdam, The Netherlands.
10. Luis F. G. Sarmenta and Satoshi Hirano: "Bayanihan: building and studying Web-based volunteer computing systems using Java". Future Generation Computer Systems, vol. 15, no. 5–6, pp. 675–686, 1999.
11. Hiromitsu Takagi et. al.: "Ninflet: A migratable parallel objects framework using Java". Concurrency: Practice and Experience, vol. 10, no. 11–13, pp. 1063–1078, 1998.
12. Steve Tuecke et. al.: "Open Grid Services Infrastructure". Global Grid Forum, June 2003.
13. B. Wilkinson and M. Allen: "Parallel programming: techniques and applications using networked workstations and parallel computers". Prentice-Hall, 1999.
14. Richard Wolski et. al.: "The network weather service: a distributed resource performance forecasting service for metacomputing". Future Generation Computer Systems, vol. 15, no. 5–6, pp. 757–768, 1999.

Connecting Condor Pools
into Computational Grids by Jini*

Gergely Sipos and Péter Kacsuk

MTA SZTAKI Computer and Automation Research Institute,
Hungarian Academy of Sciences
1518 Budapest, P.O. Box 63., Hungary
{sipos,kacsuk}@sztaki.hu

Abstract. The paper describes how Condor-pools could be joined together to form a large computational cluster-grid. In the architecture Jini provides the infrastructure for resource lookup, while Condor manages the job execution on the individual clusters. Semi on-line application monitoring is also available in this structure, moreover it works even through firewalls. Beside Condor the presented Jini based Grid can support other local jobmanager implementations, thus various types of sequential or parallel jobs could be executed with the same framework.

1 Introduction

The availability of the Condor local jobmanager within single administrative domains has been proved in several projects [4]. Other works described how Condor flocking can be applied to connect clusters together [2]. Unfortunately in such a role Condor meets neither the security, nor the functionality requirements that second generation, service oriented grids should do.

We already presented how the Java based Jini technology can be used as the middleware layer in computational Grids [5]. Jini does have service-oriented vision, and based on its Lookup Service infrastructure clients can find suitable computational services. To exploit the advantages of both Condor and Jini we integrated them into a single framework. In this system Jini acts as the information system layer, while Condor manages the running jobs on the connected clusters. Appling this structure there is no need to use Condor flocking since Jini can provide the necessary tools and protocols for the inter-domain communication. To make the cooperation of the two technologies available Condor had to be wrapped into a Jini service program, and a suitable service proxy had to be developed for it. Since neither Jini nor Condor supports application monitoring, the Mercury monitor infrastructure [1] has been integrated into the Grid as well. Our system supposes that Mercury has been accordingly installed on the machines of the Condor-pools and clients use the GRM trace collector and the PROVE visualiser tools [3].

* The work presented in this paper was supported by the Ministry of Education under No. IKTA5-089/2002, the Hungarian Scientific Research Fund No. T042459 and IHM 4671/1/2003.

M. Dikaiakos (Ed.): AxGrids 2004, LNCS 3165, pp. 110–112, 2004.

Although Condor can manage different types of sequential and parallel jobs – thus PVM, MPI and Java applications can be executed in our Grid, – the purpose of this work is to give a general pattern that developers of Jini based multi-layered Grids can follow. Later, similarly to the presented solution any other jobmanager implementation (e.g. Sun Grid Engine, Fork) can be wrapped into the same grid.

In Section 2 the structure and usage scenario of the Condor-Jini Grid is presented, while Section 3 outlines conclusions.

2   Job Execution and Monitoring in the Jini Based Condor-Grid

The developed server program wraps the job executor functionality of Condor into a Jini service. Using this service Jini enabled clients can submit sequential and parallel jobs into remote Condor-pools. In the system the job submission and result download processes are fully performed by the cooperating cluster side server program and its client side proxy, the user only has to start these procedures. Fig. 1 presents the usage scenario of the high-level job executor and monitor service.

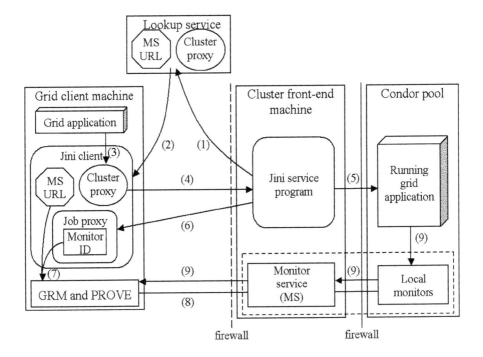

Fig. 1. The usage scenario of a Condor cluster in the Jini based Grid

The service program has to be started on the front-end machine of the Condor-pool. With this separation the security of the whole system could be significantly improved, since this machine can perform every grid-related task, the Condor nodes can stay protected. After its start-up, the service program discovers the lookup services and registers the cluster proxy together with the URL of the Mercury Monitor Service (MS URL) at them (1). When an appropriate Jini client application downloads these two objects (2), the proxy can be used to submit compiled PVM, MPI or Java programs to the Condor cluster (3). The proxy forwards the received application to the remote server (4) which submits it into the Condor-pool with native calls (5). At the same time a job proxy is returned to the client (6). This second proxy can be used to start or stop the remote grid application or to download its result files. Based on the monitor ID contained by this job proxy and on the MS URL has been downloaded from the Lookup Service the GRM tool can register for the trace of the remote job (7, 8). Applying the Mercury infrastructure (the components inside the broken lines) the instrumented grid application can forward trace events to the client side GRM trace collector and the PROVE visualiser tools (9). Since Mercury is a pre-installed service on the cluster only one port has to be opened from the front-end machine to the public network to enable trace forwarding. Beside the service program and the proxies we already developed a client application that can use the service in the described way.

3   Conclusions

The presented Condor based Jini executor service has been publicly demonstrated during the Grid Dissemination Day organised by the Hungarian Grid Competence Centre, as an important part of the JGrid project [6]. Although its automatic service discovery and usage functionalities derived from Jini resulted an easy-to-use and easy-to-install system, due to security issues the present version cannot be publicly used. The demonstrated version builds on Jini version 1, thus authentication, authorization and dynamic policy configuration could not be handled. We are already working on the next version of the service that will apply every security solution provided by Jini 2.

References

1. Z. Balaton and G. Gombás: Resource and Job Monitoring in the Grid, Proc. of EuroPar'2003 Conference, Klagenfurt, Austria, pp. 404–411, 2003.
2. D. H. J. Epema, M. Livny, R. van Dantzig, X. Evers, and J. Pruyne: A worldwide flock of condors: load sharing among workstation clusters. Technical Report DUT-TWI-95–130, Delft, The Netherlands, 1995.
3. P. Kacsuk: Performance Visualization in the GRADE Parallel Programming Environment, Proc. of the 5th international conference/exhibition on High Performance Computing in Asia-Pacific region (HPC'Asia 2000), Peking, 2000, pp. 446–450.
4. M. J. Litzkov, M. Livny, and M. W. Mutka: Condor – A hunter of idle workstations. Proc. of the 8th IEEE International Conference on Distributed Computing Systems, pp. 104–111, 1988.
5. G. Sipos and P. Kacsuk: Executing and Monitoring PVM Programs in Computational Grids with Jini, Proc. of the 10th EuroPVM/MPI Conference, Springer-Verlag, Venice, Italy, 2003, pp. 570–576.
6. JGrid project: http://pds.irt.vein.hu/jgrid

Overview of an Architecture Enabling Grid Based Application Service Provision

S. Wesner[1], B. Serhan[1], T. Dimitrakos[2], D. Mac Randal[2],
P. Ritrovato[3], and G. Laria[3]

[1] High Performance Computing Centre Stuttgart, 70550 Stuttgart, Germany
{wesner,serhan}@hlrs.de
[2] Central Laboratory of the Research Councils, Rutherford Appleton Lab, UK
{t.dimitrakos,d.f.mac.randal}@rl.ac.uk
[3] CRMPA – University of Salerno, Italy
{ritrovato,laria}@crmpa.unisa.it

Abstract. In this short paper we examine the integration of three emerging trends in Information Technology (Utility Computing, Grid Computing, and Web Services) into a new Computing paradigm (Grid-based Application Service Provision) that is taking place in the context of the European research project GRASP. In the first part of the paper, we explain how the integration of emerging trends can support enterprises in creating competitive advantage. In the second part, we summarise an architecture blueprint of Grid-based Application Service Provision (GRASP), which enables a new technology-driven business paradigm on top of such integration.

1 From Application Service Provision to Utility Computing

Application Service Provision (ASP) is a business model, originally derived from the idea to use the Internet or other wide area networks to provide online application services on a rental basis-commercially delivering computing as a service.

As indicated in [1], [2], one can distinguish two different types of ASPs: the "traditional" ASP and the Internet Business Service Provider (IBSP also referred to as the "network-centric" ASP). In contrast to traditional ASPs, providing application services that are Internet-enabled by design, IBSPs build their applications instead of adapting the source code of their applications via changes in the configuration of the application rather than changing the source code of its components. IBSPs therefore move closer to building their businesses on a utility model than traditional ASPs.

Utility computing presents a paradigm where shared infrastructure can be provided on demand to multiple customers [3]. It describes a system that lets companies pay for IT services as needed. Beside the technological developments that enable utility computing as a paradigm for ASPs also new business interaction models and fine-grained accounting models for utility computing getting possible.

M. Dikaiakos (Ed.): AxGrids 2004, LNCS 3165, pp. 113–118, 2004.

2   Grid Services: An Enabling Technology

The following sections will assume as background knowledge: the basic principles of the Service Oriented Architecture paradigm, the Open Grid Service Architecture [4] and their partial realization in the Grid Service specification [5] via the Open Grid Service Architecture vision [6], [7].

3   GRASP:
Towards Grid-Based Application Service Provision

The EU GRASP project [8] is an industry driven European research project, which is exploring the use of Grid Services paradigm as a means of providing a timely and effective technological basis supporting the evolution of the ASP market towards a sustainable Utility Computing model.

3.1   New Business Interaction Models for IBSPs

To achieve this GRASP is developing an architectural framework for Grid-based Application Service Provision (GRASP), a prototype realization of this framework in a GRASP platform and "proof-of-concept" implementations of "federated" and "many-to-many" ASP models in different domains such as e-Learning and Biomedical Attention Management.

- The "federated" model, which is concerned with the on-demand creation of dynamic virtual organizations of service providers, which share resources, capabilities and information for a limited period of time and responding to a specific market need.
- The "many-to-many" model, essentially an evolution of the classic one-to-many model achieved by evolving its foundation from client-server to a service-oriented paradigm: the entity can take the role of either a consumer or a service provider in the context of the same application depending on the required interactions. Users may count their material contribution to the provision of the overall application provision as a means of payment towards using that application.

The GRASP architectural framework closes the gap between the effective deployment of Grid infrastructures, Web Service based enabling technologies, and enterprise models for application service provision. Our intention is to improve enterprise application service provision models so as to be able to take full advantage of the flexibility offered by Web Services as a standardized means of integrating components of heterogeneous systems both within local, as well as wide area networks, and of the additional functionality and reliability offered by Grid Services for supporting dynamic resource allocation, life-time management of dynamic service instances, resources integration and efficient distributed computation. We expect that when properly integrated within a business workflow this bundle can soften enterprise borders, giving way to new, more flexible ways of secure and reliable collaboration.

4   Main Subsystems of the GRASP Architecture

One of the key architectural elements of GRASP is the distinction between the Application Service delivered to a client and the component Grid services that are used to implement this. The component Grid services are provided on demand by 3rd party Service Providers running Virtual Hosting Environments (VHE), which of course may consist of many individual hosts actually running the services. From a management perspective each VHE uses a Gateway server responsible for creation and management of the Grid services within it. This architecture enables the VHE manager to control the operation of and access to their services as necessary in a fully commercial environment while still exploiting the power of the underlying Grid technology (including direct P2P communication between services) to actually deliver the overall Application Service. The basic business functionality that Application and Service Provider require is built into the Grasp Framework, simplifying the job of building Grid-based Application Services.

The GRASP prototype exploits the functionality of the OGSI.NET toolkit [9] which is a full implementation of the most recent OGSI specification [10]. However for the realisation of business applications further higher level services are needed. The following sections outline the key services identified missing in OGSI needed for business oriented applications.

4.1   Service Location

This component enters the picture in case the ASP provider is setting up a new dynamic application and is seeking for the appropriate services. Another possibility is that in an existing operational dynamic application problems have been detected and services must be either replaced or accompanied by additional services.

So we assume the ASP Provider to be one party within a Virtual Organizations (VO) grouping together several Service Providers that offer a list of services. The client of the Service Locator can specify the characteristics of needed services including pricing and QoS requirements. The Service Locator queries its Service Directory for potential Service Providers and also forward the request to other known Service Locators. As a result the Service Locator returns a list of Service Providers that potentially could be integrated into the dynamic application. This model assumes that the client receives by other means the connection data for the Service Locator. This is proved approach also used in other Grid frameworks such as UNICORE [11].

4.2   Filter and Instantiation Service

The Service Instantiator is located on the Gateway machine within a Virtual Hosting Environment (VHE) as outlined above. The Service Instantiator (a Grid Service hosted by the Gateway machine) is responsible for all requests for instantiating a new service. The Filter service is present at the start of the standard server pipeline in order to elaborate the incoming requests and forward them to the right process. In case of a request for creating a new service the access rights of the requestor are verified and the GRASP Service Container is queried if the service already exists. If the service does not yet exist the Service Instantiator chooses the appropriate factory within the HE and invokes it. The Factory creates the new service instance and returns to Service Instantiator a valid reference to this instance (ServiceLocator, SL, in OGSI terminology). The Instantiator generates a modified SL in order to hide the real reference, and calls the Container to update a table maintaining the mapping between SL and SL* (modified SL). The external reference (SL*) for the new service instance is then returned to the requestor by the Service Instantiator.

If the service requestor invokes an already existing service instance the request is intercepted by the Filter service forwarding the request to the Container (performing a SL* to SL mapping). This additional intermediate SL allows the VHE to replace or move a service instance within the VHE (e.g. due to anticipated problems with the SLA) without renegotiating with the service requestor and enables local solutions without affecting the virtualisation concept.

4.3   Service Orchestration

As outline in section 1 the IBSP model assumes that applications are build from several components allowing dynamic reconfiguration. Within GRASP this concept has been extended to build dynamic applications out of distributed services. Such dynamic applications include not only Grid Services but also plain Web Services (e.g. for checking the creditability of a credit card). This means that ideally a workflow engine capable of orchestrating web and grid services in a dynamically changing workflow is needed.

For the first version of the GRASP prototype a standard BPEL4WS [12] workflow engine has been chosen in favour of existing Grid specific workflow languages such as GSFL [13]. However the BPEL compliant engine is not capable of handling the dynamicity of the Grid Services such as the on-demand service location and instantiation and the transient nature of Grid Services. Another problem is the potentially different organisation of workflows due to the statefulness of Grid Services. These problems has been solved with Web Service proxies providing the needed static reference towards the BPEL engine and handling the Grid specifics.

For the second version of the prototype BPEL extensions with a pre-parsing process or the extension of BPEL engines in general are considered in order to integrate Grid Services more seamless in hybrid WebService/GridService workflows.

4.4   SLA Management

Commercial usage of SOA is typically closely connected with a demand for assured Quality of Services (QoS). Such QoS are negotiated between a service provider and a service consumer and are specified in Service Level Agreements (SLA).

An appropriate SLA management system must support the the set-up process by allowing an automated negotiation and parsing of SLAs. During the operation phase the SLAs must be supervised on a per service basis. The basic architecture considers a Locator capable of searching for SLAs, support for an external SLA language and a monitoring concept that allows future extensions regarding QoS prediction.

Regarding the observation of a single SLA we try to exploit the dynamics of the grid in the way, that for every grid service running on behalf of a client, we instantiate an accompanying SLA grid service that contains and validates a specific SLA to be fulfilled by the related grid service. We are encouraged by the fact that the first draft of OGSI-Agreement [14] introduces a similar approach, using Agreement Services. The first prototype of this concept is currently under implementation.

4.5   Security

All of the GRASP security rests on top of OGSA-compliant Grid security mechanisms, and is orthogonal to Web Services security protocols, such as WS-Security. The ASP security context is addressed using a public key certificate scheme based on GSI, and will exploit ASP securization technologies. For the Grasp infrastructure context, a novel dynamic security perimiter model is proposed (see also [15] [16] [17]) where a protective shell is introduced around each of the Grasp components involved in delivering the Application service in order to secure each component individually and the group as a whole. As this short paper does not allow to explain this concept in enough detail and we like to direct the interested reader to [18].

5   Conclusion

The European GRASP project complements Grid infrastructure development projects such as [19], [20], [11], Web technology deployment projects such as [21] and ASP business model assessment and risk management projects such as [22] by providing a tangible "proof-of-concept" for Grid-based Application Service Provision.

Building on top of OGSI the GRASP project has already prototype implementations of some of the missing elements filling the large gap between the basic functionality of OGSI and the overall picture of the Open Grid Service Architecture enabling the exploitation of the Grid Service concept in a commercial context.

References

1. Strategies, S.: Market analysis report, traditional isvs: Moving along the software-as-services curve (2002) http://store.yahoo.net/summitresearch/sofasser.html
2. Strategies, S.: Market analysis report, out of the box: Top nine net-native software-as-services design differentiators (2002) http://store.yahoo.net/summitresearch/sofasser.html
3. Machiraju, V., Rolia, J., van Moorsel, A.: Quality of business driven service composition and utility computing. Technical report, Software Technology Laboratory, HP Labs Palo Alto, HPL-2002-66 (2002)

4. Foster, I., Kesselmann, C., Tuecke, S.: The anatomy of the grid
5. Tuecke, S., Czajkowski, K., Foster, I., Frey, J., Graham, S., Kesselman, C.: Grid service specification. Technical report, Open Grid Service Infrastructure WG, Global Grid Forum (2003).
6. Foster, I., Kesselman, C., Nick, J., Tuecke, S.: The physiology of the grid: An open grid services architecture for distributed systems integration. Technical report, Open Grid Service Infrastructure WG, Global Grid Forum (2002), http://www.globus.org/research/papers/ogsa.pdf
7. Foster, I., Kesselman, C., Nick, J., Tuecke, S.: Grid services for distributed system integration. Volume 35 of Computer (2002), http://www.gridforum.org/ogsiwg/drafts/GS_Spec_draft03_2002-07-17.pdf
8. GRASP: (The grasp project) http://www.eu-grasp.net
9. Wasson, G., Beekwilder, N., Humphrey, M.: A technical overview of the ogsi.net system (2003).
10. Tuecke, S., Czajkowski, K., Foster, I., Frey, J., Graham, S., Kesselmann, C., Maquire, T., Sandholm, T., Snelling, D., Vanderbilt, P.: Open grid service infrastructure (ogsi). Technical report (2003).
11. UNICORE: (The unicore project), http://www.unicore.org
12. Andrews, T., Curbera, F., Dholakia, H., Goland, Y., Klein, J., Leymann, F., Liu, K., Roller, D., Smith, D., Thatte, S., Trickovic, I., Weerawarana, S.: Business process execution language for web services version 1.1 (2003).
13. Krishnan, S., Wagstrom, P., von Laszewski, G.: Gsfl: A workflow framework for grid services (2002).
14. Czajkowski, K., Dan, A., Rofrano, J., Tuecke, S., Xu, M.: Agreement-based grid service management (ogsi-agreement) (2003).
15. Dimitrakos, T., Dordjevic, I., B.M.Matthews, J.C.Bicarregui, Phillips, C.: Policy-driven access control over a distributed firewall architecture. In: Proc. of the 3rd IEEE International Workshop on Policies for Distributed Systems and Networks, IEEE Press (2002).
16. Dimitrakos, T., Djordjevic, I., Milosevic, Z., Jøsang, A., Phillips, C.: Contract performance assessment for secure and dynamic virtual collaborations. In: Proceedings of EDOC'03, 7th IEEE International Enterprise Distributed Object Computing Conference, IEEE Press (2003).
17. Djordjevic, I., Dimitrakos, T., Phillips, C.: An architecture for dynamic security perimeters of virtual collaborative networks. In: Accepted for publication in Proc. 9th IEEE/IFIP Network Operations and Management Symposium (NOMS 2004), IEEE Press (2004).
18. Djordjevic, I., Dimitrakos, T.: Dynamic service perimeters for secure collaborations in grid-enabled virtual organisations: Overview of a proposed architecture (2004).
19. GLOBUS: (The globus project), http://www.globus.org
20. LEGION, AVAKI: (The legion project), http://www.cs.virginia.edu/~legion and http://www.avaki.com
21. The SWAD Project: (The Semantic Web Advanced Development in Europe project), http://www.w3.org/2001/sw/Europe/
22. ALTERNATIVE: (The alternative project), http://www.alternativeproject.org

A Grid-Enabled Adaptive Problem Solving Environment*

Yoonhee Kim[1], Ilkyun Ra[2], Salim Hariri[3], and Yangwoo Kim[4]

[1] Dept. of Computer Science, Sookmyung Women's University, Korea
yulan@sookmyung.ac.kr
[2] Dept. of Computer Science & Engineering,
The University of Colorado at Denver, USA
ikra@carbon.cudenver.edu
[3] Dept. of Electrical and Computer Engineering, University of Arizona, USA
hariri@ece.arizona.edu
[4] Dept.of Information & Telecommunication Engineering, Dongguk University, Korea
ywkim@dongguk.edu

Abstract. As complexity of computational applications and their environments has been increased due to the heterogeneity of resources; complexity, continuous changes of the applications as well as the resources states, and the large number of resources involved, the importance of problem solving environments has been more emphasized. As a PSE for metacomputing environment, Adaptive Distributed Computing Environment (ADViCE) has been developed before the emergence of Grid computing services. Current runtime systems for computing mainly focus on executing applications with static resource configuration and do not adequately change the configuration of application execution environments dynamically to optimize the application performance. In this paper, we present an architectural overview of ADViCE and discuss how it is evolving to incorporate Grid computing services to extend its range of services and decrease the cost of development, deployment, execution and maintenance for an application. We provide that ADViCE optimize the application execution at runtime adaptively optimize based on application requirements in both non-Grid and Grid environment with optimal execution options. We have implemented the ADViCE prototype and currently evaluating the prototype and its adaptive services for a larger set of Grid applications.

1 Introduction

High performance problem solving computing environments capitalize on the emerging high speed network technology, parallel and distributed programming tools and environments, and the proliferation of high performance computers. Recently, there has been an increased interest in building large scale high performance distributed computing (i.e. metacomputing). These metacomputing

---

* This Research was supported by the Sookmyung Women's University Research Grants 2004.

M. Dikaiakos (Ed.): AxGrids 2004, LNCS 3165, pp. 119–128, 2004.
© Springer-Verlag Berlin Heidelberg 2004

projects provide large scale applications with computing and storage power that was once available only in traditional supercomputers.

The concept of Grid computing has been investigated and developed to enlarge the concept of distributed computing environment to create infrastructure that enables integrated services for resource scheduling, data delivery, authentication, delegation, information service, management and other related issues [1]. As the Grid provides integrated infrastructure for solving problems, interfacing services such as web portal to access Grid services, PSEs (Problem Solving Environments) have been developed to improve the collaboration among Grid services and reduce significantly the time and effort required to develop, run, and experiment with large scale Grid applications. However, most PSEs to support parallel and distributed computing focus on providing environments for successful execution of applications and providing reasonable resource scheduling schemes. Due to the lack of adaptability on creating dynamic application configurations due to changes of resource status, the execution of these applications is inefficient.

There have been several application-specific tools and PSEs to utilize Grid environment efficiently. ASC Grid Portal [2] is a PSE for large-scale simulation in astrophysics. Hotpage [3] is another PSE targeted toward high performance computing applications. Cactus [4] provides a problem-solving environment for developing large-scale distributed scientific applications. GrADS [5] is a toolkit to help users to build applications over heterogeneous resources with ease of use. Similarly, UNICORE [6] provides graphical user interface to access heterogeneous resources uniformly. However, providing adaptive application execution environment by changing the application configurations at runtime has not been investigated extensively. The Adaptive Distributed Virtual Computing Environment (ADViCE) [10] was developed to support adaptive PSE for component-based applications. The ADViCE provides an efficient web-based approach for developing, running, evaluating and visualizing large-scale parallel and distributed applications that utilize computing resources connected by local and/or wide area network.

In this paper, we describe the architecture of ADViCE, which has ADViCE interface over non-Grid and Grid environment. ADViCE provides a parallel and distributed programming environment; it provides an efficient web-based user interface that allows users to develop, run and visualize parallel/distributed applications running on heterogeneous computing resources connected by networks. To support Grid services through ADViCE, the ACS that creates adaptive application configurations using Resource Specification Language (RSL), which runs over the Globus toolkit [7]. We show that our approach to generate adaptive application configurations can improve the application performance significantly with non-Grid and Grid services.

The organization of the remaining sections of the paper is as follows. We present an overview of the ADViCE architecture in Section 2. In Section 3 we describe the porting approach of ADViCE over Globus. We also describe in detail how the ACS can adaptively change the application configuration at runtime.

Section 4 shows the experimental results on ADViCE over non-Grid environment and preliminary experimental results and we conclude the paper in Section 5.

2   Overview of the ADViCE Architecture

The ADViCE (Adaptive Distributed Virtual Computing Environment) [10] is a web-based computing environment and provides transparent computing and communication services for large scale parallel and distributed applications. It offers access transparency, configuration transparency, fault-tolerance transparency, and performance transparency:

- Access Transparency: The users can login and access all the ADViCE resources (mobile and/or fixed) regardless of their locations. "Mobile Transparency: ADViCE supports in a transparent manner mobile, fixed users, and resources.
- Configuration Transparency: The resources allocated to run a parallel and distributed application can be dynamically changed in a transparent manner; that is the applications or users do not need to make any adjustment to reflect the changes in the resources allocated to them.
- Fault Tolerance Transparency: The execution of a parallel and distributed application can tolerate failures in the resources allocated to run that application.
- Performance Transparency: The resources allocated to run a given parallel and distributed application might change dynamically and in a transparent manner to improve the application performance.

The ADViCE architecture consists of two independent web-based servers: Application Visualization Editing Server (VES) and Application Control and Management Server (CMS). The VES provides Application Editing Service (AES), Application Visualization Service (AVS), and CMS offers Application Resource Service (ARS), Application Management Service (AMS), Application Control Service (ACS) and Application Data Service (ADS). The ADViCE provides three important services/capabilities (refer to Figure 1): 1) Evaluation Tool: to analyze the performance of parallel and distributed applications with different machine and network configurations; 2) Problem Solving Environment: to assist in the development of large scale parallel and distributed applications, and 3) Application-Transparent Adaptively: to allow parallel and distributed applications to run in a transparent manner when their clients and resources are fixed or mobile.

3   Poring ADViCE on Grid

As ADViCE provides a graphical Application Editing Service (AES) and runtime execution environment, integrating it to Grid environment gives many advantages for Grid applications. First, ADViCE supports computation oriented

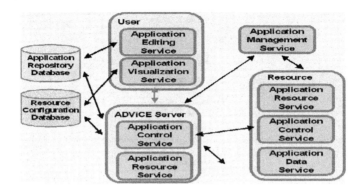

Fig. 1. The Architecture of ADViCE

dataflow models. AES helps users to build an application easily using choosing built-in modules and connecting them with links easily. Second, it has an adaptive runtime framework, which supports adaptive runtime configurations based on application profiling. In this Section, we explain how we achieve the advantages from ADViCE when it was ported over Globus.

3.1   Supporting Dataflow Models with AES

The Grid portal is a web interface to access Grid services and resources. It consists of three layers: a front-end program for web client, Grid service interface, and grid services. The front-end program for a web client is a graphical user environment for accessing Grid services, executing applications and visualizing results. The Grid service interface is developed by using Grid Portal Development Kit (GPDK) [8], which is a web-based Grid portal toolkit that provides web and java interface over Globus toolkit. As it doesn't provide a problem-solving environment, a Grid PSE built with GPDK has been investigated. Most existing PSEs are limited on specific application domains, and are not flexible to support various application domains. In addition, current Globus [7] version does not include PSE tools, to allow users to access grid services and grid-enabled libraries through an easy-to-use interface. Therefore, it is necessary to develop a PSE with an integrated and flexible interface to developing applications and accessing grid services. Figure 2 shows the overall framework to integrate Grid web portal and ADViCE.

ADViCE supports to build an application with a computational dataflow models, which is a set of tasks connected with dataflow links; each task consists of input, and output computation. With control of execution, the model is executed automatically when its input data is ready to feed in. To support this model, current version of Globus needs outside control support as its Resource Specification Language (RSL) is not sufficient to express the dataflow and control flow. To get over this limitation, ADViCE provides dataflow management scheme with Application Flow Graph (AFG), which is generated from AES.

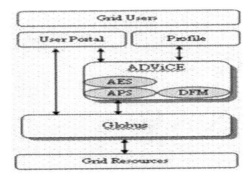

Fig. 2. Integrated Framework of Grid Portal and ADViCE

When an application is composed, the application developer can specify the properties of each task of the application. Just a double click on the task icon generates a popup panel that allows the user to specify (optional) preferences such as computational mode (sequential or parallel), machine type and the number of processors to be used in a parallel implementation of a given task. The user needs to save it first and then submit it for execution simply by clicking on the 'run' button on the main menu. The job gets submitted to the site server which then saves the Application Flow Graph. In effect, this is done by another servlet that is responsible for execution of the application. At this point of time, the servlet calls the Globus execution environment to execute the application. This servlet is also responsible for using the Globus Resource Management Service (GRAM) to generate a dataflow script which is a set of RSLs after checking the dependency among tasks and source of data to transfer. After each task gets allocated to a machine depending on the dataflow script, a corresponding RSL file is executed over Globus. Figure 3 is an algorithm of generating a dataflow script.

3.2   Adaptive Application Configuration

Application Profiling Service (APS) includes analyzing the application characteristics and their previous execution information and generating appropriate parameter information to improve the application performance. The information would be adaptively included in the application configuration, which is controlled by the dataflow manager in ACS. That is, the adaptive application configuration is generated from the Application Flow Graph and the Profile information including application characteristics. As PSE service, ADViCE is integrated into the Grid portal as java components. AES in ADViCE provides application development environment. An application is represented by an Application Flow Graph (AFG) and attributes of its modules in the graph. AFG information is used as input for the Application Profiling Service (APS) to select the appropriate application configuration and execution environment. The application configuration is created by the Dataflow Manger (AFM) based on

```
       procedure Generate_Dataflow
       begin
1          Dataflow manager receives AFG.
2          Dataflow manager invokes APS.
3          Check application wish list includes operating system,
               memory size, CPU speed, and network bandwidth.
4          Check application history includes total execution time,
               response time, us-age of memory, and network throughput from APS.
5          Check dependency among tasks and classify the sets of tasks being executed in parallel.
6          while the dataflow script do
7              For each parallel set,
                   generate a RSL with a Globus command after locating input data.
8              Locates potential output data.
9          endwhile
10         APS collects the runtime history of the application.
11         ARS collect the runtime history information.
12         Send information to the APS.
       end Generate_Dataflow
```

Fig. 3. Generating Dataflow Algorithm

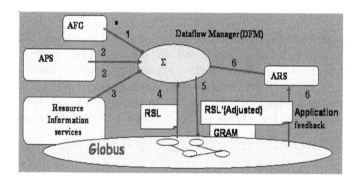

Fig. 4. Adaptive Application Configuration

an application performance model and the application requirements as specified by the user as shown in Figure 4.

The main feature of the ADViCE over Grid is the adaptive application profiling service that identifies the best resources that are currently available to run the application. The Dataflow Manager generates an RSL(Resource Specification Language) script file which will be processing by the GRAM (Globus Resource Allocation Manager) [11] along with the AFG. It selects the application configuration based two factors: the load status of available Grid resources and the application requirements. When the Dataflow Manager receives the AFG (Step 1), it invokes the APS to get the application requirement information which contains both application wish list and the application history list if available (Step 2). The application wish list includes application requirements specified by application users and task module developers such as operating system, memory size, CPU speed, network bandwidth, etc. The application history list contains previously executed application's total execution time, response time, usage of

memory, and network throughput, etc. While the Dataflow Manager is waiting the reply from the APS, it requests resource information from the resource
information service, MDS (Metacomputing Directory Service) [12], via LDAP
(Lightweight Directory Access Protocol) (Step 3). The request resource information includes static host information (operating system version, CPU type,
number of processors, total of RAM, etc.), dynamic host information (current
load average, queue length, etc.), storage system information (total disk size, free
disk space, etc.), and network information (network bandwidth and latency).
Once the Dataflow Manager collects all necessary information (Step 4 & Step
5), the Dataflow Manager is now creating the RSL (Resource Specification Language) [11] script file, adjust and add RSL information adaptively and submit
it to GRAM for execution (Step 6, Step 7, & Step 8). The application runtime history information is collected by the ARS and sent to the APS when the
application is completed (Step 10, Step 11 & Step 12).

4   Experimental Results

This section presents the performance results of ADViCE in terms of two aspects:
(1) benefits of using dataflow model, and (2) benefits from adaptive generation of
application configuration. In the former experiment, we show how the dataflow
model used in ADViCE can help programmers develop applications with ease
and improve the application performance. In the latter experiment, we present
the performance gain from the adaptive generation of application configuration
data.

4.1   Experiment 1:
Problem Solving Environment with Dataflow Model

A distributed application can be viewed as an Application Flow Graph (AFG),
where its nodes denote computational tasks and its links denote the communications and synchronization between these nodes. Without an application development tool, a developer or development team must make much effort and spend
much time to develop the distributed application from scratch. To overcome
these difficulties, the ADViCE provides an integrated problem solving environment to enable novice users to develop large-scale, complex, distributed applications using ADViCE tasks. The Linear Equation Solver (LES) application has
been selected as a running example. The problem size for this experiment is 1024
x 1024 and its execution environment consists of five SGI Origin 2000 machines
with 400-MHz IP35 processors running IRIX 6.5.15F.

Table 1 compares the timing of several software phases when we develop
the LES application using MPICH-G2 and ADViCE. When users have enough
knowledge about parallel programming and the MPICH-G2 tool, they usually
spend 1456 minutes for an LU task, 1686 minutes for an INV task, and 1274
minutes for MULT task. The total time to develop this application is approximately 4416 minutes, (i.e., around 74 hours). Using ADViCE, a novice user

Table 1. Performance comparison of Linear Equation Solver application for each software phase

Phase	MPICH-G2			ADViCE		
	LU	INV	MULT	LU	INV	MULT
Design and Development	1456 min (728 lines)	1686 min (843 lines)	1274 min (637 lines)	2.10 min	1.57 min	2.30 min
Compilation	4.92 sec	6.10 sec	5.25 sec	0 sec	0 sec	0 sec
Runtime Setup	Data transmission time: 35.404 sec			Data transmission time: 34.32 sec		
	Executable transmission time: 15.527 sec			Executable transmission time: 15.232 sec		
	File and script creating time and launching time:95 sec			File and script creating time and launching time: 0.45 sec		
Task Execution	16.409 sec	148.658 sec	34.776 sec	17.327 sec	135.484	34.437 sec
Application Execution	383.277 sec			315.140 sec		
Application Visualization	3200 sec			0.155 sec		

spends around six minutes to develop such an application. There is no compile time in ADViCE, but an MPICH-G2 application needs about 16 seconds for compilation. The ADViCE setup time for the LES application is 50.002 seconds, while the MPICH-G2 user spends around 59 seconds for creating machine files, transmitting the data and executable files, and launching them in order. Since the ADViCE is based on the dataflow model and executes the application tasks concurrently, the application execution time, including the setup time, is less than the summation of all the individual task execution times. In our experiment with the LES application, the total execution time of the MPICH-G2 implementation using four nodes is 383.277 seconds. The ADViCE implementation with the same configuration is approximately 315.140 seconds, which outperforms the MPICH-G2 by about 17.8 %.

4.2   Experiment 2: Adaptive Application Configuration

In this experiment we benchmarked two applications used in the Linear Equation Solver (LES), Matrix Inversion (INV) and Matrix Multiplication (MULT), to evaluate and analyze the performance of our adaptive approach. The problem size for this experiment is 10241024 and they run over five node high-performance cluster at the University of Arizona. The Globus 2.0 and MPICH-G2 are also used for this experiment. In order to demonstrate adaptive application configuration, we compare the execution times of two scenarios: 1) when the applications run with minimum amount of memory required to finish their executions; 2) when the applications run without any requirements for the memory size. The specification of the minimum memory size was implemented by extending the RSL string, which will be submitted to the Globus resource management architecture. Figure 5 compares the performance of the two scenarios as we increase the minimum memory size required to run the INV application. The adaptive version of INV application (INV (Adaptive)) performs better and the performance gap becomes wider as we increase the minimum memory size. For exam-

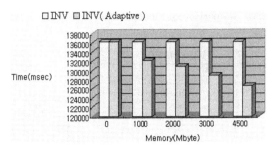

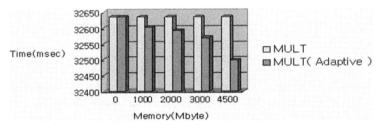

Fig. 5. Performance Comparison between adaptive and non-adaptive execution of INV task

Fig. 6. Performance Comparison between adaptive and non-adaptive execution of MULT task

ple, with the minimum memory size of 4500 Mbytes, the execution time of INV is 136240 msec, while the execution time of INV (Adaptive) is 126611 msec. Figure 6 shows the performance comparison when the same scenarios are applied to the MULT application. Similarly to the INV task scenario, the adaptive version of MULT (MULT (Adaptive)) also outperforms the MULT application and the performance gain becomes larger as we increase the minimum memory size.

From the two applications discussed above, their clear that the application performance can be improved significantly if the application execution environment can be changed dynamically when the application performance degrades due to changes in computing and network loads. The adaptive runtime layer in our approach automatically analyzes the characteristics of a given application and adaptively generates the appropriate configuration parameters to optimize its performance at runtime.

5   Conclusion

We describe the architecture of ADViCE, which has ADViCE interface over non-Grid and Grid environment. ADViCE provides a parallel and distributed programming environment; it provides an efficient web-based user interface that allows users to develop, run and visualize parallel/distributed applications running on heterogeneous computing resources connected by networks. To support Grid services through ADViCE, the ACS that creates adaptive application configurations using RSL, which runs over the Globus toolkit. We show that our approach to generate adaptive application configuration can improve the application performance significantly with non-Grid and Grid services in the experiments. Our consideration of next generation of PSEs over Grid environments is adopting standard protocols to create interoperable, reusable middleware and a service-oriented computing infrastructure for scientific applications.

References

1. I. Foster, C. Kesselman, "The Grid: Blueprint for a New Computing Infrasteructure," Morgan-Kaufmann, 1998.
2. Astrophysics Simulation Collaboratory: ASC Grid Portal, http://www.ascportal.org
3. HotPage, http://hotpage.npaci.edu
4. Cactus Code, http://www.cactuscode.org
5. GrADS Project, http://nhse2.cs.rice.edu/grads/index.html
6. Romberg,M., "The UNICORE Architecture Seamless Access to Distributed Resources," High Performance Distributed Computing, 1999.
7. Globus Project, http://www.globus.org
8. J. Novotny, "The Grid Portal Development Kit," Concurrency: Practice and Experience, Vol.00, pp1-7, 2000.
9. Gregor von Laszewski, "A Java Commodity Grid Kit," Concurrency: Practice and Experience, vol. 13, pp.645-662, 2001.
10. Dongmin Kim, Ilkyeun Ra and S. Hariri, Evaluation and Implementation of Adaptive Distributed Virtual Computing Environment2 (ADViCEII), Proc. of IASTED International Conference, Boston, MA, November 1999, pp. 677-682.
11. K. Czajkowski, I. Foster, N. Karonis, .etal, A Resource Management Architecture for Metacomputing Systems, Proc. IPPS/SPDP '98 Workshop on Job Scheduling Strategies for Parallel Processing, pp. 62-82, 1998.
12. K. Czajkowski, S. Fitzgerald, I. Foster, C. Kesselman, Grid Information Services for Distributed Resource Sharing, Proceedings of the Tenth IEEE International Symposium on High-Performance Distributed Computing (HPDC-10), IEEE Press, August 2001.

Workflow Support for Complex Grid Applications: Integrated and Portal Solutions*

Róbert Lovas, Gábor Dózsa, Péter Kacsuk,
Norbert Podhorszki, and Dániel Drótos

MTA SZTAKI, Laboratory of Parallel and Distributed Systems,
H-1518 Budapest, P.O. Box 63, Hungary
{rlovas,dozsa,kacsuk,pnorbert,drdani}@sztaki.hu
http://www.lpds.sztaki.hu

Abstract. In this paper we present a workflow solution to support graphically the design, execution, monitoring, and performance visualisation of complex grid applications. The described workflow concept can provide interoperability among different types of legacy applications on heterogeneous computational platforms, such as Condor or Globus based grids. The major design and implementation issues concerning the integration of Condor tools, Mercury grid monitoring infrastructure, PROVE performance visualisation tool, and the new workflow layer of P-GRADE are discussed in two scenarios. The integrated version of P-GRADE represents the thick client concept, while the portal version needs only a thin client and can be accessed by a standard web browser. To illustrate the application of our approach in the grid, an ultra-short range weather prediction system is presented that can be executed in a grid testbed and visualised not only at workflow level but at the level of individual parallel jobs, too.

1   Introduction

The workflow concept is a widely accepted approach to compose large scale applications by connecting programs into an interoperating set of jobs in the Grid [6][12][17][19][20].

Our main aim was to develop a workflow solution for complex grid applications to support the design, execution, monitoring, and performance visualisation phases of development in a user-friendly way. In the presented approach the interoperability among different types of legacy applications executed on heterogeneous platforms, such as Condor [1] or Globus [14] based computational grids, is the particularly addressed issue beside the efficient monitoring and visualisation facilities in the grid.

Several achievements of different grid-related projects have been exploited in the presented work to hide the low-level details of heterogeneous software components as well as to provide a unified view for application developers. These

---

* The work presented in this paper was partially supported by the following grants: EU-GridLab IST-2001-32133, Hungarian SuperGrid (IKTA4-075), IHM 4671/1/ 2003, and Hungarian Scientific Research Fund (OTKA) No. T042459 projects.

targets are crucial for the successful utilisation of grid environments by the users from other scientific areas, such as physics, chemists, or meteorology. The design and implementation issues concerning the integration of Condor/Condor-G/DAGman tools [1][2][20], Mercury/GRM grid monitoring infrastructure [3], PROVE performance visualisation tool [4], and the new high-level workflow editor and manager layer of P-GRADE programming environment [10] are discussed in Section 2 and Section 3.

As the main result a new extension of P-GRADE graphical programming environment was developed; the integrated workflow support enables construction, execution, and monitoring of complex applications on both Condor and Globus based grids (see Section 2 and Section 3). The portal version of workflow layer offers similar facilities via web interface to the integrated version but the occasionally slow and unreliable network connection must be taken into consideration more rigorously during the separation of client and server side functionalities. (see Section 4).

To illustrate the application of our approach in the grid, an ultra-short range weather prediction system is presented that can be executed on a Condor-G/Globus based testbed and visualised the execution not only at workflow level but at the level of individual jobs, too.

2   Component Based Grid Programming by Workflow

The presented workflow connects existing sequential or parallel programs into an interoperating set of jobs. Connections define dependency relations among the components of the workflow with respect to their execution order that can naturally be represented as graphs. Such representation of a meteorological application is depicted in Fig. 1.

Nodes (labelled as delta, visib, etc. in Fig. 1) represent different jobs from the following four types: sequential, PVM, MPI, or GRAPNEL job (generated by P-GRADE programming environment).

Small rectangles (labelled by numbers) around nodes represent data files (dark grey ones are input files, light grey ones are output files) of the corresponding job, and directed arcs interconnect pairs of input and output files if an output file serves as input for another job. In other words, arcs denote the necessary file transfers between jobs.

Therefore, the workflow describes both the control-flow and the data-flow of the application. A job can be started when all the necessary input files are available and transferred by GridFTP to the site where the job is allocated for execution. Managing the file-transfers and recognition of the availability of the necessary files is the task of our workflow manager that extends the Condor DAGMan capabilities.

For illustration purpose we use a meteorological application [5] called ME-ANDER developed by the Hungarian Meteorological Service. The main aim of MEANDER is to analyse and predict in the ultra short-range (up to 6 hours) those weather phenomena, which might be dangerous for life and property. Typically such events are snowstorms, freezing rain, fog, convective storms, wind gusts, hail storms and flash floods. The complete MEANDER package consists of more than ten different algorithms from which we have selected four ones to compose a workflow application for demonstration purpose. Each calculation algorithm is computation intensive and implemented as a parallel program containing C/C++ and FORTRAN sequential code.

The first graph depicted in Fig. 1 (see Workflow Layer) consists of four jobs (nodes) corresponding four different parallel algorithms of the MEANDER ultra-short range weather prediction package and a sequential visualisation job that collects the final results and presents them to the user as a kind of meteorological map:

- Delta: a P-GRADE/GRAPNEL program compiled as a PVM program with 25 processes
- Cummu: a PVM application with 10 processes
- Visib: a P-GRADE/GRAPNEL program compiled as an MPI program with 20 worker processes (see the Application window with the process farm and the master process in Fig. 1)
- Satel: an MPI program with 5 processes
- Ready: a sequential C program

This distinction among job types is necessary because the job manager on the selected grid site should be able to support the corresponding parallel execution mode, and the workflow manager is responsible for the handling of various job types by generating the appropriate submit files.

Generally, the executables of the jobs can be existing legacy applications or can be developed by P-GRADE. A GRAPNEL job can be translated into either a PVM or an MPI job but it should be distinguished from the other types of parallel jobs since P- GRADE provides fully interactive development support for GRAPNEL jobs; for designing, debugging, performance evaluation and testing the parallel code [10]. By simply clicking on such a node of the workflow graph P-GRADE invokes the Application window in which the inter-process communication topology of the GRAPNEL job can be defined and modified graphically [23] (see Fig. 1, Application window) using similar notations than that at workflow level. Then, from this Application window the lower design layers, such as the Process and the Text levels, are also accessible by the user to change the graphically or the textually described program code of the current parallel algorithm (see the Process and Text window of visibility calculation in Fig. 1). It means that the introduced workflow represents a new P-GRADE layer on the top of its three existing hierarchical design layers [13].

Besides the type of the job and the name of the executable (see Fig. 1), the user can specify the necessary arguments and the hardware/software requirements (architecture, operating system, minimal memory and disk size, number of processors, etc.) for each job. To specify the resource requirements, the application developer can currently use either the Condor resource specification syntax and semantics for Condor based grids or the explicit declaration of grid site

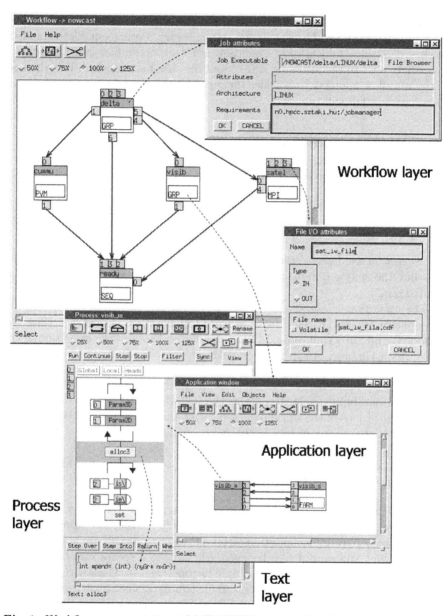

Fig. 1. Workflow representation of MEANDER meteorological application and the underlying design layers of P-GRADE parallel programming environment

where the job is to be executed for Globus based grids (see Fig. 1, Job Attributes window, Requirement field). In order to define the necessary file operations (see Fig. 1) of the workflow execution, the user should define the attributes of the file symbols (ports of the workflow graph) and file transfer channels (arcs of the workflow graph). The main attributes of the file symbols are the file name, and its type. The type can be permanent or temporary. Permanent files should be preserved during the workflow execution but temporary files can be removed immediately when the job using it (as input file) has been finished. It is the task of the workflow manager to transfer the input files to the selected site where the corresponding job will run.

3   Execution and Monitoring of Workflow

Two different scenarios can be distinguished according to the underlying grid infrastructure:

- Condor-G/Globus based grid
- Pure Condor based grid

In this section we describe the more complex Condor-G/Globus scenario in details but the major differences concerning the pure Condor support are also pointed out.

The execution of the designed workflow is a generalisation of the Condor job mode of P-GRADE [9]; but to execute the workflow in grid we utilise the Condor-G and DAGMan tools [1][2] to schedule and control the execution of the workflow on Globus resources by generating

- a Condor submit file for each node of the workflow graph
- a DAGman input file that contains the following information:
  1. List of jobs of the workflow (associating the jobs with their submit files)
  2. Execution order of jobs in textual form as relations
  3. The number of re-executions for each job's abort
  4. Tasks to be executed before starting a job and after finishing the job (implemented in PRE and POST scripts).

The PRE and POST scripts generated automatically from the workflow description realise the necessary input and output file transfer operations between jobs. In the current implementation GridFTP commands [19] are applied to deliver the input and output files between grid sites in a secure way (in the pure Condor scenario it can be done by simple file operations). These scripts are also responsible for the detection of successful file transfers, since a job can be started only if its all input files are already available. In order to improve the efficiency the data files are transferred in parallel if the same output file serves as an input file of more than one jobs.

Additionally, before the execution of each job a new instance of GRM monitor [3] is launched and attached (via a subscription protocol) to Mercury main monitor [4] located at the grid site where the current job will be executed. In order to visualise the trace information, collected on jobs by the GRM/Mercury monitor infrastructure, PROVE performance visualisation tool [4] is used (see Fig. 2). Furthermore, these scripts also generate a PROVE-compliant tracefile

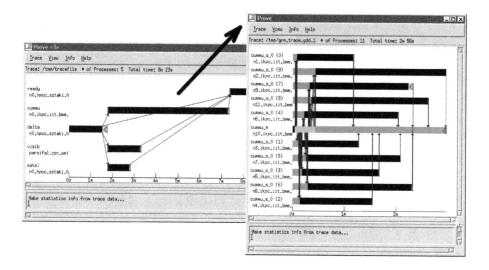

Fig. 2. Space-time diagram of the whole workflow and one of its component jobs

for the whole workflow including events regarding the start/finish of job as well as file transfers.

Notice that currently we use Condor DAGman as the base of workflow engine. However, in the near future we are going to create a general Grid Application Manager that takes care of possible optimisations concerning the selection of computing sites and file resources in the grid, controlling the migration of jobs of the workflow among different grid resources, handling the user's control request during the execution, etc.

During the execution, job status information (like submitted, idle, running, finished) of each component job is reflected by different colour of the corresponding node in the graph, i.e. the progress of the whole workflow is animated within the editor.

PROVE visualisation tool provides much more detailed view of the progress of the whole workflow and each component job than that shown by the status animation within the workflow editor. PROVE co-operates with the Mercury/GRM grid monitor system (developed within the EU GridLab project [15]) to collect the trace events generated by any of the component jobs running on any of the grid resources if the corresponding programs are instrumented and linked against the GRM library and Mercury is installed on each grid site. Having accessed the appropriate trace events, PROVE displays them on-line in separated space-time diagrams for each component job. An overall view on the progress of workflow execution is also displayed as the same kind of space-time diagram. Fig. 2 depicts the space-time diagram of our workflow-based meteorological application and one of its parallel component job cummu.

In the workflow space-time diagram, horizontal bars represent the progress of each component job in time (see the time axis at the bottom of the diagram)

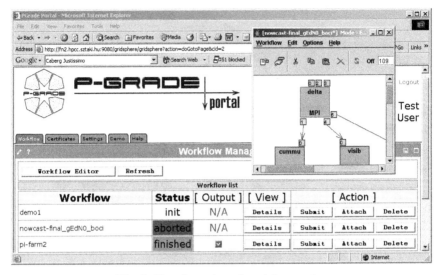

Fig. 3. Portal version of workflow system

and the arrows among bars represents the file operations performed to make accessible the output file of a job as an input of another one. Interpretation of the same diagram elements is a bit different in case of (parallel) component jobs (like job cummu in Fig. 2). Here the horizontal bars represent the progress of each process comprising the parallel job whereas arrows between bars represent (PVM or MPI) message transfers among the processes.

4   Grid Portal Support

The aim of our Grid portal – developed partly within the EU GridLab [15] project and partly within national Hungarian Supercomputing Grid [8] projects – is to provide the potential users a high-level graphical interface to build up and execute workflow like grid applications.

The portal is relying on the GridSphere portal technology [15] that is the result of the EU GridLab project. We have implemented three different portlets in GridSphere to provide services for:

- Grid certificate management,
- creation, modification and execution of workflow applications on grid resources available via Globus, and
- visualisation of workflow progress as well as each component job.

The certificate management portlet co-operates with a MyProxy server in order to assist the user in creating, storing and retrieving proxy certificates for the various Globus resources.

The workflow editor portlet (see Fig. 3) provides a graphical workflow editor client – on the basis of the WebStart technology – for the user to create new workflow application and to modify existing ones. The workflow editor client can upload all the executable and input files as well as the description of the workflow to the server from the client machine and can also submit the whole workflow for execution.

The visualisation portlet (see Fig. 3) provides similar facilities to PROVE tool as it was described in Section 3, but this part of the system is mainly running on the server side due to the large amount monitored information to be collected and processed; the collection of trace files might require high network bandwidth and their visualisation might be computationally intensive calculation. In the implemented visualisation portlet, only the raw image must be downloaded to the client side, which is more reasonable from the thin client's view.

5   Related and Future Work

Some other workflow solutions, such as Unicore [12], Triana [6] and Pegasus [17] provide sophisticated control facilities at workflow level, such as loops and conditional branches, or hierarchical design layers. Another advantage of Unicore is the pluggable graphical user interface, where the application developer can implement an application oriented front-end, making the Unicore environment configurable and user-friendly. In our integrated solution, the user can easily access and also modify the parallel program code of a workflow node using the hierarchical layers of GRED graphical editor [23] in case of GRAPNEL jobs (see Fig. 1).

Triana is a problem solving environment (PSE) based on Java technology including workflow editor and resource manager. Recently it has been extended to enable the invocation of legacy code [11]. The workflow support in MyGrid [16] has been demonstrated in bioinformatics based on web service technology but there is a lack of integration of local applications and toolkits in their native form. Our workflow system has been already demonstrated with a wide range of legacy applications including PVM and MPI applications written in Fortran, C or C++.

Pegasus workflow manager (developed within GriPhyN project [18]) addresses data intensive applications based on Condor-G/DAGman and Globus technology. On the other hand, our workflow solution gives efficient support for calculation intensive parallel applications (utilizing the existing tools of P-GRADE programming environment in case of GRAPNEL jobs) as well as for monitoring and performance visualisation in the grid relying on the results of GridLab project [15]. The monitoring facilities allow the user to focus on either the global view of workflow execution, or the individual jobs running on a grid site, or even the behaviour of component processes including their interactions. Moreover, the presented workflow tool can be executed either:

– as the part of P-GRADE parallel programming environment taking the advantages of all the integrated tools in P-GRADE at each stage of program development life-cycle, or

– via a web browser providing easy access for the workflow editor, and the underlying execution manager, and monitoring/visualisation facilities.

Another advantage of the presented system is the existing migration support for parallel jobs between grid sites [21] that will be exploited and integrated in the workflow manager during the further development. It will offer a more dynamic and more efficient runtime support for workflow execution of certain types of application (e.g. long-running parallel simulations) than the current workflow solutions can provide.

6   Conclusions

The developed workflow layer, workflow manager and Grid portal can be used to create and to execute workflow like complex grid applications by connecting existing sequential and parallel programs. Furthermore, it is capable of executing such workflows on a Globus or Condor based grid and observing the execution both at the level of workflow and at the level of each individual (parallel) component job if Mercury/GRM service is installed on the grid resources.

Our workflow solutions have been developed and evaluated on a grid testbed consisting of three different Linux clusters – located at MTA SZTAKI (Budapest), at BUTE (Budapest) and at University of Westminster, CPC (London) – which are equipped by Globus Toolkit 2 as grid middleware, by Mercury as monitoring infrastructure, and by MPICH and PVM as message passing libraries.

The developed workflow portal has been demonstrated successfully at different forums (ACM/IEEE Supercompting 2003, IEEE Cluster 2003) by a complex meteorological program, which performs ultra-short range weather forecasting. This workflow solution is to be used in several national grid projects, e.g. the Hungarian SuperGrid [8] project (Globus based grid), the Hungarian Chemistry Grid project [22], and Hungarian ClusterGrid project [7], which is a Condor based nation-wide computational grid infrastructure.

References

1. D. Thain, T. Tannenbaum, and M. Livny, Condor and the Grid, in Fran Berman, Anthony J.G. Hey, Geoffrey Fox, editors, Grid Computing: Making The Global Infrastructure a Reality, John Wiley, 2003
2. James Frey, Todd Tannenbaum, Ian Foster, Miron Livny, and Steven Tuecke: Condor-G: A Computation Management Agent for Multi-Institutional Grids, Journal of Cluster Computing volume 5, pages 237-246, 2002
3. Z. Balaton and G. Gombás: Resource and Job Monitoring in the Grid, Proc. of EuroPar'2003, Klagenfurt, pp. 404-411, 2003
4. Z. Balaton, P. Kacsuk, and N. Podhorszki: Application Monitoring in the Grid with GRM and PROVE, Proc. of the Int. Conf. on Computational Science – ICCS 2001, San Francisco, pp. 253-262, 2001
5. R. Lovas, et al.: Application of P-GRADE Development Environment in Meteorology, Proc. of DAPSYS'2002, Linz, pp. 30-37, 2002

6. I. Taylor, et al.: Grid Enabling Applications Using Triana, Workshop on Grid Applications and Programming Tools, June 25, 2003, Seattle.
7. P. Stefán: The Hungarian ClusterGrid Project, Proc. of MIPRO'2003, Opatija, 2003
8. P. Kacsuk: Hungarian Supercomputing Grid, Proc. of ICCS'2002, Amsterdam. Springer Verlag, Part II, pp. 671-678, 2002
9. P. Kacsuk, R. Lovas, et al: Demonstration of P-GRADE job-mode for the Grid, In: Euro- Par 2003 Parallel Processing, Lecture Notes in Computer Science, Vol. 2790, Springer- Verlag, 2003
10. P-GRADE Graphical Parallel Program Development Environment: http://www.lpds.sztaki.hu/projects/pgrade
11. Yan Huang, Ian Taylor, David W. Walker and Robert Davies: Wrapping Legacy Codes for Grid-Based Applications, to be published in proceedings on the HIPS 2003 workshop.
12. www.unicore.org
13. P. Kacsuk, G. Dózsa, R. Lovas: The GRADE Graphical Parallel Programming Environment, In the book: Parallel Program Development for Cluster Computing: Methodology, Tools and Integrated Environments (Chapter 10), Editors: P. Kacsuk, J.C. Cunha and S.C. Winter, pp. 231-247, Nova Science Publishers New York, 2001
14. Globus Toolkit, www.globus.org/toolkit
15. GridLab project, www.gridlab.org
16. Matthew Addis, et al: Experiences with eScience workflow specification and enactment in bioinformatics, Proceedings of UK e-Science All Hands Meeting 2003 (Editors: Simon J. Cox)
17. Ewa Deelman, et al: Mapping Abstract Complex Workflows onto Grid Environments, Journal of Grid Computing, Vol.1, no. 1, 2003, pp. 25-39.
18. GriPhyN project, www.griphyn.org
19. W. Allcock, J. Bester, J. Bresnahan, A. Chervenak, L. Liming, S. Meder, and S. Tuecke: Gridftp protocol specification, Technical report, Global Grid Forum, September 2002
20. Condor DAGman, http://www.cs.wisc.edu/condor/dagman/
21. J. Kovács, P. Kacsuk: A migration framework for executing parallel programs in the Grid, Proc. of the 2nd AxGrids Conf., Nicosia, 2004
22. Hungarian ChemistryGrid project, http://www.lpds.sztaki.hu/chemistrygrid
23. P. Kacsuk, G. Dózsa, T. Fadgyas and R. Lovas: The GRED Graphical Editor for the GRADE Parallel Program Development Environment, Journal of Future Generation Computer Systems, Vol. 15(1999), No. 3, pp. 443-452.

Debugging MPI Grid Applications
Using Net-dbx

Panayiotis Neophytou[1], Neophytos Neophytou[2], and Paraskevas Evripidou[1]

[1] Department of Computer Science, University of Cyprus,
P.O. Box 20537, CY-1678 Nicosia, Cyprus
{cs99pn1,skevos}@ucy.ac.cy
[2] Computer Science Department, Stony Brook University,
Stony Brook, NY 11794-4400, USA
nneophyt@cs.sunysb.edu

Abstract. Application-development in Grid environments is a challenging process, thus the need for grid enabled development tools is also one
that has to be fulfilled. In our work we describe the development of a Grid
Interface for the Net-dbx parallel debugger, that can be used to debug
MPI grid applications. Net-dbx is a web-based debugger enabling users
to use it for debugging from anywhere in the Internet. The proposed
debugging architecture is platform independent, because it uses Java,
and it is accessible from anywhere, anytime because it is web based. Our
architecture provides an abstraction layer between the debugger and the
grid middleware and MPI implementation used. This makes the debugger
easily adaptable to different middlewares. The grid-enabled architecture
of our debugger carries the portability and usability advantages of Net-
dbx on which we have based our design. A prototype has been developed
and tested.

1   Introduction

The rapidly growing demand on computational and storage resources has made
the development of Grids of various kinds and sizes, of different scopes and objectives, a common yet difficult task. A lot of different factors need to be considered
in the development and deployment of a Grid, the most important being the application domain on which it is going to be used. The requirements of a Grid are
provided by the set of people that are resource providers and resource consumers
that share common interests. These sets of people are what are called Virtual
Organizations (VO) [3]. So far a lot of Grids have been developed with different uses to serve a wide variety of researchers as well as business corporations.
In this process, developers of such distributed systems for large-scale research
have formed a community that has developed good quality middleware (Globus,
EDG, etc.) that allows resource providers to interconnect their resources and
efficiently and securely share them with other users, to solve common problems.

The next task is the development of the Grid applications that lie atop of
the middleware's infrastructure. These applications make the Grid accessible

M. Dikaiakos (Ed.): AxGrids 2004, LNCS 3165, pp. 139–148, 2004.

and of service to its users. While the analysis and design of such applications is quite an important part of the process, their implementation is the most challenging part of this development cycle. These large-scale, resource demanding applications may have their data and processing widely distributed across a Grid system. Powerful tools and IDEs (Integrated Development Environments), specifically debugging tools are becoming even more necessary. In this work we have developed a grid-aware debugger targeted to the Message Passing Interface (MPI) [12], a well-known low level parallel programming paradigm that is now being used as an additional alternative model for grid programming.

In this paper we describe our architecture for debugging Grid applications. Our architecture relies on an MPI enabled grid development and runtime environment, a Grid enabled MPI implementation, and an existing debugging tool (Net-dbx) that enables debugging of MPI applications across the internet. We have developed an architecture that addresses the heterogeneity associated with Grid environments, with the help of a communications proxy server and the use of abstraction layers. We call this architecture Net-dbx Grid Interface (Net-dbx GI). We have tested this architecture on our local test bed using the Globus Toolkit 2.4, MPICH-G2 and Netdbx. Support for other Grid enabled MPI implementations, such as PACX-MPI and LAM-MPI will be tested in the near future.

Net-dbx [14] utilizes WWW capabilities in general and Java applets in particular for portable, parallel and distributed runtime source-level debugging across the Internet. It can be used with MPI programs written in C, C++ and FORTRAN. Its design is based on a framework that utilizes gdb [16] to attach the application processes on the individual nodes, and the additional facilities provided by the underlying MPI implementation to provide a complete picture of the topology and communication aspects of the debugged application. Net-dbx GI extends this existing architecture and lays the necessary interfaces for proper initialization, communication and collaboration of the resources needed to participate in the debugging process for applications deployed on the Grid. Other similar architectures to Net-dbx are TotalView [2], p2d2 [9,1], Panorama [11] and others.

In the rest of this paper, we will show the improvements and changes made to the existing Net-dbx architecture. In Section 2 we present the Net-dbx debugging tool. In section 3 of the paper we describe the layered architecture and the interfaces which are needed to adapt Net-dbx GI architecture to any Grid MPI environment. In section 4 we describe the testing procedure of the architecture using the Globus Project [4] middleware and MPICH-G2 [10] MPI platform.

2   Net-dbx

Net-dbx's approach to achieving distributed debugging is based on individually attaching every process to a local debugger at the lowest level and then integrating the individual debuggers into a device-independent, interactive, user-friendly environment [13]. For each process to be monitored, the integration environment interacts with the local debugger. As the user defines global and individual operations to be applied to all or some of the processes, these are translated by the integration tool into interaction with each of the local debuggers individually. To attach all the required processes to the local debuggers, an initialization scheme has been implemented as described in [14]. The overall architecture of Net-dbx is based on a three-layer design: the lower layer, which resides on the MPI-Nodes, the communications layer, which is implemented on the client side, and the integration layer, which coordinates the communication objects and provides the graphical environment to the user.

The communications and integration layers, which rely on the client side, are implemented in Java. As a Java applet, the system is capable of running in the user's Internet Browser display. Having the requirement for a Java-enabled browser as its only prerequisite, the Net-dbx applet can be operated uniformly from anywhere on the Internet using virtually any client console.

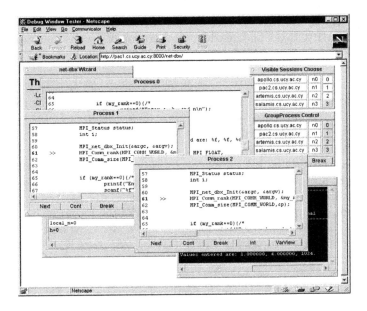

Fig. 1. Net-dbx User Interface at debugging time

Net-dbx gives you the ability to select which processes to debug. In the example shown in Figure 1 we have a multicomputer that consists of 4 nodes, with a process running on each one of them. The visual components available to the user at debugging time are also shown in Figure 1. All the components are controlled by a process coordinator. When the user chooses a process from the Visible Sessions Choose window the coordinator opens the corresponding process window visualizing that particular process. The user can open as many process windows as the number of processes running. Through these windows the user can set breakpoints, individually control the progress of a process etc. The user also has the choice of controlling groups of processes from the Group Process control. The complete functionality of Net-dbx is described in detail in [14].

We have chosen Net-dbx over any other of the tools mentioned in the Introduction because of some important advantages it has for usage on Grid environments. Firstly, it is web based, which makes it portable and available from anywhere. Secondly, it is supported by low-bandwidth connections (as low as 33Kbps) which makes it ideal for distant debugging through anywhere in the internet in contrast with the other debuggers that are designed mostly for local use.

3   Architecture of Net-dbx Grid Interface

The Net-dbx GI architecture is based on the same principles of layered design as Net-dbx. In order to make the new architecture portable, the previous design has been enriched with basic components and methods that are required to support most Grid implementations. An initialization scheme is required in order to be able to locate and attach all the participating processes to local debuggers, and establish a communication link between those processes and the debugging applet. This is particularly challenging in Grid implementations, as the inherent architecture of the grid does not allow external users to login directly into the Grid nodes, but rather submit computational jobs asynchronously. The initialization scheme and communications layers have been tailored to address these constraints, and establish direct links to all participating nodes, using an intermediate proxy server.

At the lowest level, our implementation relies on the vendor-dependent MPI implementation and local debugging tools on each node. These will then communicate with higher communication abstraction layers, and at the topmost part everything is integrated into the debugging GUI applet, which is hosted at the remote user's web browser. In the following section we describe Net-dbx GI architecture, with particular focus on the communications and middleware interface layers that enable this tool to operate on Grid implementations.

3.1   Layered Architecture

Net-dbx GI architecture is depicted in Figure 2. Following the Net-dbx architecture, the lower layers are defined as the set of resources that all together with the help of Grid services collaborate and constitute the Virtual Organization's grid network, which with the help of the local vendor-MPI implementation and a grid enabled MPI implementation work as a large MPI multi-computer. It consists of simple tools that are required on each Node and can be used for individually debugging the processes running on that Node. These tools include the local vendor-MPI runtime environment. A grid enabled MPI implementation will help in the communication of the participating Nodes that are geographically distributed. Also included on each node are the Grid middleware tools, and a source level runtime debugger (we currently use gdb).

On the higher layers there is a client tool that integrates debugging of each Node and provides the user with a wider view of the MPI program, which runs on the selected resources on the Grid environment. The program residing in the client side is the Net-dbx Java applet enriched with a set of interfaces to Grid services. It is used to integrate the capabilities of the tools, which rely on the MPI-Nodes. Net-dbx GI architecture also includes three interfaces to the Grid services and a communications proxy server to help with the quick and easy propagation of messages. We will explain the usage of the interfaces in section 3.2 and the usage of the proxy server in section 3.3.

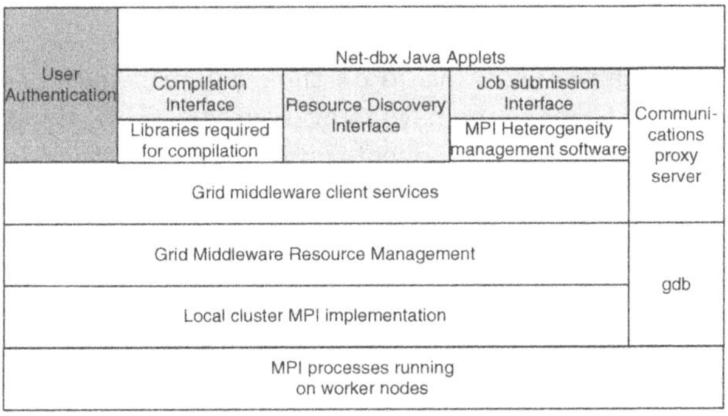

User Authentication	Net-dbx Java Applets			Communications proxy server
	Compilation Interface	Resource Discovery Interface	Job submission Interface	
	Libraries required for compilation		MPI Heterogeneity management software	
	Grid middleware client services			
	Grid Middleware Resource Management			gdb
	Local cluster MPI implementation			
	MPI processes running on worker nodes			

Fig. 2. Net-dbx Grid Interface Architecture

3.2   Abstraction Layers

Our architecture provides abstraction layers as interfaces that can be used with any standard Grid middleware and grid enabled MPI implementation. To achieve this we had to change the way Net-dbx worked to add more abstraction in the initial setup and initialization scheme as well as in the way Net-dbx communicated with the individual nodes.

The first of the three interfaces shown in Figure 2 is the Compilation Interface. This component is responsible for the correct compilation of the user's source code so that the executable can run on the desired environment. This module adds a call to our instrumentation library in the user program. This call enables the synchronization of all participating processes and makes them available to be attached for debugging. This initialization process will be described later in more detail. The instrumentation and all the functionality related to Net-dbx is only invoked when the program is run from the debugger, with a special command line argument.

The second interface is the Resource Discovery Interface. This interface consists of two main components. The Information Services Client module is responsible for connecting with the Grid Middleware Information Services component and retrieves information about available resources, and cluster configuration. The output of this component is an XML file containing cluster information about the available resources, depending on the queries made by this component. This component must be implemented in order to enable the retrieval of such information as available resources on which someone can run MPI applications and be able to debug them using gdb. The second component is the Resource configuration module that interprets the XML file and presents the results to the user so that he can make his own choices about the environment on which his application will run.

The third interface is the Job Submission Interface . This component takes its input from the User Interface containing all of the user's options and it is responsible to do all the necessary actions to fully submit the job. This component is provided with a ssh interface and it's able to send and receive data from a ssh connection with Net-dbx server. If the middleware in use doesn't provide a Java API then all the middleware's client services can be invoked using this ssh connection.

3.3   Communications Proxy Layer

Most of the changes to Net-dbx's architecture were made to the communications scheme, in order to provide full platform independence. Net-dbx uses telnet sessions to accomplish communication between the client and the gdb sessions attached to the individual processes. This is not feasible in a grid environment because a local user may have different mappings on the remote resources. Grid user has no real access to the resource itself; rather the grid middleware provides an interface to the resources and single sign-on to the whole system using different authentication methods. So to avoid having to integrate the authentication methods of every grid middleware currently available or under development, we have implemented a new method that is access independent.

Secure sockets [15] are used[1] for communication between the gdb debugging session, and the client. We also used sockets for the communication between the user and the application's I/O. Previously in Net-dbx, gdb was instantiated using a telnet session and received commands through telnet. Currently, in Net-dbx GI, gdb is spawned by the process itself using code from the instrumentation library integrated at compilation time, and its I/O is redirected to a secure socket.

The socket-handling is made by the proxy server running on Net-dbx server. This proxy server accepts connections from MPIHost (nodes that run processes) and from Net-dbx client applets. MPIhost objects send a label to the proxy server in the format "MPIHOST hostname rank" and client objects send "CLIENT hostname rank" labels to indicate the process they want to connect to. The proxy server matches these labels and binds the sockets to each other by forwarding the input and the output of these sockets. It is only required for the ip address of the proxy server to be public. Since the MPI hosts are the ones who initialize

---

[1] In Grid environments where security is not an issue then secure sockets can be used.

the connections to the proxy server they may also be within private networks with non-public ip addresses.

The proxy server also help us overcome one of the major security constraints posed in Java is the rule that applets can have an Internet connection (of any kind – telnet, FTP, HTTP, TCP, etc) only with their HTTP server host [6].

3.4   Security

There are mainly two security issues raised by Net-dbx GI architecture. The first is user authentication. A user of an implementation of the Net-dbx GI debugging architecture is automatically considered a user of the whole Virtual Organization because he is going to submit jobs on the resources. As such he must be authenticated with the correct credentials required by the VO [5]. So far Net-dbx authenticates the user using a username and password given at login time and by comparing that with a list of usernames and passwords in a database on the server. The authentication mechanisms for Net-dbx had to be revised and a security layer has been added to the architecture (Figure 1: User Authentication Layer) so the implementers of the architecture can adapt the debugger's methods to the ones required by the VO.

The second aspect of security that needs to be considered is the communication between the nodes, the client and the proxy server. The use of secure sockets [15] is required to prevent interception of the messages by malicious intruders who could manipulate the command stream to the debugger and compromise the target machine thereafter.

3.5   Initialization and Running Scheme

The initialization scheme used in Net-dbx is also preserved in Net-dbx GI. The participating processes' PIDs are used to attach the debugger. The synchronization scheme [14] ensures that all the processes of interest to the user are attached in the local debuggers right after the MPI initialization calls. Net-dbx GI extends this scheme to meet the requirements of our architecture and to overcome the heterogeneity-related difficulties encountered in a grid environment. Figure 3 shows the exact order of the initialization tasks starting from the point where the user chooses runtime parameters for his application, to the point that all the processes are fully attached and ready to be debugged using the user interface. The three main components are shown in the Figure 3. The Net-dbx applet which is the component running on the user's browser. The MPI processes that run on the MPI enabled nodes that are shared within a GRID. Finally, in between is the proxy server which is hosted on the Net-dbx web server.

At first, the system initiates an ssh session[2] with the debugger server (which is the web server) and authenticates as the Net-dbx user. The ssh session provides a command line interface initiate and control the client services of the grid. It also handles the application's standard input and output after the job submission.

---

[2] Ssh is used in Grid environments where security is not an issue.

Using the ssh session, the Net-dbx client checks to ensure the availability of the proxy server. Once the proxy is available, the user preferences are passed to the Job Submission module. Then this module can submit the job directly to the grid services or indirectly by using the ssh session and command line tools (this depends on the implementation of the module). After job submission the processes begin execution on the nodes.

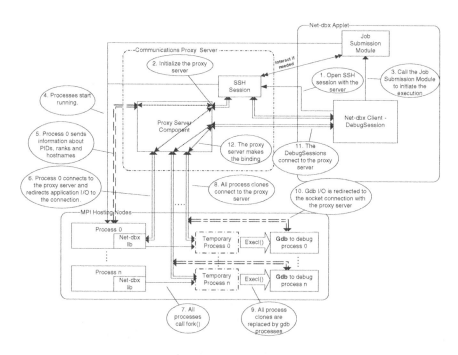

Fig. 3. Initialization and Running Scheme

The first call the processes make, after MPI_Init(), goes to the Net-dbx module added at compilation time. Process 0 gathers all the information regarding the PIDs, the hostnames and ranks of all the processes (using standard MPI commands) and sends them to the proxy server, which in turn outputs them to the ssh session for the client to collect. Then, Process 0, which is responsible for handling program's I/O, connects to the proxy server and redirects the program's standard input and output to the secure socket connection. The proxy server handles the program's input and output through the ssh session, which is now available to the user through a window in the client's applet. After that, all processes call fork() and clone themselves. The clone connects to the proxy server and immediately replaces itself with a gdb process. Then gbd's I/O is redirected to the connection. In the meanwhile, on the client side, one object is created for each process to control it (based on the information about the execution environment which includes PIDs, ranks and hostnames). Each of these objects connects to the proxy server and requests a connection with the appropriate gdb socket. If the proxy server has the requested socket it binds them together, if not it waits until the appropriate gdb connection occurs. After binding all the "interesting" (user selected) processes the program is synchronized at the point where all the processes left the initialization call, and it is ready for debugging.

4   Prototype Implementation

A working prototype of the proposed architecture has been developed and tested. The goal of this prototype was to achieve the same behavior for the debugger on both our disparate Grid clusters, as it worked on a local network.

We have tested the Grid Interface of Net-dbx using 2 clusters. The first one consists of six dual processor SuperServer machines and the second one consists of six single processor IBM PCs. The operating system used is RedHat Linux 8. The grid middleware we have chosen is the Globus Toolkit v.2.4, which supports MPI, using MPICH-G2 as the grid enabled implementation of MPI. The underlying clusters' MPI implementation we used is the MPICH p4 device [8], although any other MPI implementations may also be used as well. The services provided by the Globus Toolkit fulfill all the needs of our architecture. That is the resource management component, which is responsible for the job submission mechanism and the information services component responsible for providing information on the grid environment.

The implementation of the communications layer included the full development of the proxy server in Java and the extension of the Net-dbx instrumentation library. The proxy server was fully implemented in Java, as a portable platform independent module, and it will be used in all the future implementations of the architecture. The Net-dbx library was extended in order to enable the spawning of gdb and the I/O redirections, as described in Section 3.5. We have implemented the compilation interface by using the existing Net-dbx compilation scripts and extended them for use with MPICH-G2 and Globus. The current Resource Discovery interface just hardcoded the resources that we had available in our test-bed, as full implementation of the architecture was not our goal in this working prototype. Finally the Job Submission module was also hard-coded because it depends on the Resource Discovery interface. The hardcoded layers are currently under further development, along with some additions to the user interface.

5   Conclusions and Future Work

In this paper we have presented Net-dbx GI, our architecture for building a gridenabled debugger based on the Net-dbx tool for remote debugging of local network based MPI applications. We have tested our architecture on our local Globus MPI enabled test-bed and we have shown that our architecture can be used to debug parallel grid applications on real grid environments. We are currently working on an implementation of our architecture that will work as a debugging portal on the web. Developers will be able to use the portal to debug their parallel grid applications from anywhere with the use of a common web browser. Further additions to the user interface will provide useful runtime environment information to the user, such as message propagation delays between clusters and other grid-specific and topology aware information. We are also working on a complete security infrastructure to ensure proper access to the VO's resources.

References

1. Doreen Cheng, Robert Hood: A portable debugger for parallel and distributed programs. SC 1994: 723-732
2. "Etnus, Online Documentation for the TotalView Debugger", http://www.etnus.com/Support/docs/index.html, 2003.
3. Ian T. Foster: The Anatomy of the Grid: Enabling Scalable Virtual Organizations. Euro-Par 2001: 1-4.
4. Ian T. Foster, Carl Kesselman: The Globus Project: A Status Report. Heterogeneous Computing Workshop 1998: 4-18.
5. Ian T. Foster, Carl Kesselman, Gene Tsudik, Steven Tuecke: A Security Architecture for Computational Grids. ACM Conference on Computer and Communications Security 1998: 83-92.
6. J. Steven Fritzinger, Marinanne Mueller: Java Security white Paper, Sun Microsystems Inc., 1996.
7. Andrew S. Grimshaw, William A. Wulf: The Legion Vision of a Worldwide Computer. CACM 40(1): 39-45 (1997).
8. William Gropp, Ewing L. Lusk, Nathan Doss, Anthony Skjellum: A High-Performance, Portable Implementation of the MPI Message Passing Interface Standard. Parallel Computing 22(6): 789-828 (1996).
9. Robert Hood, Gabriele Jost: A Debugger for Computational Grid Applications. Heterogeneous Computing Workshop 2000: 262-270.
10. Nicholas T. Karonis, Brian R. Toonen, Ian T. Foster: MPICH-G2: A Grid-enabled implementation of the Message Passing Interface. Journal of Parallel and Distributed Computing 63(5): 551-563 (2003).
11. John May, Francine Berman: Retargetability and Extensibility in a Parallel Debugger. Journal of Parallel and Distributed Computing 35(2): 142-155 (1996).
12. Message Passing Interface Forum. MPI: A message-passing interface standard. International Journal of Supercomputer Applications, 8(3/4):165-414, 1994.
13. Neophytos Neophytou, Paraskevas Evripidou: Net-dbx: A Java Powered Tool for Interactive Debugging of MPI Programs Across the Internet. Euro-Par 1998: 181-189.
14. Neophytos Neophytou, Paraskevas Evripidou: Net-dbx: A Web-Based Debugger of MPI Programs Over Low-Bandwidth Lines. IEEE Transactions on Parallel and Distributed Systems 12(9): 986-995 (2001).
15. "Secure Sockets Layer", http://wp.netscape.com/security/techbriefs/ssl.html, 2003.
16. Richard M. Stallman, Roland Pesch, Stan Shebs, et al., Debugging with GDB: The GNU Source-Level Debugger, Ninth Edition, for GDB version 5.1.1, Free Software Foundation.

Towards an UML Based Graphical Representation of Grid Workflow Applications*

Sabri Pllana[1], Thomas Fahringer[2], Johannes Testori[1],
Siegfried Benkner[1], and Ivona Brandic[1]

[1] Institute for Software Science, University of Vienna
Liechtensteinstraße 22, 1090 Vienna, Austria
{pllana,testori,sigi,brandic}@par.univie.ac.at
[2] Institute for Computer Science, University of Innsbruck
Technikerstraße 25/7, 6020 Innsbruck, Austria
Thomas.Fahringer@uibk.ac.at

Abstract. Grid workflow applications are emerging as one of the most interesting programming models for the Grid. In this paper we present a novel approach for graphically modeling and describing Grid workflow applications based on the Unified Modeling Language (UML). Our approach provides a graphic representation of Grid applications based on a widely accepted standard (UML) that is more amenable than pure textual-oriented specifications (such as XML). We describe some of the most important elements for modeling control flow, data flow, synchronization, notification, and constraints. We also introduce new features that have not been included by other Grid workflow specification languages which includes broadcast and parallel loops. Our UML-based graphical editor Teuta provides the corresponding tool support. We demonstrate our approach by describing a UML-based Grid workflow model for an advanced 3D medical image reconstruction application.

1 Introduction

In the past years extensive experience has been gained with single site applications and parameter studies for the Grid. For a short time, Grid workflow applications are emerging as an important new alternative to develop truly distributed applications for the Grid. Workflow Grid applications can be seen as a collection of activities (mostly computational tasks or user interaction) that are processed in some order. Usually both control and data flow relationships are shown within a workflow. Although workflow applications have been extensively studied in areas such as business process modeling [9], it is relatively new in the Grid computing area.

The Web Service Flow Language (WSFL) [11] focuses on the composition of Web services by using a flow model and a global model. Moreover, the order of the Web services is defined. Both flow of control and data flow are represented.

---

* The work described in this paper is supported by the Austrian Science Fund as part of Aurora Project under contract SFBF1104.

M. Dikaiakos (Ed.): AxGrids 2004, LNCS 3165, pp. 149–158, 2004.

The Web service flow language can be considered as a language to describe concrete workflows that are based on a specific implementation of workflow activities namely Web services. However, it is not an abstract workflow language that shields implementation details. There are multiple choices to represent workflow activities. Web services represent one implementation. XLANG [15] is used to model business processes as autonomous agents which supports among others exceptions, conditional and iterative statements, and transactions. The Business Process Execution Language for Web Services (BPEL4WS) [1] specifies the behavior of a business process based on Web Services. In BPEL4WS business processes provide and use functionality based on Web Service interfaces. BPEL4WS is a merge of the concepts of XLANG and WSFL.

Commonly these languages are considered to be too complex for Grid applications with extensive language features for control flow and synchronization that in many cases make only sense in the business process modeling area. Moreover, in these models workflow is commonly defined such that interaction among Web services is done via a central workflow control engine which certainly would be a bottleneck for Grid applications.

There is also some work done to introduce languages for the specification of Grid workflow applications based on the eXtensible Markup Language (XML) [5]. Grid Workflow [4] is a language for describing Grid workflow applications developed at Sandia National Laboratories. This language is missing the advanced constructs for the control flow such as branches, loops, split and join. There is no graphical representation defined for this language. Grid Services Flow Language (GSFL) [10] is an XML based language for Grid workflow applications developed at Argonne National Laboratory. It can represent only a sequence of activities, and is missing the advanced constructs for the control flow such as branches, loops, split and join.

Triana [6] supports the graphical representations of workflows. *Triana* workflows are experiment-based: each unit of work is associated with a specific experiment. A workflow – defined by a *task graph* – defines the order in which experiments are executed. *Triana* provides support for simple control-flow constructs, but for instance advanced concurrency cannot be explicitly expressed since there is no support for synchronization conditions.

In this paper we introduce a new approach that employs the Unified Modeling Language (UML) [12] for graphically modeling and describing Grid workflow applications. Workflow modeling is strongly supported by UML through activity diagrams. Moreover, UML is a widely used standard that is easier to read and understand by human beings than XML documents as commonly used by many workflow specification languages. In order to facilitate machine processing of UML diagrams, UML tools support the automatic transformation of UML diagrams into XML Metadata Interchange (XMI) [13]. We tried to incorporate all important features presented by previous workflow languages including WSFL, eliminated unnecessary complexity and introduced new concept that were missing. Our UML modeling approach covers some of the most important modeling constructs for workflow hierarchical decomposition, control and data flow, synchronization and notification. Moreover, we included workflow constructs that are not covered by existing workflow languages including parallel loops and broadcast communication. Existing work can express parallel activities which must be specified one by one through a fork mechanism. Grid applications often exploit large numbers of independent tasks which should be naturally expressed by parallel loops. Moreover, some workflow languages support some kind of message passing. But the important concept of broadcast is not provided by existing work. Our UML-based graphical editor Teuta provides the corresponding tool support. We demonstrate our approach by describing a UML-based Grid workflow model for an advanced 3D medical image reconstruction application [3].

The paper is organized as follows: Section 2 briefly describes the subset of the UML that we use in this paper. A set of concepts that may be relevant for describing Grid workflow is presented in Section 3. A case study for an advanced 3D medical image reconstruction is presented in Section 4. Finally, some concluding remarks are made and future work is outlined in Section 5.

2   Background

In this paper, UML activity diagrams are used for representing computational, communication, and synchronization operations. We use the UML1.x notation [12], because at the time of writing this paper the UML2.0 specification is not officially accepted as a standard.

An activity diagram is a variation of a state machine in which the states represent the execution of actions or subactivities and the transitions are triggered by the completion of the actions or subactivities. An action state is used to model a step in the execution of an algorithm, or a workflow process. Transitions are used to specify that the flow of control pass from one action to the next action state. An activity diagram expresses a decision when guard conditions are used to indicate different possible transitions (see Figure 1(a)). A guard condition specifies a condition that must be satisfied in order to enable the firing of an associated transition. A merge has two or more incoming transitions and one outgoing transition. Fork and join are used to model parallel flows of control, as shown in Figure 1(b). The initial and final state are, respectively, visualized as a solid ball and a solid ball inside a circle. Figure 1(c) shows the UML notation for the object flow, which we use for the representation of the data flow in a workflow.

Figure 1(a) illustrates how to model a loop by employing an activity diagram, whereas Figure 1(b) shows one option for modeling the parallel execution of two activities.

3   Graphical Representation of the Grid Workflow

In this section we describe a set of UML elements and constructs that may be used for the graphical representation of the workflow. Due to space limitation we are not able to present all relevant aspects, but nevertheless we can illustrate the expressiveness of the UML activity diagram for specification of the workflow with a set of examples.

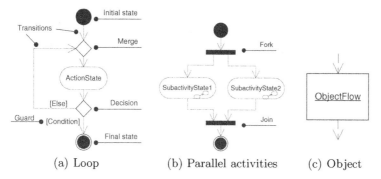

(a) Loop   (b) Parallel activities   (c) Object

Fig. 1. UML activity diagram notation

3.1   Workflow Hierarchical Decomposition

The Workflow Management Coalition [16] defines workflow as:

The automation of a business process, in whole or part, during which documents, information or tasks are passed from one participant to another for action, according to a set of procedural rules.

A Grid workflow could be defined as a flow of a set of activities. Usually, these activities represent CPU intensive computation or the transfer of the large files.

The UML stereotyping extension mechanism provide the possibility to make the semantics of a core modeling element more specific. In addition, stereotyping mechanism improves the readability of the model, by associating a specific name to a model element. The stereotype *workflow*, which is defined based on the UML modeling element *subactivity*, is used to represent the workflow (see Figure 2(a)). The compartment of the stereotype *workflow* named *Tags* specifies the list of tag definitions which include *id* and *type*. The tag *id* is used to uniquely identify the element *workflow*, whereas the tag *type* is used to describe the element *workflow*. By using tags it is possible to associate an arbitrary number of *properties* (such as *id*) to a modeling element. Analogously are defined the stereotypes that are presented in the remaining part of this paper, but because of the space limitation the stereotype definition process is not shown.

The UML modeling element *subactivity* supports hierarchical decomposition. This makes possible the description of the workflow at different levels of abstraction. Figure 2(b) shows the workflow *SampleWorkflow1*. The content of the workflow *SampleWorkflow1* which comprises a sequence of workflows *SampleWorkflow2* and *SampleWorkflow3* is depicted in Figure 2(c).

3.2   Elemental Operations

Compute, *TransferData*, and *View* are some of the elemental operations of the Grid workflow (see Figure 3). Element *Compute* (see Figure 3(a)) represents a computational intensive activity of the workflow. Element *TransferData* (see Figure 3(b)) represents the transfer of data. Properties of this element may

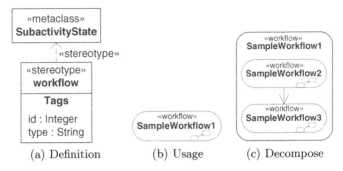

(a) Definition   (b) Usage   (c) Decompose

Fig. 2. The representation of the workflow hierarchical decomposition with the stereotype *workflow*

(a) Compute   (b) TransferData   (c) View

Fig. 3. Elemental operations

specify the source and destination of the data, and the type of the data transfer. Figure 3(c) depicts the element *View*, which represents an activity of the visualization of the data.

3.3 Control Flow

UML activity diagrams provide a reach set of elements for representing the control flow (see Section 2). Figure 4(a) shows an example of the branch. If the value of the logical expression *condition* is *True* then the activity *SampleComputation* is executed. An example of the loop is represented in Figure 4(b). The body of the loop is executed if the *condition* is true.

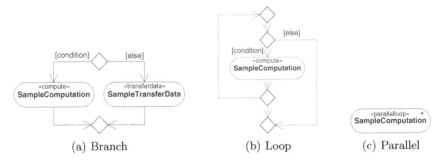

(a) Branch   (b) Loop   (c) Parallel

Fig. 4. Control flow

Existing work can express parallel activities which must be specified one by one through a fork mechanism (see Figure 1(b) in Section 2). However, Grid applications often exploit large numbers of independent tasks which should be naturally expressed by parallel loops (see Figure 4(c)). The '*' symbol in the upper right corner of the activity denotes dynamic concurrency. This means that multiple instances of the activity *SampleComputation* may be executed in parallel. The parameters of the parallel loop are specified by using the properties of the element *parallelloop*. The element *parallelloop* may be used to represent parameter studies on the Grid. The index can be used to query different input data for all concurrent running activities. In the gathering phase, all results can be for instance visualised or combined to create a final result of the parameter study.

3.4 Data Flow

One of the specific features of the Grid workflow is the moving of large amounts of data among workflow activities. Figure 5 shows an example of the graphical representation of the data flow. The output file *SampleFile* of the activity *SampleComputation1* serves as input for the activity *SampleComputation2*.

Fig. 5. Data flow

3.5 Synchronization

For the realization of the advanced synchronization workflow patterns we use *events*. Figure 6(a) shows the synchronization of parallel flows of control via events. The activity *SampleTransferData* will not begin the execution before either activity *SampleComputation1* or activity *SampleComputation2* is completed. The actions send and receive *event* are associated with transitions. An alternative notation for representing send and receive of an event is shown in Figure 6(b).

3.6 Notification

A Grid service can be configured to be a notification source, and a certain client to be a notification sink [14]. Multiple Grid clients may subscribe for a particular information in one Grid service. This information is broadcasted to all clients that are subscribed. Figure 7 shows the graphical representation of the concept *broadcast*.

Grid service notification mechanism may be used for directly sending large amounts of data. This avoids the communication via a central workflow control engine, which certainly would be a bottleneck for Grid applications.

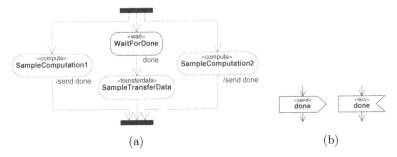

(a)   (b)

Fig. 6. Synchronization via events

Fig. 7. The *broadcast* concept

3.7   Constraints

The information specified by the user in the form of *constraints* is important to enable the workflow repair and fault tolerance. If during execution some constraints are no longer fulfilled, then the execution environment should be able to find alternative mapping. A UML constraint specifies the condition that must be true for a modeling element. A constraint is shown inside the braces ({ }), in the vicinity of the element with which is associated.

Figure 8 shows an constraint, that is associated with the activity *Sample-Computation*, which specifies that execution time of the activity should be less than 10 time units.

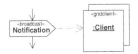

Fig. 8. Constraint specification

4   Case Study: Advanced 3D Medical Image Reconstruction

In order illustrate the work described in this paper we will develop a workflow for a real-world grid application for 3D medical image reconstruction, which is developed by the Institute for Software Science of the University of Vienna in cooperation with the General Hospital of Vienna [2]. For this case study we use our UML-based editor Teuta [7, 8], which provides the tool-support for the graphical workflow composition of Grid applications.

The application for our case study, which is also part of the GEMMS project [3], is based on a service oriented architecture to provide clients with advanced fully 3D image reconstruction services running transparently on remote parallel computers. As a service layer we will use a Generic Application Service (GAPPService). GAPPService is a configurable software component which exposes a native application as a service to be accessed by multiple remote clients over the Internet providing common methods for data staging and remote job management: the upload method uploads the input files to the service, the start method executes the start script of the application and the download method downloads the output files. Additionally, a status method can be specified which returns the current status of the application.

The particular tasks necessary to execute the image reconstruction service are done manually using the web-based ClientGUI. In the most simple use cases the manual invocation performed by the client is sufficient (e.g. if the medical doctor wants to reconstruct 2D projection data). But in some cases an additional workflow would be able to automate the execution and facilitate the handling of the reconstruction service (e.g. for instrument calibration or for testing purposes). Therefore the next step will be to develop the workflow which will allow the automatic execution of the service tasks. In the following we will model such a workflow.

In the following we consider the abstract workflow which hides the details of the implementation and the actual workflow describing the execution details.

On the right-hand side of Figure 9 is depicted the abstract workflow which can be used in almost all use cases as general workflow. First of all the user has to upload an input file. Next the user has to execute the start script which starts the reconstruction software. Finally after the reconstruction has finished the download method can be executed and the output files can be downloaded. Now the received 3D image can be visualized.

On the left-hand side of Figure 9 is shown an activity diagram with the details hidden from the user. The workflow described below describes a very specific use case where the user can validate the quality of the images and start a new reconstruction with new parameters. As described in the previous activity diagram the first step is to upload the input file to the host where the GAPPService is installed. In the second step the user can execute the StartScript. The image reconstruction stars after the execution of the StartScript. If the StatusScript is specified, the user can invoke the getStatus method as long as the reconstruction job is executing and obtain the current status of the application. After finishing the processing, the reconstruction application has to generate the finish file which is especially necessary if the StatusScript is not specified. The generation of the finish file informs the client that the application has finished processing. After the reconstruction has finished, the output file can be downloaded and visualized. If the reconstruction result is not satisfying, the reconstruction could be started again with new reconstruction parameters. This could be repeated until the visualized image has the acceptable quality.

5   Conclusions and Future Work

In this paper we have described an approach for graphically modeling and describing Grid workflow applications based on the UML standard. We have pre-

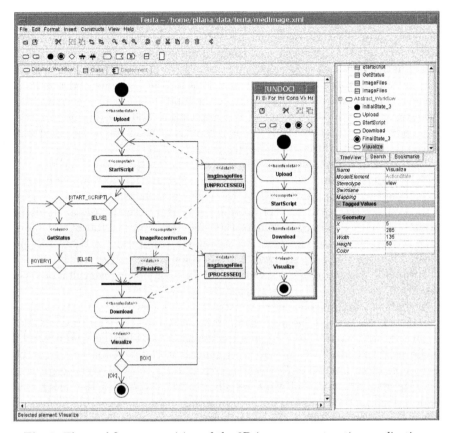

Fig. 9. The workflow composition of the 3D image reconstruction application

sented a set of concepts for modeling control flow, data flow, synchronization, notification, and constraints. We have demonstrated our approach by describing a Grid workflow model for an advanced 3D medical image reconstruction application.

The upcoming UML2.0 specification provides a richer set of concepts for behavioral modeling. We plan to extend our tool Teuta for supporting of the new concepts and notation of UML2.0.

References

1. T. Andrews, F. Curbera, H. Dholakia, Y. Goland, J. Klein, F. Leymann, K. Liu, D. Roller, D. Smith, S. Thatte, I. Trickovic, and S. Weerawarana. Business Process Execution Language for Web Services. Version 1.1, BEA, IBM, Microsoft, SAP, and Siebel, May 2003.
2. W. Backfrieder, M. Forster, S. Benkner, and G. Engelbrecht. Locally Variant VOR in Fully 3D SPECT within A Service Oriented Environment. In *International Conference on Mathematics and Engineering Techniques in Medicine and Biological Sciences*, Las Vegas, USA, June 2003. CSREA Press.

3. G. Berti, S. Benkner, J. Fenner, J. Fingberg, G. Lonsdale, S. Middleton, and M. Surridge. Medical Simulation Services via the Grid. In *17th International Parallel and Distributed Processing Symposium (IPDPS 2003)*, Nice, France, April 2003. IEEE Computer Society.

4. H. Bivens. Grid Workflow. Sandia National Laboratories, http://vir.sandia.gov/~hpbiven/, April 2001.

5. T. Bray, J. Paoli, C. Sperberg-McQueen, and E. Maler. Extensible Markup Language (XML) 1.0 (Second Edition). http://www.w3.org/TR/REC-xml, October 2000.

6. Department of Physics and Astronomy, Cardiff University. Triana, 2003. http://www.triana.co.uk/.

7. T. Fahringer, S. Pllana, and J. Testori. Teuta. University of Vienna, Institute for Software Science. Available online: http://www.par.univie.ac.at/project/prophet.

8. T. Fahringer, S. Pllana, and J. Testori. Teuta: Tool Support for Performance Modeling of Distributed and Parallel Applications. In *International Conference on Computational Science. Tools for Program Development and Analysis in Computational Science.*, Krakow, Poland, June 2004. Springer-Verlag.

9. Business Process Management Initiative. Business Process Modelling Language. www.bpmi.org/bmpi-downloads/BPML-SPEC-1.0.zip, June 2002.

10. S. Krishnan, P. Wagstrom, and G. Laszewski. GSFL : A Workflow Framework for Grid Services. Preprint ANL/MCS-P980-0802, Argonne National Laboratory, August 2002.

11. F. Leymann. Web Services Flow Language (WSFL 1.0). Technical report, IBM Software Group, May 2001.

12. OMG. Unified Modeling Language Specification. http://www.omg.org, March 2003.

13. OMG. XML Metadata Interchange (XMI) Specification. http://www.omg.org, May 2003.

14. B. Sotomayor. The Globus Toolkit 3 Programmer's Tutorial. http://www.casa-sotomayor.net/gt3-tutorial/, July 2003.

15. S. Thatte. XLANG: Web services for Business Process Design. Technical report, Microsoft Corporation, 2001.

16. The Workflow Management Coalition. http://www.wfmc.org/.

Support for User-Defined Metrics in the Online Performance Analysis Tool G-PM[*]

Roland Wismüller[1], Marian Bubak[2,3], Włodzimierz Funika[2],
Tomasz Arodź[2,3], and Marcin Kurdziel[2,3]

[1] LRR-TUM, Institut für Informatik, Technische Universität München,
D-85747 Garching, Germany
[2] Institute of Computer Science, AGH, al. Mickiewicza 30, 30-059 Kraków, Poland
[3] Academic Computer Centre – CYFRONET, Nawojki 11, 30-950 Kraków, Poland
phone: (+48 12) 617 39 64, fax: (+48 12) 633 80 54, phone: (+49 89) 289 17676
{bubak,funika}@uci.agh.edu.pl, wismuell@in.tum.de

Abstract. This paper presents the support for user-defined metrics in the G-PM performance analysis tool. G-PM addresses the demand for aggressive optimisation of Grid applications by using a new approach to performance monitoring. The tool provides developers, integrators, and end users with the ability to analyse the performance characteristics of an application at a high level of abstraction. In particular, it allows to relate an application's performance to the Grid's performance, and also supports application-specific metrics. This is achieved by introducing a language for the specification of performance metrics (PMSL) and the concept of probes for providing application specific events and data. PMSL enables an easy specification of performance metrics, yet allowing an efficient implementation, required for the reduction of monitoring overhead.

Keywords: Grid, performance monitoring, user-defined metrics

1 Introduction

With Grid computing, a new level of complexity has been introduced to the development process of distributed applications. Grid enabled applications are presumed to be run not only in geographically distributed locations, but also on a diverse set of hardware and software platforms. At the same time, the emphasis is on the computing being as cost effective as possible. This leads to the requirements for the applications to utilise the available resources in the optimal way. Usually, performance degradations emerge as a result of an imbalance in computation distribution, flaws in the schema of application synchronisation operations, or suboptimal allocation of resources. Such conditions can be fully observed only during an application run in an environment that closely resembles the one in which the application is to be deployed. The best approach would

---

[*] This work was partly funded by the European Commission, project IST-2001-32243, CrossGrid.

M. Dikaiakos (Ed.): AxGrids 2004, LNCS 3165, pp. 159–168, 2004.

be to observe the application directly on the Grid. Consequently, Grid oriented performance monitoring systems become necessary tools for development of high performance Grid applications. These tools should work in on-line mode – it is a necessary prerequisite not only for the monitoring of applications with a very long execution time, but also for non-batch programs, like interactive applications or services. Moreover, the monitoring should not introduce a noticeable overhead as this might disturb the application's execution, thus rendering the measured performance properties useless.

A performance monitoring tool for Grid applications, G-PM, designed to fulfil the above-stated demands is being developed in the CrossGrid project [5]. For gathering of the raw performance data, both application- and Grid-related, the G-PM tool uses the OCM-G monitoring service[1]. The performance data are requested from the OCM-G and then analysed by G-PM during the application's execution. On top of the data returned by OCM-G, a set of standard, built-in metrics is defined, like communication volume and delay, or overhead of file I/O.

The tool differs from related approaches (see Sect. 3) in the respect that it combines the support for on-line standard performance measurements with the support for user-defined metrics and application-specific instrumentation. This enables to adjust the tool's operation to the specific analysis needs meaningful in the context of the application. Once such a metrics, specified with a simple definition language, has been entered in the tool's user interface, it can be used in the same way as the built-in ones.

This paper focuses on the support for user-defined metrics in the G-PM tool. The main part of the article (Section 2) presents the Performance Metrics Specification Language PMSL and two usage examples. Furthermore, an approach to the efficient implementation of the measurements based on user-defined metrics is described. Section 4 presents concluding remarks along with information on the current state of G-PM.

2   User-Defined Metrics

In the following, we present the technical details on how user-defined metrics are specified and how they are implemented in a distributed on-line fashion. Due to space limitation, we must refer the reader to [3, 13] for the detailed motivation, design goals, and the basic concepts behind this work.

2.1   Specification of Metrics

A user-defined, application specific metrics in G-PM is based on already existing metrics, plus some minimal, specific information from the user's application:

- Occurrences of important events in the application's execution,
- associations between related events, and
- (optionally) performance data computed by the application itself.

---

[1] For more details please see [1, 2].

```
1  IO_volume_for_interaction_vt(Process[] processes, File[] partners,
                                 VirtualTime vt)
2  {
3      PROBE end(Process p, VirtualTime vt);
4      PROBE begin(Process p, VirtualTime vt);
5      Process p;
6      Value[] volume;
7      volume[p] = IO_volume(p, partners, [START, NOW]) AT end(p, vt)
                 - IO_volume(p, partners, [START, NOW]) AT begin(p, vt);
8      return SUM(volume[p] WHERE p IN processes);
9  }

10 IO_volume_for_interaction(Process[] processes, File[] partners,
                             TimeInterval time)
11 {
12     VirtualTime vt;
13     Value[] volume;
14     volume[vt] = IO_volume_for_interaction_vt(processes, partners, vt);
15     return SUM(volume[vt] WHERE volume[vt].time IN time);
16 }
```

Fig. 1. PMSL specification for the example metrics

This information is provided via *probes*, i.e. special function calls, which receive a *virtual time* and the optional performance data as parameters. The virtual time is an arbitrary, but monotonically increasing integer value, which is used to specify associations between different events, i.e. probe executions.

Using this concept, it is possible to derive new metrics from existing ones (e.g. by relating two metrics to each other) or to measure a metrics only for specific program phases. For example, in an interactive, parallel application, the programmer may provide two probes (called **begin** and **end**), marking the beginning and end of the processing of a certain class of user interactions[2]. Probe calls belonging to the same interaction are identified by receiving the same value for the virtual time.

With this preparation, G-PM can e.g. be used to measure the amount of data transferred to/from disk for each interaction. Obviously, this amount is simply the total amount of data at the end of the interaction, minus the amount at its beginning. Rules like this are the means by which a G-PM user can specify new metrics at runtime.

Since no suitable specification mechanism existed for this purpose, we had to design a new language. It should be simple to use and should not force the user to think about the *implementation* of the metrics. The result, called PMSL therefore is a *declarative, functional language*. It only provides single assignment variables and does neither include control flow constructs nor alterable state. To support metrics based on events, PMSL includes a *special operator* (**AT**), which takes the value of an expression at the time of an event occurrence. Finally, the language provides a couple of *set operations* used for data aggregation.

---

[2] For the sake of simplicity of demonstration we assume an SPMD-style program, thus, these probes will be executed in each process. See [13] for a more detailed discussion.

Instead of formally introducing the syntax and semantics of PMSL, we will just discuss the specification for the example metrics introduced above, which demonstrates most of the language's features. Fig. 1 shows the specification of our example metrics. In general, each metrics has parameters that define

1. the object(s) to be measured (e.g. `Process[] processes`: a list of processes),
2. restrictions to the measurement, like partner objects or code regions (e.g. `File[] partners`: a list of files), and
3. a time specification. This can be a point in real time at which the measurement is done, a measurement interval in real time (`TimeInterval time`), or a point in virtual time (`VirtualTime vt`).

In Fig. 1 two metrics are defined: `IO_volume_for_interaction_vt` specifies a metrics for the amount of disk I/O for a point in virtual time, i.e. (in our example) for a single user interaction. Line 7 tells how to compute the contribution of one process: just subtract its total I/O volume at the `begin` event from the one at the `end` event. The term `[START,NOW]` defines the measurement time interval for the `IO_volume` metrics (which is a built-in metrics of G-PM): the lower bound is the start time of the whole measurement, the upper bound is the current time, i.e. the time of the event. Line 8 finally states that the return value is the sum of the contributions of all measured processes. `IO_volume_for_interaction` is a metrics that refers to a given interval of (real) time. Its result is the I/O volume caused by all user interactions in the specified measurement time interval. Since all measurement values in G-PM are time-stamped, this metrics can be computed by considering the results of `IO_volume_for_interaction_vt` for all virtual times and by summing up all results whose time-stamps lie in the measurement interval.

The examples show that the metrics are specified at a rather high level of abstraction, thus, users of G-PM should be able to define their own metrics according to their needs. Nevertheless, the specifications still can be converted to efficient, distributed on-line measurements, as we will show in the next section.

2.2   Implementation of Measurements

There are two reasons why the measurements must be implemented in a distributed fashion: First, the `AT` construct in PMSL requires a measurement value to be determined when an event occurs. In order to avoid communication delays which would adulterate the results, determining the measurement value must happen at the same place where the event occurs. Second, distributed processing of measurement data often significantly reduces the amount of data that must be sent to the G-PM tool via the network, thus reducing the perturbation of the measured system and increasing scalability.

The way from a PMSL specification to a distributed on-line measurement consists of five phases:

1. When the user defines the new metrics, it is parsed into an intermediate representation (IR).

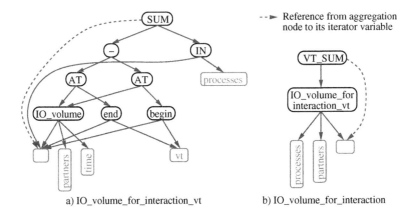

a) IO_volume_for_interaction_vt   b) IO_volume_for_interaction

Fig. 2. IR of the example metrics

2. Later, when the user defines a measurement of this metrics, the IR is partially evaluated, using the now known parameter values (i.e. objects to measure, measurement restrictions).
3. The partially evaluated IR is optimised in order to reduce the measurement's perturbation.
4. The necessary inferior measurements and the monitoring requests for all probe events are defined. At the same time, a dataflow graph is created, which controls the computation of the final measurement results.
5. The dataflow graph is distributed to the components of the OCM-G monitoring system and the measurements is started.

Parsing PMSL into an IR. As an intermediate representation for PMSL specifications we use simple expression-DAGs (directed acyclic graphs), where inner nodes are operations, while leaf nodes are variables or constants. Fig. 2 shows the IRs for the example metrics of Fig. 1. Note that using an expression-DAG as IR is only possible since PMSL is a functional language. Most of the translation process is relatively straightforward, with three notable issues:

- Assignments are handled by subsequently replacing all uses of the assigned variable with the DAG of the assignment's right hand side. For indexed variables, this replacement includes an index substitution. Thus, local variables like the `volume` arrays in Fig. 1 are completely eliminated.
- Variables used as iterators in aggregation functions (e.g. p in line 8 of Fig. 1) are substituted by anonymous, private copies. This is necessary to avoid conflicts when the same variable is used in different aggregations.
- After creating the IR, we perform a common subexpression elimination. This avoids multiple definitions of the same inferior measurements later. In our example, the two references to the `IO_volume` metrics are unified in Fig. 2a.

The main problem at this stage, however, is the handling of the time parameters. While they are explicit input parameters in the specification, this is not the case in the implementation. An on-line performance analysis tool just requests a measurement value from time to time. Thus, the actual time of a measurement is the time when the underlying monitoring system processes this request. Fortunately, the use of time is rather limited in PMSL:

- A virtual time parameter can not be modified, but just passed to inferior metrics and probes. Thus, in the implementation we can convert it from an input to an output parameter. However, we must then ensure that all "uses" of the parameter provide the same value (e.g. in line 7 of Fig. 1 both probes must provide the same value for vt). This is done by taking the virtual time into account in the firing rules of the dataflow nodes created in phase 4.
- Real time (and time interval) parameters can not be modified, too. Like virtual time, they can be passed to inferior metrics. This case is simply handled by requesting the values for these metrics at (approximately) the same time.

  But a time interval can also be used as an operand to an IN operator inside an aggregation function, like in line 15 of Fig. 1. This case is detected via pattern matching in the IR, which checks for constructs of the form

  aggregation_function (*expr* WHERE *expr*.time IN *time_interval*)

  We then introduce special aggregation nodes (e.g. VT_SUM in Fig. 2b) which later handle this case.

Of course, the time can also used to compute the value of the metrics. However, this is done using a special metrics Time, which returns the current time, instead of using the time parameters. Thus, there are no difficulties during the evaluation.

Partial Evaluation of the IR. Once the user defines a measurement based on the specified metrics, all the parameters of this metrics are fixed[3]. Thus, we can assign values to some of the leaf nodes in the DAG and evaluate its inner nodes. For each node, the evaluation either results in a constant or – if some of the node's operands still have unknown values – in a new DAG. The result of this phase is shown in Fig 3a, where we assumed that a measurement of IO_volume_for_interaction should be performed for two processes (*p1* and *p2*), restricted to consider only I/O to a file named *file1*.

The figure shows that besides the actual evaluation, a couple of other transformations is applied in this phase:

- Uses of metrics, which have been specified via PMSL, are "inlined", i.e. the node has been replaced with the partially evaluated DAG of this metrics. In our example, the node IO_volume_for_interaction_vt of Fig. 2b has been replaced in this way.
- Since the parameters of all used metrics must evaluate to constants in this phase, there is no need anymore to represent them as explicit child nodes. Instead, the metrics nodes for built-in metrics directly contain the full measurement specification.

---

[3] With the exception of the time parameters, which are handled as described before.

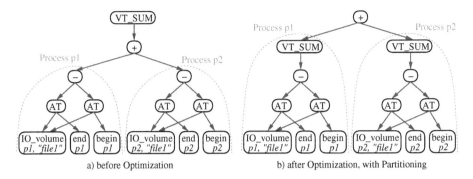

Fig. 3. Partially evaluated IR

- Similarly, probe nodes now directly contain the information needed to request the monitoring of this probe.
- Aggregation nodes are replaced by simple operations when the iteration set is known. E.g. the "SUM" node of Fig. 2a is replaced by a "+" node with two operands, one for each process considered.

Optimisation of the Partially Evaluated IR (PEIR). The PEIR can be optimised in several ways to improve the quality of the resulting measurement. The main goal is to reduce the frequency and volume of data which needs to be sent over the network. This can be achieved by moving nodes aggregating over virtual time down towards the leaves. E.g. in Fig. 3a, the labelled sub-DAGs can be evaluated locally in the context of the monitored processes. However, the "+" node combines data from different processes. This means that whenever an **end** event occurs, some communication is necessary. By interchanging the "+" and "VT_SUM" nodes, as shown in Fig. 3b, the aggregation over time can now also be done locally. Communication is only required when the aggregated values are needed because the result of the measurement has been requested.

Definition of Measurements and Monitoring of Probes. In this phase, a measurement is defined for each metrics node in the PEIR. Likewise, the monitoring of all probes used in the PEIR is requested. The latter results in a callback function being invoked when a probe is executed. This function usually will read some of the inferior measurements. Their results are again delivered via a callback. Since we will get these results at different times, because they are triggered by different probes, the best way to combine them into the final result is by using a dataflow approach. Thus, we also create a proper dataflow graph in this phase.

The result for our example is shown in Fig. 4. It shows both the dataflow graph and the activities performed by the different callbacks. The tokens flowing through the dataflow graph consist of a measurement value, its time stamp, and optionally a virtual time stamp and a requester identification. The latter is needed when the same measurement is read by different probe callbacks. In

Dataflow graph:

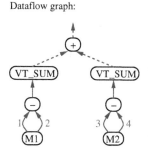

Callback	Actions performed
p_i : begin (i = 1,2)	get vt from event notification request a result of measurement i with callback data = (vt, 2+2*(i−1))
p_i : end (i = 1,2)	get vt from event notification request a result of measurement i with callback data = (vt, 1+2*(i−1))
measurement$_i$ (i = 1,2)	get (value, time) from measurement result get (virtualTime, requesterID) from callback data pass (value,time,virtualTime,requesterID) to node M$_i$

➤ data flow is triggered by execution of probes
⇢ data flow is triggered by requesting the measurement's result

measurement$_i$: measurement of
IO_volume for process p_i

Fig. 4. Implementation of measurement

these cases, the requester identification is used to determine the dataflow arc to which the result is sent. E.g. in Fig. 4, node "M1" will forward its result token to the arc labelled 2 when the result was requested by the **begin** callback, and to arc labelled 1 when requested by the **end** callback.

A big advantage of this dataflow scheme is that it immediately supports distributed processing. An arc between dataflow nodes processed on different hosts just translates to a communication link.

Measurement. During the measurement, tokens are created in the dataflow graph either when a probe is executed or when the measurement result is requested. Usually, a dataflow node fires, i.e. performs its operation and produces a result token, when a token is available on each of its input arcs. In our implementation, there are two extensions to this general rule:

- If an input token contains a virtual time stamp, the operation waits until it has a complete set of operands with identical virtual time stamps (e.g. the "−" nodes in Fig. 4).
- When a dataflow node aggregating over virtual time (e.g. the "VT_SUM" node) triggers, it does not produce a result token but rather updates an internal summary value. The node produces a result token only upon a special request. In our example, this request is issued when the result of the complete measurement is requested.

3   Related Work

There already exist several tools which offer a user-definable data evaluation. One example are visualization systems like AVS[4], which allow the user to customize the data processing by connecting modules to a dataflow pipeline. A similar approach, specifically targeted to performance analysis, has been taken

---

[4] http://www.avs.org

by Pablo [11]. Paraver [6] offers a menu-driven specification of user-defined metrics. However, all of these approaches only support a *centralized* and *off-line* data analysis, where large amounts of raw data (event traces in case of Pablo and Paraver) have to be sent to a single computer and have to be analysed there. In contrast, G-PM targets a *distributed on-line* analysis, where the raw data is processed at its origin, which greatly reduces the load of the network and the computer executing the tool's user interface. Only this kind of analysis allows to provide an immediate feedback on the behaviour of an application.

Some other performance analysis tools also use languages to define metrics. Examples are Paradyn [10] with its measurement definition language MDL [9], EXPERT [15] with the trace analysis language EARL [14], and the JavaPSL property specification language [8]. In contract to PMSL, these languages are used only *internally* in the tools; they are not suited for being exposed to the user. MDL and EARL are *imperative*, rather than *declarative* languages, i.e. a metrics is defined by exactly specifying the implementation of its measurement. JavaPSL is declarative, but aims at different goals. In fact, JavaPSL and PMSL have a common root in the APART Specification Language ASL [7]. A major contribution of PMSL is that it allows to combine *events* with existing metrics.

Finally, our approach of using expression DAGs has some similarity to dynamic instrumentation techniques as implemented by Dyninst [4] and DPCL [12]. The main difference is that the DAG created from a PMSL specification *combines information from distributed sources*, i.e. its evaluation must be spread across several processes. In contrast, in Dyninst and DPCL the DAGs are local, i.e. they are always executed by a single process. However, the concepts fit together rather well: In an advanced implementation, we could use Dyninst or DPCL to efficiently implement the local sub-DAGs marked in Fig. 3.

4   Conclusions

The paper presented a method to support user-defined metrics for monitoring of Grid enabled, distributed applications, which relies on the PMSL performance metrics specification language. The language allows to combine information from event occurrences, application specific data, and existing metrics in order to define new, higher-level metrics. These metrics may summarize information from different processes of the distributed application; the necessary data processing is performed on-line, using an efficient distributed dataflow scheme. Consequently, applications can be monitored with minimal additional overhead.

The PMSL language and its translation have been implemented as a first prototype, where the optimizations of the PEIR and the distribution of the dataflow graphs are not yet included. This implementation is integrated into the current version of the G-PM tool, which will be released inside the CrossGrid project in Spring 2004. The implementation of optimizations and the fully distributed evaluation based on the OCM-G monitoring system is work in progress.

References

1. Baliś, B., Bubak, M., Funika, W., Szepieniec, T., and Wismüller, R.: An Infrastructure for Grid Application Monitoring. In: *Recent Advances in Parallel Virtual Machine and Message Passing Interface, 9th European PVM/MPI Users' Group Meeting*, Sept. - Oct. 2002, Linz, Austria, LNCS 2474, pp. 41-49, Springer-Verlag, 2002.
2. Baliś, B., Bubak, M., Funika, W., Szepieniec, T., and Wismüller, R.: Monitoring and Performance Analysis of Grid Application. In: *Computational Science - ICCS 2003*, June 2003, St. Petersburg, Russia, LNCS 2657, pp. 214-224, Springer-Verlag, 2003.
3. Bubak, M., Funika, W., Wismüller, R., Arodz, T., and Kurdziel, M.: The G-PM Tool for Grid-oriented Performance Analysis. In: *1st European Across Grids Conference*, Santiago de Compostela, Spain, Feb. 2003, LNCS 2970, Springer-Verlag, 2004
4. Buck, B. and Hollingsworth, J.K.: An API for Runtime Code Patching, *The International Journal of High Performance Computing Applications*, **14(4)**, Winter 2000, pp. 317–329.
5. *CrossGrid - Development of Grid Environment for interactive Applications*, EU Project, IST-2001-32243, Technical Annex. http://www.eu-crossgrid.org
6. European Center for Parallelism of Barcelona. *Paraver*. http://www.cepba.upc.es/paraver/
7. T. Fahringer, M. Gerndt, G. Riley, and J. L. Träff: Knowledge Specification for Automatic Performance Analysis. APART Technical Report, ESPRIT IV Working Group on Automatic Performance Analysis, Nov. 1999. http://www.fz-juelich.de/apart-1/reports/wp2-asl.ps.gz
8. T. Fahringer and C. Seragiotto: Modeling and Detecting Performance Problems for Distributed and Parallel Programs with JavaPSL. In *9th IEEE High-Performance Networking and Computing Conference, SC'2001*, Denver, CO, Nov. 2001.
9. J. R. Hollingsworth, B. P. Miller, M. J. R. Gonçalves, Z. Xu, O. Naim, and L. Zheng: MDL: A Language and Compiler for Dynamic Program Instrumentation. In *Proc. International Conference on Parallel Architectures and Compilation Techniques*, San Francisco, CA, USA, Nov. 1997. ftp://grilled.cs.wisc.edu/technical_papers/mdl.ps.gz.
10. Miller, B.P., et al.: *The Paradyn Parallel Performance Measurement Tools*. IEEE Computer, 28(11): 37-46, Nov. 1995.
11. University of Illinois. *Pablo Performance Analysis Environment: Data Analysis*. http://www-pablo.cs.uiuc.edu/Project/Pablo/PabloDataAnalysis.htm
12. University of Madison, Wisconsin. *Dynamic Probe Class Library (DPCL)*. http://www.cs.wisc.edu/paradyn/DPCL/
13. Wismüller, R., Bubak, M., Funika, W., and Baliś, B.: A Performance Analysis Tool for Interactive Applications on the Grid. *International Journal of High Performance Computer Applications*, Fall 2004, SAGE Publications. In print.
14. F. Wolf and B. Mohr: EARL - A Programmable and Extensible Toolkit for Analyzing Event Traces of Message Passing Programs. In: *Proc. of the 7th International Conference on High- Performance Computing and Networking (HPCN 99)*, LNCS 1593, pp. 503–512, Amsterdam, 1999. Springer-Verlag.
15. F. Wolf and B. Mohr: Automatic Performance Analysis of MPI Applications Based on Event Traces. In: *Euro-Par 2000 Parallel Processing, 6th International Euro-Par Conference*, LNCS 1900, pp. 123–132, Munich, Germany, Aug. 2000. Springer-Verlag.

Software Engineering
in the EU CrossGrid Project[*]

Marian Bubak[1,2], Maciej Malawski[1,2], Grzegorz Młynarczyk[3],
Piotr Nowakowski[2], Robert Pająk[2], Katarzyna Rycerz[1,2], and Michał Turała[2,4]

[1] Institute of Computer Science, AGH, al. Mickiewicza 30, 30-059 Kraków, Poland
[2] Academic Computer Centre – CYFRONET, Nawojki 11, 30-950 Kraków, Poland
[3] Websoft Ltd., Kraków, Poland
[4] Institute of Nuclear Physics, Kraków, Poland
phone: (+48 12) 617 39 64, fax: (+48 12) 633 80 54
{bubak,malawski,kzajac}@uci.agh.edu.pl, Michal.Turala@cern.ch,
{ymnowako,ympajak}@cyf-kr.edu.pl, Grzegorz.Mlynarczyk@websoft.pl

Abstract. This paper details the software engineering process utilized by the CrossGrid project, which is a major European undertaking, involving nearly two dozen separate organizations from 11 EU member and candidate countries. A scientific project of this magnitude requires the creation of custom-tailored procedures for ensuring uniformity of purpose and means throughout the Project Consortium.

Keywords: software engineering, grid, CrossGrid, quality indicators

1 Introduction

CrossGrid is one of the largest European projects in Grid research [2], uniting 21 separate institutions and funded by the 5th European Framework Programme. The primary objectives of CrossGrid is to further extend the Grid environment to a new category of applications of great practical importance and to involve more countries (including EU candidate states) in European Grid research [12]. The applications developed within CrossGrid are characterized by the interaction with a person in a processing loop. They require a response from the computer system to an action by the person in different time scales; from real through intermediate to long time, and they are simultaneously compute- as well as data-intensive. Examples of these applications are: interactive simulation and visualization for surgical procedures, flooding crisis team decision support systems, distributed data analysis in high-energy physics, air pollution combined with weather forecasting. A visualization engine should be developed and optimized for these applications.

[*] This research is partly funded by the European Commission IST-2001-32243 Project "CrossGrid" and the Polish State Committee for Scientific Research, SPUB-M 112/E-356/SPB/5.PR UE/DZ 224/2002-2004.

M. Dikaiakos (Ed.): AxGrids 2004, LNCS 3165, pp. 169–178, 2004.

To enable efficient development of this category of applications for the Grid environment, new tools for verification of parallel source code, performance prediction, performance evaluation and monitoring are needed. This, in turn, requires extension of the Grid by new components for application-performance monitoring, efficient distributed data access, and specific resource management. Users should be able to run their applications on the Grid in an easy and transparent way, without needing to know details of the Grid structure and operation. CrossGrid will develop user-friendly portals and mobile personalized environments and will integrate new components into the Grid and application development tools.

The elaborated methodology, generic application architecture, programming environment, and new Grid services will be validated and tested thoroughly on the CrossGrid testbeds. This will result in further extension of the Grid across Europe. CrossGrid development will exploit all the available achievements of DataGrid, EuroGrid and other related projects in a way which enables their interoperability. CrossGrid closely collaborates with DataGrid.

2   Architecture

CrossGrid utilizes a layered architecture composed of three distinct software layers (applications, tools and services) and one hardware layer, similar to that defined in [11]. The individual layers of CrossGrid are reflected by the distribution of Project Work Packages (WPs): three technical WPs devoted to development of each layer separately, one testbed WP, providing hardware support for CrossGrid operations and one managerial WP. CrossGrid architecture essentially follows a layered approach in that the topmost layer (applications) relies on lower layers (support tools and Grid services), which in turn make use of the infrastructure (testbed) layer. Each type of Work Package (technical, testbed and management) is subject to a different set of operating procedures and quality assurance criteria, described below. This paper does not concentrate on the technical aspect of CrossGrid software, but rather on the management, oversight and reporting process inherent in a widely-distributed multinational undertaking that is CrossGrid.

3   Project Phases

CrossGrid is scheduled for three years, officially starting in March 2002 and lasting until February 2005. The Project is divided into five distinct phases, as depicted by Fig.1

CrossGrid utilizes an incremental software release policy, with three scheduled releases. Therefore, the timeline is arranged as follows: *Initial phase* including requirement definition and merging (Months 1-3), *First development phase* including detailed design, refinement of requirements and production of initial prototypes (Months 4-12), *Second development phase* including further refinement of prototypes and integration of components (Months 13-24), *Third*

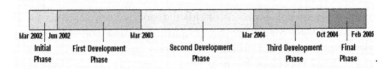

Fig. 1. Project timeline

development phase including finalization of software components and their complete integration (Months 25-32), *Final phase* including public demonstrations and preparation of final documentation (Months 33-36).

4   Standards, Conventions and Metrics

CrossGrid is expected to deliver a substantial quantity of software, integrated and tested on numerous platforms. Owing to the complexity of the Project and the multitude of partners participating in it, it is essential that the same rules are enforced for each partner and each software module produced.

Standard Operating Procedures

A special document, mentioned before, details the standards, practices, conventions and metrics enforced within the CrossGrid project – namely the Standard Operating Procedures [5] document. In short, the document consists of the following sections:

Central repository: Information related to the functioning and terms of use of the CrossGrid code repository at FZK (Karlsruhe) and its backup site at Valencia. This repository is tasked with software collection, maintenance and retention.

Tool control: A list of developer tools which should be used by all Partners. The selection of developer tools is proposed by the Technical Architecture Team in conjunction with individual Task leaders and then approved by Project Management. Tool regulations cover: compilers, automated and manual documentation tools and static code analysis tools.

Problem reporting and change request mechanisms: All participants involved in developing code for CrossGrid are to follow the same procedures. The appropriate tools for problem reporting and change requesting are integrated into the CrossGrid code repository. They are consistent with the requirements of the Standard Operating Procedures document and they are intended to facilitate smooth development of the Project.

The autobuild tool: Information relating to requirements posed by the Autobuild tool, used as a means of creating regular builds of CrossGrid software with minimum overhead for developers.

CrossGrid naming conventions for software development: The largest section of the Standard Operating Procedures document is devoted to the procedures which should be followed in the implementation of CrossGrid modules.

Other conventions: Date/time formats, measurement units etc.

5   Tests and Reviews

As specified before, the CrossGrid project is divided into five phases, three of which are termed development phases, which is where the software is actually created. However, in order to develop software that matches its creators' expectations, one must resort to formalized methods of design and control over the development process. To quote [1], we need to answer the question if we are building the right thing, if what we're building is technically feasible and what is the best mode of utilization of the available resources. These aspects are addressed by the CrossGrid software development plan and are described in the following section.

Software Requirements Review

The Software Requirements Review is conducted upon the submission of the so-called Software Requirement Specifications (SRS) by each technical task (i.e. tasks, which develop software, as opposed to management tasks, integrated within WP5). These documents contain the following information: *Overall description of module* (functionality, operations, interfaces, requirements and constraints). Where appropriate, these should be augmented by UML component and use case diagrams. *A "state of the art" document* reviewing technologies suitable for the development of each module.

In addition, the Technical Architecture Team (TAT) is responsible for preparing a preliminary draft of the general project architecture, expressing any interaction between project components. Each task must fit into this architecture and the TAT is responsible for reviewing all SRSs and deciding whether they conform to that overall Project hierarchy. Upon completion of this review, the partners responsible for each SRS are expected to make corrections in accordance with the deliverable submission policy.

Design Review

Following the submission of SRS documents, each partner is to create a Design Document, expressing in concrete terms (UML class and sequence diagrams) the exact structure of their module. The Design Document is intended as a "white box" description of module functionality and is subjected to review by the IRB and TAT. The Design Documents contain the following information: *System decomposition description:* an overview of the component breakdown of each module, accompanied by UML component diagrams. This section describes the module functionality in accordance with the IEEE-890 Standard Design Template. *Dependency description:* this section is devoted to the interaction between the module being described and other modules (those being developed by other tasks as well as those external to the Project). *Interface description:* a formal description of any interface the software will provide (both APIs and GUIs) including method declarations and descriptions along with use cases and sequence diagrams (screenshots should be provided for GUIs).*Detailed design:* class diagrams for each component of the software module being developed. This is the most low-level description of software design, with explanations regarding each attribute and method of the software being developed. The Design Documents are the basis for the implementation process, which commences upon the completion of their review. A standard Design Document template has been approved by Project Management and distributed to all relevant partners.

Implementation and Software Releases

As stated before, following the submission and acceptance of Design Documents, CrossGrid enters a phase of incremental releases, each of which is subject to a review. Three major releases are accounted for in the Technical Annex, but – as experience dictates – additional releases may prove necessary and the implementation process should be flexible enough to accommodate these releases. This issue has been addressed by the managers of the CrossGrid software repository, through the introduction of the Autobuild tool (see [7] for further details). For each release, the following procedure is intended to occur:

Coordination meeting: Involves a discussion of the previous release and develops a framework for a subsequent release. The coordination meeting is organized after each release and is open to all Project participants, but entails the participation of WP task leaders, CrossGrid steering group and representatives of the Technical Architecture Team and WP4 Integration Team. The end product of this meeting is an evaluation of the release's suitability and quality, along with a prioritized list of issues concerning the next release, including: all software and documentation modifications with regard to the previous release and versions of external software (i.e. Globus Toolkit, DataGrid middleware, compilers etc.) to be used for the next release. In preparation for the coordination meetings each task holds internal meetings to develop a common stance and deliver a cohesive presentation.

WP follow-up meetings: Individual tasks discuss the issues related to the next release and develop specific workplans. Each task holds an internal meeting in order to develop its own workplan with regard to the next release, taking into account the results of the coordination meeting. The follow-up meetings involve designations of responsibilities for individual participants. A separate meeting is held by the Architecture Team to gauge the influence of the coordination meeting on CrossGrid architecture. If significant changes are foreseen, an updated version of the architecture document is developed.

Software release workplan coordination: The CrossGrid Steering Group develops a plan for the next release, upon discussion with individual WP leaders. The plan includes a list of all third-party software units which need to be installed on testbed sites in order to satisfy the upcoming release's requirements.

Middleware integration: Applications and middleware tasks upload the latest (internally tested) versions of their software to the central repository (Karlsruhe), where they are accessed by WP4.4 (Verification and QA) for testing. Integration issues are reported and fixed through the use of mechanisms described in Section 4. The WP4 Integration Team integrates the pertinent modules with external software units and oversees the basic integration tests as per the software release test plan described in WP4 deliverables.

Acceptance testing: An integrated CrossGrid release is installed on Testbed sites for acceptance testing. Acceptance tests are created by software developers in cooperation with the Project Technical Architecture Team, basing on the SRS documents and presented as a sequence of formalized test cases. The acceptance tests are deemed to have been passed when each test case presented by the application groups is executed correctly. Interactive and distributed components are tested on a special testbed, called the Test and Validation Testbed, made up of specially-selected components of the Project's testbed infrastructure and running standardized software.

Release: The Integration Team holds a meeting to describe the release and indicate changes introduced since the last release. The release is accompanied by relevant documentation, developed by individual WPs and by the Integration Team. The types of tests and the applicable procedures are further described in Appendix 4, WP4.1 section of [10].

For each major release, technical tasks are obliged to prepare a set of documents detailing the structure and functionality of the software they are delivering. The initial prototype documentation template has been approved by Project Management and distributed to all relevant partners. The template includes descriptions of module components which have been implemented so far and the functionality of the prototype (with use cases), description of discrepancies between the structure of the prototype and the Design Documents submitted earlier (if any changes are introduced during the implementation phase, partners are expected to explain their rationality), instructions and requirements for operating the prototype (its installation and running, description of tests which the software has been subjected to (both "black box" – i.e. comparison of actual output with required output and "white box" – confirmation of expected behavior of individual components), any issues which may affect the functioning of the prototype (including any known bugs) and references to properly annotated source code, contained in the CrossGrid CVS repository at the Research center of Karlsruhe (FZK). The repository, contained in a Savannah portal, is maintained by a dedicated administrator, answerable to the Project Steering Group, and includes separate directories for each task. The administrator controls access to the repository and grants permissions in accordance with the Project's Standard Operating Procedures. The Savannah portal also integrates a tool for bug tracking – each bug is assigned by the relevant task leader to a particular programmer, who then reports on its resolution. The main CVS repository is not public, as some organizations may choose to use their proprietary code for CrossGrid, thus uploading it to the repository. There is a back-up repository located in Valencia, for storage purposes only. Each task may, in addition, operate its own internal repository – this is not governed by Project Management.

It should be noted that in between major releases, work continues within each task on a semi-separate basis. Since CrossGrid is a collection of tools and services rather than a single, tightly-knit program or application, and since it is being developed by such a wide array of institutions and organizations – each with its own internal development culture and established procedures –

it is imperative to allot some leeway to individual developers. Therefore, the project consortium has decided to forgo frequent builds of the entire Project code (as is the case with commercial enterprises) in favor of allowing developers to organize their own schedules and develop their particular modules internally. The loose coupling between tasks – limited to common, explicitly-defined interfaces – makes it possible to limit Project builds to once a month and organizing detailed integration and acceptance testing once per release. This approach has been successfully employed over the first 18 months of the Project (see final section for details).

Testbed Releases and Validation

A "testbed release" identifies a well defined and complete collection of software to be deployed on a well defined set of distributed computing resources, including the corresponding installation mechanisms. According to the CrossGrid Architecture [4], the testbed supports the software components which are being developed within the framework of the project (CG software) and those from Globus and DataGrid (collectively referred as EDG software).

The CrossGrid testbed is divided into three focused testbeds, called the development testbed, test and validation testbed and production testbed, used at various stages of the software release process. The development testbed is relatively the smallest and supports day-to-day testing of software under development at various participating institutions. The test and validation testbed is used during integration meetings and the software release preparation procedure (see previous section), while the production testbed will be used for actual operation of the completed applications and tools. EDG release packages required by CrossGrid to operate are initially downloaded from the DataGrid official CVS repository, although for convenience reasons, the full CrossGrid testbed release, including the EDG packages, is available from a single entry point at the code repository GridPortal hosted by FZK (see [7]). The current production and test and validation testbed packages can be found there, and the development testbeds will be hosted also there when required.

Quality Indicators

CrossGrid will employ a system of quality indicators (QI) during its development phase. The Project Office will be responsible for compiling and publishing the current quality indicators each month. Three groups of quality indicators are envisioned, one for development process, one for code development (these will be task-specific) and one for testbeds. For each group, the relevant Project partners are expected to submit monthly updates regarding their indicators. These reports are submitted electronically to the Work Package 5 Quality Assurance Officer. Based on the information gathered, the Project Office prepares detailed reports, including all the defined indicators and summary reports of the overall Project progress (basing on quality indicators). The main purpose of these report is to obtain a sense of how well the Project is progressing from the Quality Assurance viewpoint, without a need to analyze all indicators in detail. To this end, each indicator is accompanied by a cutoff value, which – when reached –

triggers automatic mention in the reports. All the reports prepared by CG Office are published on the intranet pages (available from the main Project portal) and accessible by authorized users only. The Project portal also contains report templates, prepared by the Project Office.

Process quality indicators. Process-related metrics are meant primarily to capture the current status of development and anticipate changes in resource requirements. The metrics proposed in this area provide executive-level summary of the Project status. Each Project Partner is responsible for creating and delivering monthly reports to the Work Package 5 Quality Assurance Officer. These reports include number of person-hours allocated by each Project Partner to development of particular tasks and number of persons allocated by each Project Partner to development of all tasks during the measurement period,

The Project Office is obliged to prepare a summary report detailing all the information and indicators submitted by each Partner and, additionally, the following global indicators: number of monthly reports delivered to CG Office on time, ratio of deliverables submitted on time/total number of deliverables submitted for each WP, ratio of deliverables approved by the EU/total number of deliverables submitted for review (measured yearly), total number of deliverables that did not pass internal reviews (i.e. performed by IRB) for each WP, ratio of total number of person-hours reported by Project Partners per task/total number of person-hours planned for the task in the Project's schedule (measured on a quarterly basis).

Code development quality indicators. Quality of code development has been divided into two groups of indicators: static source code metrics and quality indicators, and progress and effectiveness of testing.

For the latter type of indicators the collection of tests results is crucial. It should be also noted that testing policy is one of the critical factors that have major influence on the overall quality of the delivered software.

A thorough discussion of unit testing and their related quality indicators can be found in [8]. In addition to code and testing metrics described there, the following factors related to the Project's issue tracking are measured for each task on a monthly basis: amount of issues/defects reported in the project's issues tracking system (using the Bugzilla tool as explained in [5]), average time required for issue resolution (measured and calculated for every Work Package), amount of pending (i.e. unassigned) issues, amount of issues with severity defined as blocking, critical or major.

At every monthly checkpoint the following criteria are also evaluated: there must not be any open and/or pending issues of blocking or critical severity, there should not be any open and/or pending issues of major severity, there must not be any open issues that were reported as open in the previous checkpoint report, deliverable code stability,overall test effectiveness. The stability of the code and effectiveness of testing methods is measured using indicators derived from metrics described above ([8]).

Testbed quality indicators. The following are measured on a monthly basis: number of sites participating in the testbed, monthly uptime (for each testbed site), number of users (registered and active), job submittal success rate (number of successful jobs / total number of jobs).

The appropriate values of all indicators are calculated by CG Office based on measurements performed during quality checks at CG Office and reports received from Project partners (i.e. delivered by Quality Assurance Officers assigned to each WP). Based on this information, the WP5 Quality Assurance Officer can prepare a summary report which, among others, will contain graphs depicting the current status of Quality Indicators. Each report will be published and accessible internally through the Project Portal only to registered members of the Project.

Managerial Reviews

CrossGrid is subject to a number of managerial reviews. These include the twelve Quarterly Reports, scheduled every three months and three Yearly Project Reviews, conducted at the EU Brussels office. In addition, most CrossGrid quality indicators are computed on a monthly basis, along with descriptions of work submitted by each partner – their results are analysed by the Project Office and the Project Steering Group on the fly.

Indicator	July 2003	August 2003	September 2003	October 2003 (Growth since September)
Lines of code	351046	632606	651965	846484 (+29%)
Lines of comment	107730	167626	193809	230346 (+18%)
Blank lines	71839	132726	126873	162317 (+27%)
Average cyclomatic complexity number per functions	4.40	4.45	5.64	5.68
Average cyclomatic complexity number per classes	6.11	9.73	10.81	10.96 (+1%)
Number of classes	1492	2040	2019	2710 (+34%)
Number of functions	14498	20350	25292	31631 (+25%)
RSM quality notices (without the TAB-notice)	61176	84596	110493	138094 (+24%)

Fig. 2. Selected Project Quality Indicators and their changes

6   Current Status of the Project

The CrossGrid project is currently in its 19th month and, hence, has entered the second development phase, as described in Section 3. Over the past 18 months, CrossGrid has attained all the necessary milestones set out in [9]: The SRS specifications for each development task have been submitted and approved. The design documents for each development task have been submitted and approved. CrossGrid held its first annual integration meeting in February 2003, in Santiago de Compostela (Spain) and a second one in July 2003, in Poznan (Poland). These meetings saw the preparation of the first prototype release of CrossGrid tools, services and testbeds from Work Packages WP2, 3 and 4 along with demo runs of selected applications on the actual CrossGrid testbed. The Quality Indicators introduced for the initial development stages have shown consistent progress of the Project, with more lines of code added each month, as described in the relevant reports [6]. In order to provide an overview of the overall progress and complexity of the Project, Fig.2 presents some of the chief Quality Indicators and their changes over the last four months. The indicators depicted include standard code statistics (number of lines of code, number of blank lines, number of comment lines), complexity metrics (McCabe/cyclomatic complexity metric) and some general indicators of the Project's size (number of classes and methods in all technical Work Packages).

Acknowledgments. We wish to thank M. Garbacz, J. Marco, N. Meyer, P.M.A. Sloot, W. Funika, R. Wismüller, D. van Albada, and M. Hardt for their contribution to this work.

References

1. Braude E., Software Engineering: An Object-Oriented Perspective (John Wiley & Sons, Inc., 2001.
2. Bubak M., Turala M.: "CrossGrid and its Relatives in Europe". In: Kranzlmueller D. et al (Eds.) Recent Advances in Parallel Virtual Machine and Message Passing Interface, Proc. 9th European PVM/MPI Users' Group Meeting, Linz, Austria, September/October 2002, LNCS 2474, pp. 14-15.
3. Bubak, M., Marco, J., Marten, H., Meyer, N., Noga, N., Sloot, P.M.A., and Turala, M.: CrossGrid: "Development of Grid Environment for Interactive Applications", Presented at PIONIER 2002, Poznan, April 23-24, 2002, Proceedings, pp. 97-112, Poznan, 2002.
4. CrossGrid Deliverable D5.2.2 (CrossGrid Architecture Requirements and First Definition of Architecture); multipart document stored at http://www.eu-crossgrid.org/M3deliverables.htm
5. CrossGrid Deliverable D5.2.3 (Standard Operating Procedures) http://www.eu-crossgrid.org/Deliverables/M6pdf/CG5.2-D5.2.3-v1.0-CYF020-StandardOperatingProcedures.pdf
6. CrossGrid Monthly Quality Reports; confidential (available on request from the CrossGrid Project Office).
7. The CrossGrid software repository and portal, http://gridportal.fzk.de
8. CrossGrid Quality Assurance Plan, http://www.eu-crossgrid.org/Deliverables/1stYear-revised_deliverables/CG5.2-D5.2.1-v3.0-CYF055-QualityAssurancePlan.pdf
9. CrossGrid Technical Annex and Description of Work, http://www.eu-crossgrid.org/CrossGridAnnex1_v31.pdf
10. CrossGrid WP4.1 appendix 4, http://www.eu-crossgrid.org/Deliverables/M3pdf/CG-4-D4.1-004-TEST.pdf
11. Foster I., Kesselman C., Tuecke S., The Anatomy of the Grid. Enabling Scalable Virtual Organizations. International Journal of High Performance Computing Applications, 3/2001, pp. 200-222, http://www.globus.org/research/papers/anatomy.pdf
12. Foster, I., Kesselman, C. (eds.): The Grid: Blueprint for a New Computing Infrastructure. Morgan Kaufmann, 1999.
13. Foster I., Kesselman C., Nick J. and Tuecke S.: The Physiology of the Grid. An Open Grid Services Architecture for Distributed Systems Integration, January 2002, http://www.globus.org

Monitoring Message-Passing Parallel Applications in the Grid with GRM and Mercury Monitor*

Norbert Podhorszki, Zoltán Balaton, and Gábor Gombás

MTA SZTAKI, Budapest, H-1528 P.O.Box 63, Hungary
{pnorbert,balaton,gombasg}@sztaki.hu

Abstract. The combination of the GRM application monitoring tool and the Mercury resource and job monitoring infrastructure provides an on-line grid performance monitoring tool-set for message-passing parallel applications.

1 Application Monitoring with GRM and Mercury

There are several parallel applications that are used on a single cluster or a supercomputer. As users get access to an actual grid they would like to execute their parallel applications on the grid because of the limitations of their local resources. In current grid implementations, we are already allowed to submit our parallel application to the grid and let it execute on a remote grid resource. However, those current grid systems are not able to give detailed information about our application during its execution except its status, like standing in a queue, running, etc. Our target of research has been to provide a monitoring tool that is able to collect trace information about an – instrumented – parallel application executed on a remote grid resource. Combining our GRM and Mercury Monitor tools we have achieved our goal and created an infrastructure that enables the user to collect performance information about a parallel application and examine it the same way as it has been done on the local cluster in the past years.

For monitoring parallel applications on a local resource (cluster or supercomputer), the GRM tool [1] can be used. GRM provides an instrumentation library for message passing parallel applications (MPI or PVM). The user should first instrument the application with trace generation functions that provides user defined events besides the predefined event types. PVM applications should be instrumented manually but MPI applications can be just linked with a wrapper library that is instrumented for GRM.

The Mercury Grid Monitoring System [2] in the GridLab project provides a general and extensible grid monitoring infrastructure. Its architecture is based on the Grid Monitoring Architecture GMA [3]. The input of the monitoring system consists of measurements generated by sensors. Sensors are controlled by producers that can transfer measurements to consumers when requested. The Mercury Monitor supports both event-like (i.e. an external event is needed to produce a metric value) and continuous metrics (i.e. a measurement is possible whenever a consumer requests it such as, the CPU temperature

---

* The work described in this paper has been supported by the following grants: EU-DataGrid IST-2000-25182 and EU-GridLab IST-2001-32133 projects, the Hungarian Supergrid OMFB-00728/2002 project, the IHM 4671/1/2003 project and the grant OTKA T042459.

M. Dikaiakos (Ed.): AxGrids 2004, LNCS 3165, pp. 179–181, 2004.

in a host). In addition to the components in the GMA, Mercury also supports actuators (similar to actuators in Autopilot [4]) that implement controls and makes interaction with monitored entities or with the monitoring system possible. The Mercury Monitor components used for monitoring on a grid resource are shown in Fig. 1 drawn with solid lines. The figure depicts a grid resource consisting of three nodes. A Local Monitor (LM) service is running on each node and collects information from processes running on the node as well as the node itself. Sensors (S) are implemented as shared objects that are dynamically loaded into the LM code at run-time depending on configuration and incoming requests for different measurements. Requested information is sent to a Main Monitor (MM) service. The MM provides a central access point for local users (i.e. site administrators and non-grid users). Grid users can access information via the Monitoring Service (MS) which is also a client of the MM. In large sized grid resources there may be more than one MM to balance network load. The modularity of the monitoring system also allows that on grid resources where an MM is not needed (e.g. on a supercomputer) it can be omitted and the MS can talk directly to LMs. The *resource broker*, the *jobmanager* and the LRMS are other grid services involved in starting the application and they are not part of the Mercury Monitor.

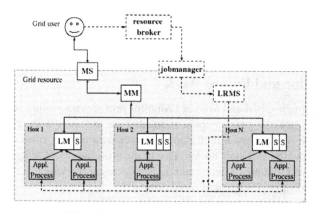

Fig. 1. Structure of the Mercury Monitor

When connecting GRM and Mercury Monitor, the trace delivery mechanism of GRM is replaced with the mechanism provided by Mercury. The GRM instrumentation library is rewritten to publish trace data using the Mercury Monitor API and to send trace events directly to LM. Application monitoring data is just another type of monitoring data represented as a metric. A special application sensor of Mercury is created that accepts incoming data from the processes on the machine, using the "extsensor" API of Mercury Monitor. GRM publishes trace data as a string data type that contains a trace event from the application process. The main process of GRM behaves as a consumer of Mercury, subscribing for trace data from producers. GRM specifies an application ID parameter to identify the application from which trace information should be transferred for the given request. If there are such metrics (coming from the application), Mercury Monitor delivers them to the main monitor of GRM in a data stream.

The use of GRM as an application monitor is not changed compared to the original usage. First, the application should be instrumented with GRM calls. Then, the job should be submitted to the resource broker, until the job is eventually started by the LRMS on a grid resource. Meanwhile, GRM can be started by the user on the local host that connects to Mercury Monitor and subscribes for trace information about the application. When the application is started and generates trace data, Mercury Monitor forwards the trace to GRM based on the subscription information.

Problems for Application Monitoring in the Grid. There are two problems that cannot be solved within this infrastructure and there is a need for a grid information system. First, GRM has to subscribe to Mercury MS on that site which executes the given job. To do that, GRM has to find out, on which grid resource the job has started. Then, the public address of the Mercury Monitoring Service on that resource has to be found out. When these two pieces of information are available for GRM, it can connect to Mercury and subscribe for the trace. Second, the application should be identified uniquely to distinguish it from other applications and prevent mixing of different traces. The grid job id, given by the resource broker is fine but Mercury Monitor receives trace records from actual application processes that are identified with their process ID (PID). The relation between the process IDs and grid job IDs should be published in the information system so that Mercury Monitor can deliver trace information for the right requests. In the EU-DataGrid (EDG) project R-GMA [5], the information system of EDG is used to deliver the necessary information to GRM.

2   Conclusion and Future Work

The combination of GRM and Mercury Monitor provides an on-line performance tool for monitoring message-passing applications that are executed in the grid. The current implementation of Mercury Monitor accepts trace data records from application processes through a UNIX domain socket. One of the most important tasks is to provide an application sensor that uses shared-memory for tracing, achieving a better performance and bringing down the intrusion of monitoring.

References

1. N. Podhorszki, P. Kacsuk: Semi-on-line Monitoring of P-GRADE Applications. In: Quality of Parallel and Distributed Programs and Systems, special issue of Journal of Parallel and Distributed Computing Practices, PDCP Vol.4, No. 4, Eds: P.Kacsuk, G.Kotsis, pp. 365-380, 2001.
2. Z. Balaton, G. Gombás. Resource and Job Monitoring in the Grid. Proc. of EuroPar'2003 Conference, Klagenfurt, Austria, pp. 404-411, 2003.
3. B. Tierney, R. Aydt, D. Gunter, W. Smith, V. Taylor, R. Wolski, and M. Swany. A grid monitoring architecture. GGF Informational Document, GFD-I.7, GGF, 2001, URL: http://www.gridforum.org/Documents/GFD/GFD-I.7.pdf
4. R. Ribler, J. Vetter, H. Simitci, D. Reed. Autopilot: Adaptive Control of Distributed Applications. Proc. 7th IEEE Symposium on High Performance Distributed Computing, Chicago, Illinois, July 1998.
5. S. Fisher et al. R-GMA: A Relational Grid Information and Monitoring System. 2nd Krakow Grid Workshop, Krakow, Poland, 2002.

Lhcmaster – A System for Storage and Analysis of Data Coming from the ATLAS Simulations

Maciej Malawski[1,2], Marek Wieczorek[1],
Marian Bubak[1,2], and Elżbieta Richter-Wąs[3,4]

[1] Institute of Computer Science, AGH, al. Mickiewicza 30, 30-059 Kraków, Poland
{malawski,bubak}@uci.agh.edu.pl
[2] Academic Computer Centre – CYFRONET, Nawojki 11, 30-950 Kraków, Poland
[3] Henryk Niewodniczanski Institute of Nuclear Physics,
ul. Radzikowskiego 152, 31-342 Kraków, Poland
[4] Jagiellonian University, Institute of Physics,
ul. Reymonta 4, 30-059 Kraków, Poland
phone: (+48 12) 617 39 64, fax: (+48 12) 633 80 54
Elzbieta.Richter-Was@cern.ch, cage@student.uci.agh.edu.pl

Abstract. This paper presents the Lhcmaster system designed to aid the physicist in the work of organizing and managing the large number of files that are produced by simulations of High Energy Physics experiments. The implemented system stores and manages data files produced by the simulations of the ATLAS detector, making them available for physicists. We will also present an outline of the Lhcmaster-G, a Grid version of the system, that may be implemented in the future in order to subsistute the Lhcmaster for a more effective and powerful tool.

Keywords: high-energy physics, particle detectors, fast simulation, data storage, Grid, CrossGrid

1 Introduction

High Energy Physics (HEP) is an important research domain that provides many compute- and data-intensive challenges for computer science. In the near future, CERN will complete the construction of the Large Hadron Collider (LHC). Currently, scientific collaborations performing the above mentioned experiments take advantage of specialized software to simulate the physical processes and performance of the detectors. The ATLAS Experiment [2] is one of four large experiments [12] within the LHC, which will be brought online in 2007 at CERN - the most prominent European organization for nuclear reseach. Because of the large amount of data which is going to be produced within the experiment, the ATLAS is currently one of the most data-intensive computing challenges. Since the particle detector at the core of experiment is not yet complete, the members of the ATLAS Collaboration team take advantage of software detector simulators in order to produce the data necessary to conduct their research. The simulators cooperate with event generators which produce data on simulated events in the same way as the accelerator itself. One of these simulators is the ATLFAST

M. Dikaiakos (Ed.): AxGrids 2004, LNCS 3165, pp. 182–190, 2004.
© Springer-Verlag Berlin Heidelberg 2004

[1], designed to perform so-called fast simulation. Although the amount of data produced by the simulators is much less than in the case of a real detector, its management is also a serious challenge.

The Lhcmaster system presented in this paper, was created in order to aid the storage of output data from the ATLFAST. Data stored in the system should be easily available for physicists intending to use it. In a typical analysis there are many processes to simulate and each of them can be simulated by using one of the available Monte Carlo event generators (e.g. Pythia, Herwig [5, 6]). There are also several options for each process, as well as additional parameters like the number of events generated in each run, the filters applied, etc. The problem was how to store hundreds of large files that vary with regards to many physical properties and simulation parameters. The files should be easily searchable by their contents, at best by means of histograms representing the contents of each file.

A further part of this paper presents the idea of Lhcmaster-G, an equivalent system designed to work on the Grid, that might be implemented in the future. We will show why a Grid-based architecture is optimal for such a system.

The specification of these two systems is enriched by the descriptions of other projects performed by physicists in order to solve similar problems.

2   Specification of Requirements for the Lhcmaster

The requirements for the Lhcmaster have been formulated by members of the ATLAS Collaboration group working at the INP[1]. The system should be a network-accessible database system meant for storing data files coming from the ATLFAST detector simulator [1], and making them available for external users to download. It should also provide a legible graphical representation of data in the form of collection of standard histograms generated for each data file.

The system should provide the following basic functionalities:

 – storage of files in the databases in a compact and coherent way; the stored data should be ordered in a hierarchical structure based on the origin of files,
 – a basic authentication facility protecting data collections, based on a scheme of authorized users and groups, supervising data access permissions,
 – unlimited read-only multi-user access from outside the system to files stored in the system, and
 – on-the-fly generation of histogram sets for the data files inserted into the system; each set of histograms should represent the physical characteristics of data stored in a specific file; the corresponding histograms in each set should represent the same physical quantity - as a result we should receive a kind of Graphical File Index (GFI) characterizing each file in the system.

---

[1] Henryk Niewodniczanski Institute of Nuclear Physics, Cracow

The system should provide for at least two types of users:

- *Administrator*: a user authorized to modify the data stored in the system,
- *External user*: an ordinary user, permitted only to read the index of files and the files stored in the system.

A model of the specified system is depicted in Fig. 1.

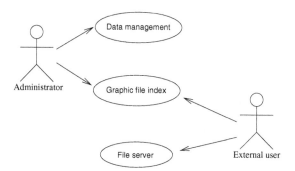

Fig. 1. Model of specified system

3   Related Work

High-energy physics is a large domain of computing and data-storage problems similar to the one presented in the current paper. Several of them are mentioned below. Two non-Grid projects, and two Grid-based projects [13] are used as an inspiration for the design of the Lhcmaster-G system.

The MC-tester [10] is a simple tool designed to compare the outputs produced by distinct event generators. Like the Lhcmaster, the MC-tester useshistograms to express the results of its work in a graphical manner. However, the usage of both tools differs greatly.

The Detector Construction Database (DCDB) system [11] is a tool closely connected with particle detectors. DCDB is a part of another LHC-related project, ALICE [4]. It supports the detector construction process, managing the distributed production of its components. However, the system is not focused on the problem of detector simulation and the data produced by detectors.

AliEn is a project which involves a complete Grid framework for the ALICE experiment and makes it possible to store commands, applications and data in a tree-like distributed catalogue. The objects stored in this core structure may be used by the users to create their own Grid applications. The AliEn environment also provides many other typical Grid elements useful in implementing Grid projects (e.g., Resource Broker, Queue Server, Information Server, Authentication Server, Virtual Organizations support).

The Simulation for LHCb and its Integrated Control Environment (SLICE) is an application connected with the LHCb experiment [3]. The goal that SLICE aims for, is to manage a distributed Monte Carlo production (event generation) performed by many physicists. The time- and resource-consuming character of the problem leads one to consider Grid technology as the proper computing environment. Therefore, SLICE is aimed at computing problems rather than data storage problems. However it could provide a good example for the Lhcmaster-G, if its future development plans include data production.

Thus, none of presented projects realises the guidelines specified for the system proposed in this paper. The problem described here undoubtedly calls for a custom solution.

4   Architecture of Lhcmaster

Lhcmaster has been designed as a system consisting of three parts: *Database Subsystem*, *Web Subsystem*, and *Data-access Subsystem*. There are three types of users in the system: *Administrator* and *External user* defined at the requirements specification stage, as well as the superuser *Root* managing the Administrators, groups of Administrators, and their rights in the system. Key elements of Lhcmaster and the interactions between the system and its users are depicted in Fig. 2.

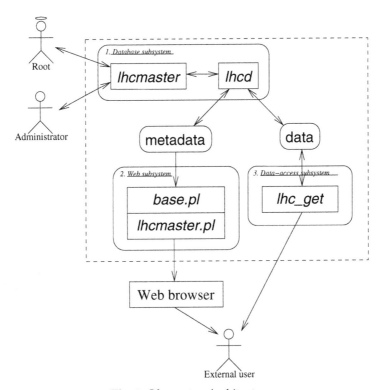

Fig. 2. Lhcmaster Architecture

The Database Subsystem is responsible for storage and management of data stored by the Administrators. The subsystem operates as a daemon (*lhcd*) that is connected to the backend database. Users can connect to the daemon by the means of the *lhcmaster* client program. The Database Subsystem is also responsible for creation of the Graphical File Index (GFI). Updating of the GFI is performed whenever the corresponding data files are modified. The analysis procedure is based on the ROOT framework and generates basic histograms in the GIF format. It is implemented as a dynamically-loaded library so it can be easily replaced by another procedure.

The Web Subsystem consists of Perl scripts and makes the GFI available for external users. Users connect to the system using a Web browser, and may scan the index in search of files that interest them. When the files are selected, the system can generate a script for downloading them. This script is the input for the Data Access Subsystem.

The Data Access Subsystem is based on an FTP server delivered with the ROOT framework. The command line client (*lhc_get*) provides a user interface.

Lhcmaster has been implemented with the use of simple and popular tools, such as the MySQL database system and CGI scripts written in Perl. This assures the simplicity and portability of the system, but also creates some obstacles for future development.

5   Feasibility Study

Lhcmaster has been successfully installed and tested. The goal was to check its conformity with requirements. The testbed was a PC, Intel Celeron 1.7 GHz, 512 MB RAM. Several series of data were stored and removed from the system. For instance, it took 245 seconds to store 386 MB of data, creating 20 histograms for each data file.

Following this, several exercises were performed. The goal was to select and download previously stored files, meeting the specific requirements imposed on physical data properties and simulation parameters. The files could be successfully selected with the use of a Web browser, and downloaded through the HTTP client provided by the system. Fig. 3 shows a sample screenshot of the GFI, with files organized in a hierarchical tree and sample histograms corresponding to one of selected files.

6   Towards the Lhcmaster-G

As shown in advance, Lhcmaster is a working system that fulfills the established requirements. However, there are several reasons that make us believe that the current implementation may not be flexible and scalable enough for future applications. In particular:

- The existing architecture produces a noticeable system load, which makes work difficult when the system is stressed to a medium or even small extent. It is not currently possible to physically distribute the Database Subsystem, which stands as the most resource-consuming part of the system.

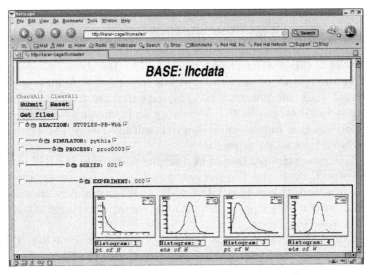

Fig. 3. Histograms corresponding to a data file

- The existing model of data storage based on local file copying lacks flexibility and generates a significant system load. A logical solution of the problem is to replace this model with an efficient network file transfer protocol (e.g., GridFTP).
- The current, centralized architecture of the system does not scale and may cause bottlenecks when new functionalities are introduced. New features, which might supplement existing ones, include:
  - allowing the production of data within the system, i.e. interfacing with the Monte Carlo event generators and detector simulations like ATLFAST, and
  - allowing the users to perform their own, custom-designed analysis of data stored within the system.

The solution we believe will meet all these requirements is to implement the system in a Grid environment. Such implementation might take place in the future, according to the design described below.

Table 1 describes the solutions that will be applied in the Lhcmaster-G, in place of existing ones.

The architecture of Lhcmaster-G is depicted in Fig. 4. The Lhcmaster-G environment will consist of several types of elements. The Storage Elements (SEs) and the Computing Elements (CEs) distributed among the nodes of the Grid will provide basic system functionalities. The Metadata Storage Elements (MSE) will be equivalent to the Web Subsystem. The Resource Broker (RB) and Replica Management (RM) providing typical Grid functionalities, will be adopted from the European DataGrid (EDG) [9] and the CrossGrid [16, 17] projects. This seems to be the best existing environment providing an integrated set of Grid solutions for applications such as Lhcmaster-G. The central

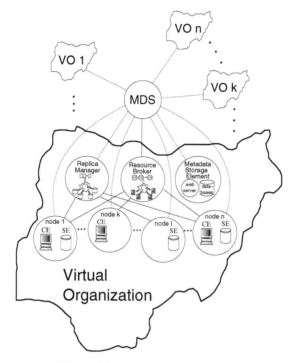

Fig. 4. Lhcmaster-G Architecture

Table 1. Grid equivalents of existing solutions

Existing solution	Equivalent Grid solution
simple login-and-password authentication of users	Grid users identified by their GSI certificates
groups of administrators	virtual organizations
data management based on simple OS file operations	GridFTP
a central database server for the stored data	distributed data management based on Replica Management including many Storage Elements

point of the Lhcmaster-G environment will be the Metadata Directory Service (MDS) or equivalent system, storing both the persistent information about the Grid structure, and the dynamic information derived continuously during system operation.

The tool can be integrated into the CrossGrid framework for interactive applications and take advantage of the roaming access, scheduling, data access and monitoring services developed in that project. Taking into account the increasing popularity of the service-oriented architectures for the Grid (like OGSA [15]) we propose to implement our system basing on the Grid Services framework.

7 Summary

High-energy physics is a broad domain that provides a field of development for many different computing and data-storage initiatives. We pointed out that Lhcmaster meets all the requirements specified in this paper. The system was tested in a real environment, and successfully performed the scheduled actions. For as long as fast simulations of the ATLAS detector are being performed, Lhcmaster will remain a valuable tool to support the work of many physicists.

However, we also showed, that further development requires a change of solutions and technologies used to implement the system. We pointed at the Grid technology as the best environment for a future implementation. The Lhcmaster-G tool, outlined in the paper is a project of a Grid-based system equivalent to Lhcmaster, and furthermore capable of providing many new functionalities.

Acknowledgements. We wish to thank M. Turała, P. Malecki, K. Korcyl for their comments and also P. Nowakowski for consultations. This work was partly funded by the European Commission, Project IST-2001-32243, CrossGrid [7], Project IST-2001-34808, GRIDSTART [8] and the Polish State Committee for Scientific Research, SPUB-M 112/E-356/SPB/5.PR UE/DZ 224/2002-2004. E. R.-W. partially supported by EC FP5 Centre of Excellence "COPIRA" under the contract No. IST-2001-37259.

References

1. Richter-Was, E., Froidevaux, D., and Poggioli, L.: ATLFAST 2.0 - a fast simulation for ATLAS, ATLAS Physics Note ATL-PHYS-98-131.
2. ATLAS Collaboration http://atlas.web.cern.ch/atlas/
3. The Large Hadron Collider beauty experiment for precise measurements of CP violation and rare decays http://lhcb.web.cern.ch/lhcb/
4. A Large Ion Collider Experiment at CERN. LHC http://alice.web.cern.ch/Alice/
5. Sjöstrand, T., Edén, P., Friberg, C., Lönnblad, L., Miu, G., Mrenna, S. and Norrbin, E.: Computer Phys. Commun. 135 (2001) 238
6. Corcella, G., Knowles, I.G., Marchesini, G., Moretti, S., Odagiri, K., Richardson, P., Seymour, M.H. and Webber, B.R.: HERWIG 6.5, JHEP 0101 (2001) 010
7. CrossGrid Project: http://www.eu-crossgrid.org
8. GRIDSTART Project: http://www.gridstart.org
9. European DataGrid Project: http://www.eu-datagrid.org
10. Golonka, P., Pierzchala, T., and Was, Z.: MC-Tester, a uniwersal tool for comparisons of Monte Carlo predictions for particle decays in high-energy. CERN-TH-2002-271. Compt. Phys. Commun. in print.
11. Traczyk, T.: Zastosowanie XML w heterogenicznej rozproszonej bazie danych wspierającej wielki eksperyment fizyki jądrowej. In: Grabara, J. K., Nowak, J. S.: PTI, Systemy informatyczne. Zastosowania i wdrożenia, Tom I, Warszawa-Szczyrk: WNT 2002, pp. 129-140

12. Bethke, S., Calvetti, M., Hoffmann, H. F., Jacobs, D., Kasemann, M., Linglin, D.:
    Report of the steering group of the LHC Computing review, 22/02/2001
    http://lhc-computing-review-public.web.cern.ch/
    lhc-computing-review-public/Public/Report_final.PDF
13. Harrison, K., Soroko, A.: Survey of technology relevant to a user-Grid interface for
    ATLAS and LHCb
    http://ganga.web.cern.ch/ganga/documents/pdf/technology_survey.pdf
14. Brun, R., Rademakers, F.: ROOT - An Object Oriented Data Analysis Framework,
    Proceedings AIHENP'96 Workshop, Lausanne, Sep. 1996, Nucl. Inst. & Meth. in
    Phys. Res. A 389 (1997) 81-86. See also http://root.cern.ch/
15. Foster, I., Kesselman, C., Nick, J.M., and Tuecke, S.: The Physiology of the Grid.
    An Open Grid Services Architecture for Distributed Systems Integration, January
    2002, http://www.globus.org
16. Bubak, M., M. Malawski, K. Zajac: Towards the CrossGrid Architecture. In: D.
    Kranzlmueller et al.: Recent Advances in Parallel Virtual Machine and Message
    Passing Interface, Proc. 9th European PVM/MPI Users' Group Meeting, Linz,
    Austria, 2002, LNCS 2474, pp. 16-24.
17. Bubak, M., Malawski, M., Zajac, K., Architecture of the Grid for Interactive Ap-
    plications. In. Sloot, P. M. A.; Abramson, D.; Bogdanov, A. V.; Dongarra, J. J.;
    Zomaya, A. Y.; Gorbachev, Y. E. (Eds.): (2003) Computational Science - ICCS
    2003, International Conference, Melbourne, Australia and St. Petersburg, Russia,
    June 2-4, 2003. Proceedings

Using Global Snapshots to Access Data Streams on the Grid

Beth Plale

Indiana University, Bloomington IN 47405, USA
plale@cs.indiana.edu
http://cs.indiana.edu/~plale

Abstract. Data streams are a prevalent and growing source of timely data. As streams become more prevalent, richer interrogation of the contents of the streams is required. Value of the content increases dramatically when streams are aggregated and distributed global behavior can be interrogated. In this paper, we demonstrate that access to multiple data streams should be viewed as one of deriving meaning from a distributed global snapshot. We define an architecture for a data streams resource based on the Data Access and Integration [2] model proposed in the Global Grid Forum. We demonstrate that access to streams by means of database queries can be intuitive. Finally, we discuss key research issues in realizing the data streams model.

Keywords: grid computing, data stream systems, publish-subscribe, continuous queries, OGSA-DAI, data management, dQUOB

1 Introduction

Data streams are a prevalent and growing source of timely data [12]. Stream applications are broad: sensor networks monitor traffic flow on US Interstates; NEXRAD Doppler radars continuously generate streamed data for weather forecasting and prediction. Network traffic, financial tickers, and web servers continuously generate data of interest. The literature describes numerous systems in existence that handle streaming data. But whereas existing applications are often designed explicitly to serve the data streams, in the future we expect data streams to be viewed as yet another input source to be consulted at will and upon demand. Just as it is common today to read starting conditions for an environmental simulation from a file, it should be equally as easy to draw those starting conditions on demand from live data streams.

These on-demand applications will be distributed and will have either significant computational needs or significant data access needs. As such, the Grid is an attractive computing framework because it promotes modularity through a service-oriented computing model, and provides scalability by virtue of its ability to amass resources that cross administrative domains. Early grids, those in existence today that span multiple departments on a university campus or sites on a company intranet, demonstrate the benefits attained from harnessing disparate and widely disbursed computational resources. Existing efforts to date to

M. Dikaiakos (Ed.): AxGrids 2004, LNCS 3165, pp. 191–201, 2004.

integrate stream systems into the grid have been ad hoc in nature [5]. Needed is a general architecture under which existing stream systems can be brought onto the grid. The model needs to be closely aligned with the specifications under development in the Global Grid Forum (GGF) because these specifications are defining the future direction of data access in grid computing.

Flexible access to real-time streaming data on the Grid is based on three requirements:

- *Aggregation of data streams:* as streams become more prevalent, richer interrogation over the streams is required. The value of the stream system increases dramatically when streams can be aggregated and global behavior can be interrogated.
- *Stream access through database operations:* database query languages are an intuitive way to think about stream access. The recent burgeoning interest in the database research community on data streams reinforces this view.
- *Grid service-based access to data streams:* grid service access to data streams should be organized around coherent meaning of a set of distributed entities such as sensors, not physical hardware.

The contribution of this paper is severalfold. We demonstrate that access to multiple data streams can be viewed as deriving meaning from a distributed global snapshot. We define an architecture for a data streams resource based on the Data Access and Integration [2] model proposed in the Global Grid Forum. We demonstrate that access to streams by means of database queries can be intuitive. Finally, we discuss key research issues in realizing the data streams model. Our current effort is to realize this architecture using our dQUOB system [18].

The term "streams" is very broadly defined. Section 2 addresses this ambiguity by categorizing streaming systems along orthogonal axes in order to expose the essential defining characteristics. In Section 4 we define the virtual stream store as a collection of domain related streams. In Section 5 we identify key research issues. The paper concludes with a discussion of related work and conclusions, Sections 6 and 7 respectively.

2   Data Stream Systems

The term "streams" can mean many things. Results stream from a database a row at a time; a sequence of requests streams to a web server; a stock ticker, a click stream, and keystrokes from a keyboard are all streams. We distinguish a *data stream* as an indefinite sequence of time-sequenced events (also called "messages" or "documents".) Events are marked with a timestamp indicating the time at which the event is generated, and often include a logical time indicating the time at which the application specific event occurred. We refer to the act of interrogating a stream as *decision-making*. Data streams differ from message passing systems in that data streams loosely couple distributed components with asynchronous time sequenced data whereas message passing systems support parallel or tightly coupled systems where communication is often synchronous. Data streams differ from mouse or keyboard events because the latter tightly couple an I/O device to a process.

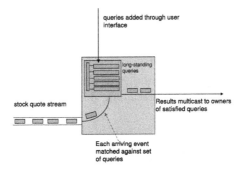

Fig. 1. Stream routing system example

Data stream systems are middleware systems that operate on data streams. These systems fall into three general categories: stream routing systems, data manipulation systems, and stream detection systems. Each is discussed below.

Stream routing systems. Stream routing systems disseminate events (or documents or information about events) to interested recipients. These systems are known by many names: publish/subscribe systems such as ECho [8], NaradaBroker [10], and Bayeux [23]; selective data dissemination system such as XFilter [1], document filtering system such as Xyleme [16], message-oriented middleware (MOM) [13]. Stream routing systems are distinguished by the locality of the information needed to make the decision. Decisions are made based almost exclusively upon the arriving event. Though some history may be maintained for instance to optimize performance, decision-making is largely localized to the immediate event at hand. The high delivery rates expected of such systems ensure that the decisions are kept simple.

A simple stream routing system is illustrated in Figure 1. A remote broker is shown receiving and distributing stock quote events. Users register their interest in particular stocks through submission of a query to the broker. The query might be, for instance, a Boolean expression, path expression, or Xpath query. Event arrival triggers query evaluation. This is quite unlike a database where query evaluation is triggered by query arrival. An arriving event is matched against the long-standing queries, and then is routed to the consumers indicated by the set of matching queries. The queries are long lived and are executed repeatedly. The expectation of these systems is that millions of queries can be active at any time. Key to achieving timeliness is the efficient matching of arriving events against a large number of long standing queries.

Data manipulation systems. Data manipulation systems are general stream processing systems that transform, filter, and aggregate data streams. Processing often results in the generation of new streams. There are looser timeliness requirements on the results on these systems than for stream routing or stream detection systems. For example, a large-scale instrument or set of instruments that generates large data sets can make the data sets available to the science community on the scale of hours later, and after having undergone extensive transformative processing. The types of decisions in data manipulation systems can be framed as requests for data and for manipulation of the data, thus the language used to express the requests must be flexible enough to express these complex requests [4, 15, 18, 17]. Data manipulation systems can be based on the assumption of periodic streams, that is, the assumption of periodicity for all streams in the system. Sensor network systems display this characteristic.

Data flow programming problems are another form of data manipulation system wherein data flows that originate at one or more data generators, are consumed at one or more consumers, and undergo filtering and transformation along the way. This functionality is provided in systems such as dQUOB [18] and DataCutter [6]. In work done at Cornell on ad hoc wireless networking, intermediate nodes aggregate information flowing from sensors to source [22].

Detection systems. Detection systems detect anomalous or changed behavior in remote distributed entities. In these systems asynchronous streams are the norm, that is, no assumptions about periodicity can be made. Stream detection systems are used to monitor performance, such as in R-GMA [9], Autopilot [19], Gigascope [7], changes in HTML pages, such as in Conquer [14], or safety critical systems, such as dQUOB [20]. Though overlap exists between detection systems and data manipulation systems, the focus of the system drives the kind of support provided to users. A detection system that provides timely detection of anomalous behavior might put an emphasis on temporal operators.

3   Distributed Global Snapshot of Stream System

We assert that data manipulation and detection systems taken together form a class of stream systems that meet the criteria of a data resource. A *data resource* is a collection of information that satisfies the properties of coherence and meaning. A relational database has coherence and meaning in that the tables in the database are related to one another and the relationships have meaning. As such, the database is amenable to rich interrogation, analysis, and manipulation.

Stream applications are organized around the production and consumption of data and as such, they export their state or behavior. Unlike a distributed application wherein a distributed global snapshot consists of a snapshot of the processes in a distributed application plus all messages in progress between processes, the distributed global snapshot of a data stream application can be determined from examining the data streams alone. That is, *we can safely draw conclusions about behavior of the distributed application simply by examining the streams*. This defining characteristic makes stream systems quite different from stream routing systems and from distributed systems in general in that embodied in their data streams is a global snapshot. This condition is sufficient for these systems to be considered a data resource in the same way as a database is considered a data resource. That is, the global snapshot over a set of streams satisfies the requirements of coherence and meaning.

4   Architecture for Stream Resource

Data-driven applications require access to data resident in files, databases, and streams. Access to data in streams should be as intuitive and uniform as access to these other mediums. We believe that this goal is best achieved within the grid services framework by viewing the data streams generated by data manipulation and detection systems as a data resource that is accessible through a grid service interface by means of a database query language. By modeling a data stream system as a data resource, we provide rich query access to the global snapshot that is inherent in these stream collections. This leads to a definition of a virtual data resource for streams management.

We define the "virtual stream store" as a *collection of distributed, domain-related data streams that satisfy the properties of meaning and coherence. Supporting the stream store is a set of computational resources located in physical proximity to data streams on which query processing can be carried out. The virtual stream store is accessed by means of a grid service that provides query access to the data streams. Event stream providers are external to the virtual store. The streams they generate are external to the store unless explicitly published to it. Data streams produced as a product of data stream processing (i.e., views) are automatically part of the virtual stream store.*

An example data stream store, illustrated in Figure 2, consists of nine data streams and associated computational resources. The computational resources, C_i, are contained within the virtual stream store but can be physically widely disbursed. Computational resources are located in physical proximity to data streams. The definition does not prohibit a computational resource from also being a provider. The providers, which include the radar in the lower left, and six sensors, two per sensor node for nodes C_1, C_2, and C_4, are excluded from the virtual stream store. This is an important feature of the model. Through the feature, the model can accommodate a database implementation of a data streams system, that is, where data streams are resident in a database and are serviced by long running queries managed through extensions to the database management system [4, 11]. Exclusion of providers benefits the provider by allowing it to retain control over which data streams are visible to a virtual stream store and when the streams become visible. In the following section we probe more deeply into the suitability of a database access interface for a data stream store and define open research issues.

5   Details

We have demonstrated that the virtual stream store architecture supports an important class of data streaming problems on the grid. From the numerous systems cited in Section 2 based on database concepts, it should be clear that database queries are a viable way to access stream data. For example, a practical solution to distributed monitoring is for a nuclear reactor monitoring system to feed its streaming data into a time-based database and perform post mortem

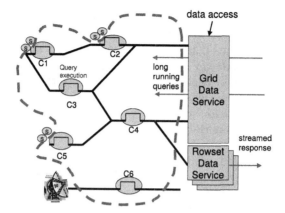

Fig. 2. Virtual stream store within thick dotted lines accessed through a grid service. The data providers are external to the store

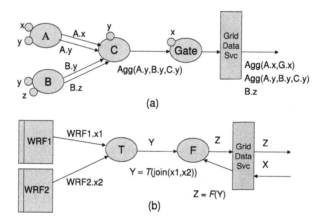

Fig. 3. Data distribution in a sensor network

processing of the data by means of issuing queries. The difference between this approach and an on-line approach should be one of implementation, not access interface. In this section we identify open research issues, but first set the stage by giving two examples from existing data stream systems.

In an example taken from [22], sensor nodes are limited computational devices equipped with several kinds of sensors (e.g., temperature, light, PIR). Nodes are connected to neighbors in an ad hoc wireless network and use a multi-hop routing protocol to communicate with nodes that are spatially distant. Special gateway nodes connect to components outside the sensor network through long- range communication such as cables or satellite links; all communication with users goes through the gateway node.

Queries are long running and periodic; streams are assumed to be synchronous. The query sensor network aggregates readings of the distributed sensors at each timestep. In Figure 3(a), four sensor nodes are depicted, A, B, C, and Gate. Gate is the gateway node that communicates with the Grid Data Service to return a stream of aggregated values, one per timestep, for each sensor in the system. As can be seen, the periodic output from the sensor network is an aggregation of values for sensors x, y, and z at each timestep. The user in this example might be a portal interface that graphically displays results in real time.

The second example is visualization flow processing as provided in dQUOB [18] where compute nodes are located on the path between the parallel model (WRF1, WRF2) and its visualization; see Figure 3. Each node on the path performs filtering, transformation, or aggregating. Transformation might convert the data from spectral domain to grid domain by application of an FFT. Another might join data streams from the model with a stream from the user and filter according to the user preference in a particular region of 3D space. Figure 3(b) depicts two model components, WRF1 and WRF2, that push data through a transformation node (T) and filter node (F). At node T the streams WRF1.x1 and WRF2.x2 are joined and the function T applied to the result. The resulting stream of events, Y, are streamed to node F where the function F is applied, resulting in stream Z. The user in this example could be a visualization tool enabled for application steering.

5.1 Research Issues

Integrating data streams from instruments and sensors into grid computing raises a number of research issues in query distribution, data distribution, query management, and query instantiation.

Query distribution. The virtual stream store will in most cases be a distributed resource that provides location transparency. That is, the user writes a single query as if all streams (tables) were centrally located. But since the streams are distributed, some form of query distribution must be provided. As this kind of functionality is nearly universal in all stream systems we examined, it could be provided as a pluggable component in the Grid Data Service. The OGSA-DAI [3] reference implementation, for instance, is structured to handle pluggable modules in the Grid Data Service.

Data distribution. Data distribution models differ across the systems we examined. For instance, in the sensor network example of Figure 3(a), records of the same sensor type but from different nodes have the same schema, and collectively form a distributed table. Where sensor nodes A, B, and C export the stream of their sensor y. The distributed table Y is the union of all A.y, B.y, and C.y. The operation performed on that distributed table is the aggregation of events based on timestamp. This is seen by the result streamed from C, namely Agg(A.y,B.y,C.y). Not shown is that C acts as an intermediate node also for streams A.x and B.z but does not operate on these. In the sensor network, data is distributed.

In other examples, such as the flow model of dQUOB [18], the data is federated in that the data from each node is treated as a separate table. While neither approach is superior, the virtual stream store and its grid service interface should be flexible enough to handle different distribution schemes.

Query distribution in databases often includes assembling results from distributed sources. This functionality is less important in a stream system because aggregation of results is often done within the system itself. In the flow-programming example, the query is broken into subqueries and placed in the virtual stream store in relation to other subqueries based on proximity to the sources. The results are returned from the stream system in their completed form.

Management of long running queries. The queries themselves reside for an extended period in the virtual stream store so lifetime is an issue. Query lifetime is often specified by means of extensions to the query language. If this support is not provided within the stream store, it would need to be provided by the grid service interface. The result of a long running query is a series of tuples generated over time that must be delivered by means of a stream delivery mechanism. These asynchronous requests are accommodated by the GGF DAIS grid service [2] by means of a special handling agent called a Rowset Data Service.

Query instantiation. Query instantiation is the realization of a query in the virtual stream store. The user specifies a query as say, an ASCII SQL statement, but the query must then be transformed into an executable entity in the virtual stream store. This instantiation is typically handled in a stream system-specific way thus support in the grid service must be modular and pluggable. To illustrate, suppose a set of hosts are available for use. In the Gigascope system [7], queries are pre-compiled into the executables that run on each of the nodes. In the case of dQUOB, the user submits a query that is compiled into a Tcl script that is then sent to the remote host. At the host are a runtime system and a dQUOB library. The runtime system receives the script and invokes a Tcl interpreter. Through the process of interpretation the script calls the dQUOB library which instantiates the query as C++ objects of operators (e.g., select, project) connected as a DAG. Thus the query is transported as a compact script, but runs efficiently as compiled code at the node. Further, the dQUOB query language allows definition of a user-defined procedures to be executed as part of the query. These code chunks are dynamically linked into the query execution environment at runtime.

Updates. An update is the act of publishing to a data stream in a virtual stream store. For reasons of performance and flexibility, data publication from devices, sensors, and instruments must be independent of the grid services interface. That is, the streams and query nodes within the virtual stream store should not bound by the requirement to understand web service interface descriptions (*i.e.*, WSDL) and use the SOAP transport protocol. Sensor nodes on an ad hoc wireless network, for instance, do not have sufficient resources or protocol support to support the communication overhead inherent in the grid service model.

6   Related Work

Numerous stream systems have been cited in Section 2. Related efforts in grid services for stream data are smaller in number. The OGSA-DAI project [3] has developed a set of services for connecting databases to the grid based on the GGF Grid Data Services specification. The OGSA-DAI work is complementary to our work and in fact will serve as a key component in our implementation of the streaming architecture proposed in this paper. In the Antarctic monitoring project [5], the authors propose a grid services architecture for interacting with an environment sensing device located in Antarctica. The grid services architecture provides access to and control of the sensor device, and accepts the data stream from the remote device via an iridium satellite phone network. The work differs from ours in that the service supports the combined functionalities of device management and access a stream of data.

Narayanan *et al* [21] discuss a services oriented software infrastructure that provides database support for accessing, manipulating, and moving large scale scientific data sets. The service model differs from our work in that the target data resource is a database of large scale data sets. R-GMA [9] is a stream detection system for performance monitoring of the grid middleware. It could be cast into the architecture described in this paper, however we envision the data stream store as having value to application users, not grid middleware services. Additionally, R-GMA supports a more limited access language than is provided by our system.

7   Conclusion

Data streams are a prevalent and growing source of timely data. As streams become more prevalent, richer interrogation of the contents of the streams are required. We argue in this paper that the value of the streamed content can be dramatically increased when a collection of streams is viewed as interrogating a distributed global snapshot. We define an architecture for a virtual stream store as embodying the global snapshot, and provide access to the store through a grid services Data Access and Integration [2] model. Our current effort is focused on defining access semantics to the virtual stream store, and on providing access to the results for clients who demand highly asynchronous streams and extremely timely results.

References

1. Mehmet Altmel and Michael J. Franklin. Efficient filtering of XML documents for selective dissemination of information. In *Proceedings of 26th VLDB Conference*, 2000.
2. Mario Antonioletti, Malcolm Atkinson, Susan Malaika, Simon Laws, Normal Paton, Dave Pearson, and Greg Riccardi. Grid data service specification. In *Global Grid Forum GWD-R*, September 2003.

3. Mario Antonioletti, Neil Chue Hong, Ally Hume, Mike Jackson, Amy Krause, Jeremy Nowell, charaka Palansuriya, Tom Sugden, and Martin Westhead. Experiences of designing and implementing grid database services in the ogsa-dai project. In *Global Grid Forum Workshop on Designing and Building Grid Services*, September 2003.

4. Shivnath Babu and Jennifer Widom. Continuous queries over data streams. In *International Conference on Management of Data (SIGMOD)*, 2001.

5. Steven Benford and et al. e-Science from the antarctic to the GRID. In *Proceedings of UK e-Science All Hands Meeting*, September 2003.

6. M. Beynon, R. Ferreira, T. Kurc, A. Sussman, and J. Saltz. Datacutter: Middleware for filtering very large scientific datasets on archival storage systems. In *Eighth Goddard Conference on Mass Storage Systems and Technologies/17th IEEE Symposium on Mass Storage Systems*, College Park, Maryland, March 2000.

7. Chuck Cranoe, Theodore Johnson, Vladislav Shkapenyuk, and Oliver Spatscheck. Gigascope: a stream database for network applications. In *International Conference on Management of Data (SIGMOD)*, 2003.

8. Greg Eisenhauer. The ECho event delivery system. Technical Report GIT-CC-99-08, College of Computing, Georgia Institute of Technology, 1999. http://www.cc.gatech.edu/tech_reports

9. Steve Fisher. Relational model for information and monitoring. In *Global Grid Forum, GWD-Perf-7-1*, 2001.

10. Geoffrey Fox and Shrideep Pallickara. An event service to support grid computational environments. *Journal of Concurrency and Computation: Practice and Experience. Special Issue on Grid Computing Environments.*, 2002.

11. Dieter Gawlick and Shailendra Mishra. Information sharing with the Oracle database. 2003.

12. Lukasz Golab and M. Tamer Ozsu. Issues in data stream management. *SIGMOD Record*, 32(2):5–14, June 2003.

13. Ashish Kumar Gupta and Dan Suciu. Stream processing of Xpath queries with predicates. In *International Conference on Management of Data (SIGMOD)*, 2003.

14. Ling Liu, Calton Pu, and Wei Tang. Continual queries for internet scale event-driven information delivery. *IEEE Transactions on Knowledge and Data Engineering, Special issue on Web Technologies*, January 1999.

15. Sam Madden and Michael J. Franklin. Fjording the stream: An architecture for queries over streaming sensor data. In *International Conference on Data Engineering ICDE*, 2002.

16. Benjamin Nguyen, Serge Abiteboul, Gregory Cobena, and Mihai Preda. Monitoring XML data on the web. In *International Conference on Management of Data (SIGMOD)*, 2001.

17. Clara Nippl, Ralf Rantzau, and Bernhard Mitschang. Streamjon: A generic database approach to support the class of stream-oriented applications. In *International Database Engineering and Applications Symposium IDEAS*, 2000.

18. Beth Plale and Karsten Schwan. Dynamic querying of streaming data with the dQUOB system. *IEEE Transactions in Parallel and Distributed Systems*, 14(4):422–432, April 2003.

19. Randy Ribler, Jeffrey Vetter, Huseyin Simitci, and Daniel Reed. Autopilot: Adaptive control of distributed applications. In *IEEE International High Performance Distributed Computing (HPDC)*, August 1999.

20. Beth (Plale) Schroeder, Sudhir Aggarwal, and Karsten Schwan. Software approach to hazard detection using on-line analysis of safety constraints. In *Proceedings 16th Symposium on Reliable and Distributed Systems SRDS97*, pages 80–87. IEEE Computer Society, October 1997.

21. Narayanan Sivaramakris, Tahsin Kurc, Umit Catalyurek, and Joel Saltz. Database support for data-driven scientific applications in the grid. *Parallel Processing Letters*, 13(2), 2003.

22. Yong Yao and Johannes Gehrke. Query processing in sensor networks. In *First Biennial Conference on Innovative Data Systems Research*, Asilomar, CA, January 2003.

23. S. Zhuang, B. Zhao, A. Joseph, R. Katz, and J. Kubiatowicz. Bayeux: An architecture for scalable and fault-tolerant wide area data dissemination. In *Proceedings Eleventh International Workshop on Network and Operating System Support for Digital Audio and Video (NOSSDAV 2001)*, June 2001.

SCALEA-G: A Unified Monitoring and Performance Analysis System for the Grid*

Hong-Linh Truong[1] and Thomas Fahringer[2]

[1] Institute for Software Science, University of Vienna
truong@par.univie.ac.at
[2] Institute for Computer Science, University of Innsbruck
Thomas.Fahringer@uibk.ac.at

Abstract. This paper describes SCALEA-G, a unified monitoring and performance analysis system for the Grid. SCALEA-G is implemented as a set of grid services based on the Open Grid Services Architecture (OGSA). SCALEA-G provides an infrastructure for conducting online monitoring and performance analysis of a variety of Grid services including computational and network resources, and Grid applications. Both push and pull models are supported, providing flexible and scalable monitoring and performance analysis. Source code and dynamic instrumentation are exploited to perform profiling and monitoring of Grid applications. A novel instrumentation request language has been developed to facilitate the interaction between client and instrumentation services.

1 Introduction

Grid Monitoring is an important task that provides useful information for several purposes such as performance analysis and tuning, performance prediction, fault detection, and scheduling. Most existing Grid monitoring tools are separated into two distinct domains: *Grid infrastructure monitoring* and *Grid application monitoring*. The lack of combination of two domains in a single system has hindered the user from relating measurement metrics of various sources at different levels when conducting the monitoring and performance analysis. In addition, many existing Grid monitoring tools focus on the monitoring and analysis for Grid infrastructure; yet little effort has been done for Grid applications. To date, application performance analysis tools are mostly targeted to conventional parallel and distributed systems (e.g. clusters, SMP machines). As a result, these tools do not well address challenges in Grid environment such as scalability, diversity, dynamics and security.

To tackle above-mentioned issues, we are developing a new system named SCALEA-G. SCALEA-G is a unified system for monitoring and performance analysis in the Grid. SCALEA-G is based on the concept of Grid Monitoring Architecture (GMA) [1] and is implemented as a set of OGSA-based services [12]. SCALEA-G provides an infrastructure of OGSA-compliant grid services for online monitoring and performance analysis of a variety of Grid services including computational resources,

---

* This research is supported by the Austrian Science Fund as part of the Aurora Project under contract SFBF1104.

M. Dikaiakos (Ed.): AxGrids 2004, LNCS 3165, pp. 202–211, 2004.

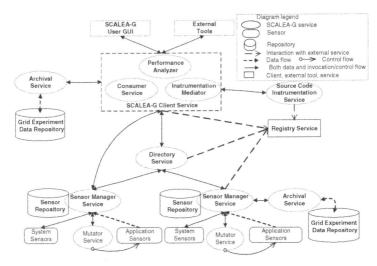

Fig. 1. High-level view of SCALEA-G Architecture

networks, and applications. Both push and pull models proposed in GMA are supported, providing a flexible and scalable way when performing the monitoring and analysis. In SCALEA-G, each kind of monitored data is described by an XML schema, allowing any client to easily access the data via XPath/XQuery. SCALEA-G supports both source code and dynamic instrumentation for profiling and monitoring events of Grid applications. A novel instrumentation request language has been devised to facilitate the interaction between client and instrumentation services. System and application specific metrics are related as close as possible in a single system, thus increasing the chance to uncover Grid performance problems.

Due to space limit, in this paper, we just describe a few selected features of SCALEA-G[1]. The rest of this report is organized as follows: Section 2 presents the architecture of SCALEA-G. In Section 3, we describe SCALEA-G sensors and Sensor Manager Service. Section 4 describes instrumentation service and instrumentation request language. We then discuss the data delivery, caching and filtering mechanism in Section 5. Security issues in SCALEA-G are outlined in Section 6. Section 7 illustrates first experiments and examples of the current prototype. We present some related work in Section 8 before going to the Conclusion and Future work in Section 9.

2   SCALEA-G Architecture

SCALEA-G is an open architecture based on OGSA [12] combined with GMA [1]. Figure 1 depicts the architecture of SCALEA-G which consists of a set of OGSA-based services and clients. *SCALEA-G Directory Service* is used for publishing and searching information about producers and consumers that produce and consume performance

---

[1] More details can be found in ftp://ftp.vcpc.univie.ac.at/projects/aurora/reports/auroratr2003-22.ps.gz and http://www.par.univie.ac.at/project/scaleag

data and information about types, characteristics of that data. *Archival Service* is a data repository which is used to store monitored data and performance results collected and analyzed by other components. *Sensor Manager Service* is used to manage sensors that gather and/or measure a variety of kinds of data for monitoring and performance analysis. The instrumentation of application can be done at source code level by using *Source Code Instrumentation Service* or dynamically at the runtime through *Mutator Service*. *Client Service* provides interfaces for administrating other SCALEA-G services and accessing data in these services. In addition, it provides facilities for analyzing performance data. Any external tools can access SCALEA-G by using Client Service. *User GUI* supports the user to graphically conduct online monitoring and performance analysis; it is based on facilities provided by Client Service. SCALEA-G services register information about their service instances with a *Registry Service*.

Interactions among SCALEA-G services and clients are divided into *Grid service operation invocations* and *stream data delivery*. Grid service operation invocations are used to perform tasks which include controlling activities of services and sensors, subscribing and querying requests for performance data, registering, querying and receiving information of Directory Service. In stream data delivery, a stream channel is used to transfer data (monitored data, performance data and results) between producers (e.g. sensors, Sensor Manager Service) and consumers (e.g. Sensor Manager Service, clients). Grid service operations use transport-level and message-level security whereas data channel is secure connection; all base on Grid Security Infrastructure (GSI) [10].

In deployment of SCALEA-G, instances of sensors and Mutator Service are executed in monitored nodes. An instance of Sensor Manager Service can be deployed to manage sensors and Mutator Services in a node or a set of nodes, depending on the real system and workload. Similarly, an instance of Directory Service can manage multiple Sensor Manager Services in an administrative domain. The client discovers SCALEA-G services through registry services which can be deployed in different domains.

3   Sensors and Sensor Manager Service

SCALEA-G distinguishes two kinds of sensors: *system sensors* and *application sensors*. System sensors are used to monitor and measure the performance of Grid infrastructure. Application sensors are used to measure execution behavior of code regions and to monitor events in Grid applications. All sensors are associated with some common properties such as sensor identifier, data schema, parameters.

3.1   System Sensors and Sensor Repository

SCALEA-G provides a variety of system sensors for monitoring the most commonly needed types of performance information on the Grid investigated by GGF DAMED-WG [9] and NMWG [13].

To simplify the management and deployment of system sensors, a *sensor repository* is used to hold the information about available system sensors. Each sensor repository is managed by a Sensor Manager Service that makes sensors in the repository available for use when requested. Figure 2 presents XML schema used to express sensors in the

```
<xsd:element name="sensorrepository"              <xsd:complexType name="Params">
              type="SensorEntry"/>              <xsd:sequence>
<xsd:complexType name="SensorEntry">             <xsd:element name="param"
 <xsd:sequence>                                   minOccurs="0" maxOccurs="unbounded">
  <xsd:element name="desc"                         <xsd:complexType>
              type="xsd:string"/>                  <xsd:attribute name="name"
  <xsd:element name="measureclass"                             type="xsd:string"/>
              type="xsd:string"/>                  <xsd:attribute name="desc"
  <xsd:element name="schemafile"                               type="xsd:string"/>
              type="xsd:string"/>                   <xsd:attribute name="dataType"
  <xsd:element name="params" type="Params"/>                   type="xsd:string"/>
 </xsd:sequence>                                  </xsd:complexType>
 <xsd:attribute name="name"                      </xsd:element>
         type="xsd:string"/>                    </xsd:sequence>
</xsd:complexType>                              </xsd:complexType>
```

Fig. 2. XML schema used to describe sensors in the sensor repository

sensor repository. The XML schema allows to specify sensor-related information such as *name* (a unique name of the sensor), *measureclass* (implementation class), *schemafile* (XML schema of data produced by the sensor), *params* (parameters required when invoking the sensor), etc. Although not specified in the repository, by default the lifetime of a sensor instance will optionally be specified when the sensor instance is created.

3.2 Application Sensors

Application sensors are embedded in programs via source code instrumentation or dynamic instrumentation. Application sensors support profiling and events monitoring.

Data collected by application sensors is also described in XML format. Figure 3 shows the top-level XML schema for data provided by application sensors. The *name* tag specifies kind of sensors, either *app.event* or *app.prof*, corresponding to event or pro-

```
<xsd:element name="sensordata"  type="SensorData"/>
<xsd:complexType name="SensorData">
<xsd:sequence>
 <xsd:element name="experiment" type="xsd:string"/>
 <xsd:element name="coderegion" type="CodeRegion"/>
 <xsd:element name="events"     type="Events"/>
 <xsd:element name="metrics"    type="Metrics"/>
</xsd:sequence>
 <xsd:attribute name="name" type="xsd:NMTOKEN"/>
</xsd:complexType>
```

Fig. 3. Top-level XML schema of data provided by application sensors

filing data, respectively. The *experiment* tag specifies a unique identifier determining the experiment. This identifier is used to distinguish data between different experiments. The *coderegion* tag refers to information of the source of the code region (e.g. line, column). The *processingunit* tag describes the context in which the code region is executed; the context includes information about *grid site, computational node, process, thread*. The *events* tag specifies list of *events*, an event consists of event time, event name and a set of event attributes. The *metrics* tag specifies a list of performance metrics, each metric is represented in a tuple of name and value.

3.3 Sensor Manager Service

The main tasks of Sensor Manager Service are to control and manage activities of sensors in the sensor repository, to register information about sensors that send data to it with a directory service, to receive and buffer data sensors produce, to support data subscription and query, and to forward instrumentation request to instrumentation service.

In Sensor Manager Service, a *Data Service* receives data collected by sensor instances and delivers requested data to consumers. It implements filtering, searching, forwarding and caching

Fig. 4. Data Service in Sensor Manager Service

data to/from various destinations/sources. In the Data Service, as shown in Figure 4, a *Data Receiver* is used to receive data from sensors and to store the received data into data buffers, and a *Data Sender* is used to deliver data to consumers. The data service uses only one connection to each consumer for delivering multiple types of subscribed data. However, an on-demand connection will be created for delivering resulting data of each query invocation and destroyed when the delivery finishes. Sensor Manager Service supports both data subscription and query. Data query requests are represented in XPath/XQuery based on XML schema published by sensors.

3.4 Interactions Between Sensors and Sensor Manager Services

The interactions between sensors and Sensor Manager Services involve the exchange of three XML messages. In *initialization phase*, the sensor instance sends a *sensorinit* XML message which contains *sensor name*, an *XML schema* of data which sensor instance produces, *lifetime* and *description* information about the sensor instance to the Sensor Manager Service which then makes these information available for consumers via directory service. In *measurement phase*, the sensor instance repeatedly performs measurement, encapsulates its measurement data into a *sensordataentry* XML message, and pushes the message to the Sensor Manager Service. The measurement data is enclosed by *<![CDATA[...]]>* tag. Thus, sensors can customize the structure of their collected data. Before stopping sending collected data, the sensor instance sends a *sensorfinal* XML message to notify the Sensor Manager Service.

4 Instrumentation Service

We support two approaches: source code and dynamic instrumentation. In the first approach, we implement a Source Code Instrumentation Service (SCIS) which is based on SCALEA Instrumentation System [17]. SCIS however simply instruments input source files (for Fortran), not addressing compilation issue. Thus, the client has to compile and link the instrumented files with the measurement library containing application sensors.

In the second approach, we exploit the dynamic instrumentation mechanism based on Dyninst [6]. A *Mutator Service* is implemented as a GSI-based SOAP C++ Web service [14] that controls the instrumentation of application processes on the host where the processes are running. We develop an XML-based instrumentation request language (IRL) to allow the client to specify code regions of which performance metrics should be determined and to control the instrumentation process. The client controls the instrumentation by sending IRL requests to Mutator Services which in turn perform the instrumentation, e.g. inserting application sensors into application processes.

```
<xsd:element name="irl"      type="IRL"/>
<xsd:complexType name="IRL">
 <xsd:sequence>
 <xsd:element name="experiment"
 type="Experiment" minOccurs="0" maxOccurs="1"/>
 <xsd:element name="request"   type="Request"
         minOccurs="0" maxOccurs="unbounded"/>
 <xsd:element name="response" type="Response"
        minOccurs="0" maxOccurs="unbounded"/>
 </xsd:sequence>
</xsd:complexType>
<xsd:complexType name="Request">
 <xsd:sequence>
   <xsd:element name="experiment"
                type="Experiment" />
   <xsd:element name="task" type="Task"/>
 </xsd:sequence>
 <xsd:attribute name="name" type="xsd:NMTOKEN"/>
</xsd:complexType>
<xsd:complexType name="Experiment">
 <xsd:sequence>
 <xsd:element name="applicationName"
               type="xsd:string"/>
 <xsd:element name="jobID"
               type="xsd:string"/>
 <xsd:element name="experimentID"
               type="xsd:string"/>
 </xsd:sequence>
```
```
</xsd:complexType>
<xsd:complexType name="Task">
 <xsd:sequence>
   <xsd:element name="coderegion"
               type="CodeRegion"/>
   <xsd:element name="metrics"
               type="ListString"/>
 </xsd:sequence>
</xsd:complexType>
<xsd:complexType name="CodeRegion">
   <xsd:attribute name="name"
               type="xsd:string"/>
   <xsd:attribute name="id"
               type="xsd:string"/>
</xsd:complexType>
<xsd:complexType name="Response">
   <xsd:sequence>
   <xsd:element name="detail"
               type="xsd:string"/>
   </xsd:sequence>
   <xsd:attribute name="name"
               type="xsd:NMTOKEN"/>
   <xsd:attribute name="status"
               type="xsd:NMTOKEN"/>
</xsd:complexType>
<xsd:simpleType name="ListString">
 <xsd:list itemType="xsd:string"/>
</xsd:simpleType>
```

Fig. 5. XML Schema of Instrumentation Request Language

4.1   Instrumentation Request Language (IRL)

The IRL is provided in order to facilitate the interaction between instrumentation requester (e.g. users, tools) and instrumentation services. IRL which is an XML-based language consists of instrumentation messages: request and response. Clients send requests to Mutator Services and receive responses that describe the status of the requests.

Figure 5 outlines the XML schema of IRL. The job to be instrumented is specified by *experiment* tag. Current implementation of IRL supports four requests including *attach, getsir, instrument, finalize*:

- *attach*: requests the Mutator Service to attach the application and to prepare to perform other tasks on that application.
- *getsir*: requests the Mutator Service to return SIR (Standardized Intermediate Representation) [11] of a given application.
- *instrument*: specifies code regions (based on SIR) and performance metrics should be instrumented and measured.
- *finalize*: notifies the Mutator Service that client will not perform any request on the given application.

In responding to a request from a client, the Mutator Service will reply to the client by sending an instrumentation response which contains the name of the request, the status of the request (e.g OK, FAIL) and possibly a detailed responding information encoded in *<![CDATA[...]]>* tag.

5   Data Delivery, Caching and Filtering

Figure 6 depicts the message propagation in SCALEA-G that uses a simple tunnel protocol. In this protocol, each sensor builds its XML data messages and sends the messages to a Sensor Manager Service which stores the messages into appropriate buffers. When a client subscribes and/or queries data by invoking operations of Consumer Service, the Consumer Service calls corresponding operations of Sensor Manager Service and passes a *ResultID* to the Sensor Manager Service. The Sensor Manager Service then builds XML messages by tagging the ResultID to the data met the subscribed/queried condition and sends these messages to the Consumer Service. At the Consumer Service side, based on ResultID, the messages are filtered and forwarded to the client.

Data produced by system sensors will be cached in circular bounded buffers at Sensor Manager Service. In the current implementation, for each type of system sensor, a separate data buffer is allocated for holding data

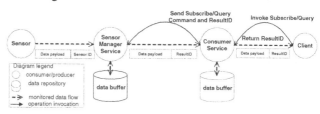

Fig. 6. Data Delivery and Caching

produced by all instances of that type of sensor. In *push* model, any new data entry met the subscribed condition will always be sent to the subscribed consumers. In *pull* model, Sensor Manager Service only searches current available entries in the data buffer and entries met conditions of consumer query will be returned to the requested consumers. Buffering data produced by application sensors is similar to that for system sensors. However, we assume that there is only one client to perform the monitoring and analysis for each application and the size of the data buffer is unbounded.

6   Security Issues

The security in SCALEA-G is based on GSI [10] facilities provided by Globus Toolkit (GT). Each service is identified by a certificate. SCALEA-G imposes controls on clients in accessing its services and data provided by system sensors by using an Access Control List (ACL) which maps client's information to sensors the client can access. The client information obtained from client's certificate when the certificate is used in authentication will be compared with entries in the ACL in the authorization process.

The security model for Mutator Service is a simplified version of that for GT3 GRAM [10] in which Sensor Manager Service can forward instrumentation requests of clients to Mutator Service. Mutator Service runs in a none-privilege account. However, if Mutator Service is deployed to be used by multiple users, it must be able to create its instances running in the account of calling users. By doing so, the instances have permission to attach user application processes and are able to perform the dynamic instrumentation. In the case of monitoring and analyzing application, when subscribing and/or querying data provided by application sensors, client's information will be recorded. Similarly, before application sensor instances start sending data to the Sensor Manager Service, the Sensor Manager Service obtains information about the client who executed the application. Both sources of information will be used for authorizing the client in receiving data from application sensors.

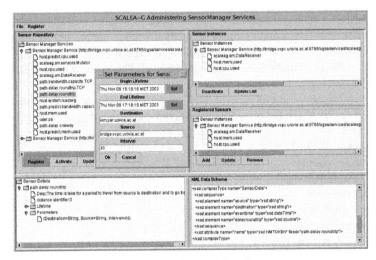

Fig. 7. SCALEA-G Administration GUI

7 Experiments and Examples

We have prototyped SCALEA-G Sensor Manager Service, Directory Service, Mutator Service, a set of system and application sensors. In this section we present few experiments and examples conducted via SCALEA-G User GUI.

7.1 Administrating Sensor Manager Services and Sensors

Figure 7 presents the administration GUI used to manage activities of Sensor Manager Services. By selecting a Sensor Manager Service, a list of available sensors and a list of sensor instances managed by that Sensor Manager Service will be shown in the top-left and top-right window of Figure 7, respectively. A user (with permission) can make a request creating a new sensor instance by selecting a sensor, clicking the *Activate* button and specifying input parameters and lifetime, e.g. Figure 7 shows the dialog for setting input parameters for *path.delay.roundtrip* sensor. An existing sensor instance can be deactivated by selecting *Deactivate* button. By choosing a sensor, detailed information of that sensor (e.g. parameters, XML schema) will be shown in the two bottom windows.

7.2 Dynamic Instrumentation Example

Figure 8 depicts the GUI for conducting the dynamic instrumentation in SCALEA-G. On the top-left window, the user can choose a directory service and retrieve a list of instances of Mutator Service registered to that directory service. The user can monitor processes running on compute nodes where instances of Mutator Service execute by invoking *Get/Update User Processes* operation as shown in the top-right window of Figure 8. For a given application process, its SIR (currently only at level of program unit and function call) can be obtained via *Get SIR* operation, e.g. the SIR of *rpp3do*

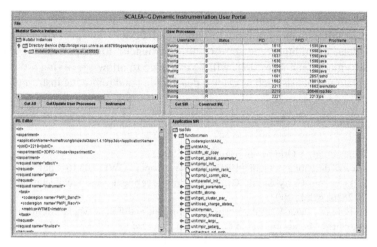

Fig. 8. SCALEA-G Dynamic Instrumentation GUI

process is visualized in the bottom-right window. In the bottom-left window, the user can edit IRL requests and send these requests to selected instances of Mutator Services.

8   Related Work

Several existing tools are available for monitoring Grid computing resources and networks such as MDS (a.k.a GRIS) [7], NWS [18], GridRM [2], R-GMA [15]. However, few monitoring and performance analysis tools for Grid applications have been introduced. GRM [3] is a semi-on-line monitor that collects information about an application running in a distributed heterogeneous system. In GRM, however, the instrumentation has to be done manually. OCM-G [4] is an infrastructure for Grid application monitoring that supports dynamic instrumentation. Atop OCM-G, G-PM [5], targeted to interactive Grid application, is used to conduct the performance analysis. However, currently the instrumentation of OCM-G is limited to MPI functions. None of aforementioned systems, except MDS, is OGSA-based Grid service. Furthermore, existing tools employ a non-widely accessible representation for monitored data. SCALEA-G, in contrast, is based on OGSA and uses widely-accepted XML for representing performance data, and provides query mechanism with XPath/XQuery-based requests.

Although there are well-known tools supporting dynamic instrumentation, e.g. Paradyn [16], DPCL [8], these tools are designed for conventional parallel systems rather than Grids and they lack a widely accessible and interoperable protocol like IRL, thus hindering other services from using them to conduct the instrumentation.

9   Conclusions and Future Work

In this paper we presented the architecture of SCALEA-G, a unified monitoring and performance analysis system in the Grid, based on OGSA and GMA concept. The main contributions of this paper center on the unique monitoring and performance analysis system based on OGSA and an instrumentation request language (IRL).

Yet, there are many rooms for improving the system. The set of sensors will be extended, enabling to monitor more resources and services, and providing more diverse kinds of data. In addition, the sensor will be extended to support monitoring based on resource model and rules. IRL will be extended to allow specifying more complex instrumentation requests such as events, deactivating and removing instrumentation.

References

1. B. Tierney et. al. A Grid Monitoring Architecture. http://www-didc.lbl.gov/GGF-PERF/GMA-WG/papers/GWD-GP-16-2.pdf
2. Mark Baker and Garry Smith. GridRM: A resource monitoring architecture for the Grid. *LNCS*, 2536: p.268, 2002.
3. Zoltan Balaton, Peter Kacsuk, Norbert Podhorszki, and Ferenc Vajda. From Cluster Monitoring to Grid Monitoring Based on GRM. In *Proceedings. 7th EuroPar'2001 Parallel Processings*, pages 874–881, Manchester, UK, 2001.
4. Bartosz Balis, Marian Bubak, Włodzimierz Funika, Tomasz Szepieniec, and Roland Wismüller. An infrastructure for Grid application monitoring. *LNCS*, 2474: p. 41, 2002.
5. Marian Bubak, Włodzimierz Funika, and Roland Wismüller. The CrossGrid performance analysis tool for interactive Grid applications. *LNCS*, 2474: p. 50, 2002.
6. Bryan Buck and Jeffrey K. Hollingsworth. An API for Runtime Code Patching. *The International Journal of High Performance Computing Applications*, 14(4):317–329, 2000.
7. K. Czajkowski, S. Fitzgerald, I. Foster, and C. Kesselman. Grid Information Services for Distributed Resource Sharing. In *Proceedings of the Tenth IEEE International Symposium on High-Performance Distributed Computing (HPDC-10)*. IEEE Press, August 2001.
8. L. DeRose, T. Hoover Jr., and J. Hollingsworth. The dynamic probe class library: An infrastucture for developing instrumentation for performance tools. In *Proceedings of the 15th International Parallel and Distributed Processing Symposium (IPDPS-01)*, Los Alamitos, CA, April 23–27 2001. IEEE Computer Society.
9. Discovery and Monitoring Event Description (DAMED) Working Group. http://www-didc.lbl.gov/damed/
10. Von Welch et all. Security for Grid Services. In *Proceedings of 12th IEEE International Symposium on High Performance Distributed Computing (HPDC'03)*, pages 48–57, Seattle, Washington, June 22 - 24 2003.
11. T. Fahringer, M. Gerndt, Bernd Mohr, Martin Schulz, Clovis Seragiotto, and Hong-Linh Truong. Standardized Intermediate Representation for Fortran, Java, C and C++ Programs. APART Working group (http://www.kfa-juelich.de/apart/), Work in progress, June 2003.
12. I. Foster, C. Kesselman, J. Nick, and S. Tuecke. Grid Services for Distributed System Integration. *IEEE Computer*, pages 37–46, June 2002.
13. GGF Network Measurements Working Group. http://forge.gridforum.org/projects/nm-wg/
14. gSOAP: C/C++ Web Services and Clients. http://www.cs.fsu.edu/~engelen/soap.html
15. R-GMA: Relational Grid Monitoring Architecture. http://www.r-gma.org
16. Paradyn Parallel Performance Tools. http://www.cs.wisc.edu/paradyn/
17. Hong-Linh Truong and Thomas Fahringer. SCALEA: A Performance Analysis Tool for Parallel Programs. *Concurrency and Computation: Practice and Experience*, 15(11-12):1001–1025, 2003.
18. R. Wolski, N. Spring, and J. Hayes. The Network Weather Service: A Distributed Resource Performance Forecasting Service for Metacomputing. *Future Generation Computing Systems*, 15:757–768, 1999.

Application Monitoring in CrossGrid and Other Grid Projects*

Bartosz Baliś[1,2], Marian Bubak[1,2], Marcin Radecki[2],
Tomasz Szepieniec[2], and Roland Wismüller[3]

[1] Institute of Computer Science, AGH, al. Mickiewicza 30, 30-059 Kraków, Poland
{balis,bubak}@uci.agh.edu.pl
[2] Academic Computer Centre – CYFRONET, Nawojki 11, 30-950 Kraków, Poland
{t.szepieniec,m.radecki}@cyf-kr.edu.pl
[3] LRR-TUM – Technische Universität München, D-80290 München, Germany
wismuell@in.tum.de
phone: (+48 12) 617 39 64, fax: (+48 12) 633 80 54, phone: (+49 89) 289-17676

Abstract. Monitoring of applications is important for performance analysis, visualization, and other tools for parallel application development. While current Grid research is focused mainly on batch-oriented processing, there is a growing interest in interactive applications, where the user's interactions are an important element of the execution. This paper presents the OMIS/OCM-G approach to monitoring interactive applications, developed in the framework of the CrossGrid project. We also overview the currently existing application monitoring approaches in other Grid projects.

Keywords: Grid, monitoring, interactive applications, CrossGrid

1 Introduction

While the current Grid technology is oriented more towards batch processing, there is a growing interest in *interactive* applications, e.g., in the European IST project CrossGrid [7]. Those applications involve a person 'in the computing loop' who can control the computation at runtime.

The user is often interested in improving performance of his application, steering it, or just in visualization of its execution. For all these purposes, specialized tools usually exist. All such tools need a *monitoring infrastructure* which collects the information about the execution of the application and possibly also offers manipulation services.

In this paper, we present an approach to monitoring interactive applications developed in the framework of the CrossGrid project. Additionally, we also overview the currently existing application monitoring approaches in other Grid projects.

---

* This work was partly funded by the European Commission, project IST-2001-32243, CrossGrid [7].

M. Dikaiakos (Ed.): AxGrids 2004, LNCS 3165, pp. 212–219, 2004.

2   Need for Monitoring Interactive Applications

In interactive applications the user usually requires a near-realtime response time, so that he can observe the results of his actions immediately. Consequently, monitoring of interactive applications requires sophisticated techniques which minimize the perturbation of monitoring.

We argue that for interactive applications we need *on-line* monitoring infrastructure. The method alternative to on-line is the off-line approach in which we generate trace files for a post-mortem analysis. Although this approach may be feasible for interactive applications, it poses many disadvantages.

– For the performance results to be useful, the user needs to be able to relate them to his individual interactions (for example "moving my head in an immerse environment resulted in the following amount of data transfer"). To enable this in the off-line approach, besides information about the application's behavior, also user's interactions must be monitored and stored in a trace file, so that a further visualization of the relation between the interactions and performance is possible. This increases monitoring intrusiveness and trace sizes. It also increases the implementation effort, since the interactions must be properly saved, and subsequently visualized, in a way smart enough to properly show the relation between interactions and performance.
– Only in on-line mode manipulations are possible. The benefits of manipulations are manifold, for example, it may be useful to stop a long-time running application to set up new measurements based on the already available results. Also, manipulations are essential for steering of the application.
– In off-line mode, information of interest can not be specified at run-time. Specifically, we cannot change measurements at run-time as a result of already available information. This again increases the amount of data which has to be gathered and monitoring intrusiveness.
– It is more convenient for the user when he can immediately see the impact of his interactions on performance.

The performance analysis of parallel programs requires a low measurement and communication overhead, both being substantially affected by traces. Event tracing is the most general technique of data collection, but it has serious disadvantages, since it causes high data rates and potential measurement perturbation. Therefore, in general, measurements cannot be based mainly on event tracing, especially in case of interactive applications.

3   OCM-G – The CrossGrid Approach

3.1   Architecture

The CrossGrid project [7] is driven by interactive applications, where the user plays an important role in steering of the execution. Our primary goal is to create a monitoring infrastructure suitable for interactive applications to support application development tools. Below we describe our approach in detail, and explain how it fulfills the requirements described in section 2.

The monitoring infrastructure developed in the CrossGrid project is the OCM-G (Grid-enabled OMIS-Compliant Monitor) [2]. The OCM-G is a distributed, decentralized, autonomous system, running as a permanent Grid service and providing monitoring services accessible via a standardized interface OMIS (On-line Monitoring Interface Specification) [13]. The architecture of the OCM-G is shown in Fig. 1. It is composed of two type of components: per-site Service Managers, and per-host Local Monitors. Additionally, some parts of the OCM-G are linked directly in the monitored application (Application Module).

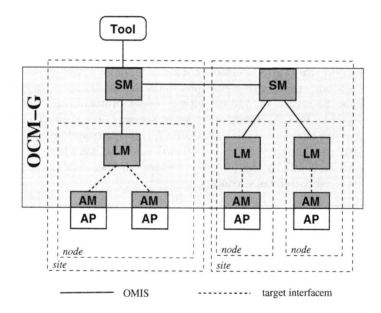

Fig. 1. Architecture of the OCM-G

3.2   Monitoring Interface

The monitoring services provided by OMIS are grouped into three basic monitoring activities:

- *get information* (e.g., 'get process status'),
- *manipulate* (e.g., 'stop a process'), and
- *detect events* (e.g., 'thread started a function call').

The first two of these service groups are referred to as *actions*. It is important to mention that the events are not saved in a trace file or immediately sent to a tool. Rather, the tool can program the necessary processing of these events inside the monitoring system.

At the level of a tool, the user is interested in *metrics* such as "delay due to synchronization", "volume of data transfer", etc. [14]. A measurement is a metric instance, i.e., the metric measured for the given application process in the given time, etc.

The philosophy of the OMIS/OCM-G approach is to provide a large set of relatively low-level monitoring services rather than high-level metrics. For example, for performance analysis OMIS does not impose any predefined semantics on metrics. Instead, using the large set of services, the tool can construct the metrics in a flexible and easy way. The latter feature is essential for the G-PM performance measurement tool [4] which uses the OCM-G for monitoring applications. G-PM allows the user to define arbitrary metrics at run-time. Only the flexibility of the OMIS/OCM-G enables this, since the high-level user's description of a metric can be translated into a sequence of lower-level monitoring requests. By contrast, other approaches, even if they define a simple monitoring protocol, also specify a list of available metrics with a fixed semantics.

Furthermore, the OMIS interface provides even more flexibility, not only with regard to available metrics. For example, in the GridLab approach, buffering of data can just be turned on and off with a proper protocol command, while in the OCM-G, the tool, by means of a set of services, has a direct control over creation and use of data storage objects, like e.g. counters and integrating timers (or trace-buffers if the tool really wants them), and thus has a better control over the buffering policy. It is the tool who decides whether to store the events in a trace or to just increment a counter.

3.3   Security

The security problems in the OCM-G are related to the fact that it is a multi-user system; specifically, Service Managers handle multiple users and applications. To ensure authenticity, integrity, and perhaps confidentiality of user's monitoring information as well as to prevent malicious users to manipulate other users' resources, all users should be properly authenticated to check if they are authorized to access the requested information or resources. In our solution, each component of the OCM-G is able to identify itself. Local Monitors and tools use the user's certificate for that, while Service Managers must have a special certificate with a unique Distinguished Name.

However, as we have shown in [3], all above is not enough to prevent from all security threats. The reason for this is site administrators have access to Service Managers' certificates (and likely the source code, too), thus they can perform a *forged-SM* attack. This attack potentially allows site administrators to access information and resources of other users on other sites. We have solved this problem by introducing a special protocol to gain access to users' resources. The protocol is roughly as follows. For each application being monitored, a virtual monitoring structure, called Virtual Monitoring System (VMS) is created. The VMS consists of all OCM-G components (LMs and SMs) which are involved in monitoring the application. Only those components which are able to properly identify themselves and are members of the proper VMS are allowed to monitor an application. However, to be granted membership in a VMS, a Service Manager must send a membership request which is singed by the user who owns the VMS.

4   Related Work

In this section, we provide an overview of three grid application monitoring approaches currently being developed. The mentioned projects/systems are as follows: GrADS (Autopilot), GridLab, and DataGrid (GRM).

4.1   GrADS

Within the GrADS project (Grid Application Development Software) [9], a software architecture for application adaptation and performance monitoring is being developed. It is a kind of program preparation and execution system which is supposed to replace the discrete steps of application creation, compilation, execution, and post-mortem analysis with a continuous process of adapting applications to both a changing Grid and a specific problem instance. The main goal of the system is to achieve reliably high performance.

An element responsible for performance monitoring in the framework is the Autopilot toolkit [18]. On the one hand, it can gather and analyse real-time application and infrastructure data, on the other hand, it can control the application's behavior.

The monitoring is based on sensors which may be put directly into the application's source code or embedded in an application library. The sensors register in the Autopilot Manager and can then be accessed by sensor clients to collect information. The clients can be located anywhere on the Grid. Controlling the application behavior is achieved by executing actuators which are implemented by the user in the source code.

Since the Autopilot toolkit works in a framework where definition of measurements, compilation and performance tuning is done automatically, it seems to be more oriented towards automatic steering than providing feedback to the programmer. It gives a rather general view of an application and its environment, e.g., to explore patterns in behavior instead of particular performance loss. Based on those patterns and external knowledge (e.g. user's experience), a performance optimization action is taken. It suits well the situation of a run-time system, where a special compiler creates a program, which is then automatically reconfigured at run-time depending on discovered patterns, e.g., I/O buffers may be resized for certain operations to improve performance.

4.2   GridLab

The Application Monitoring system developed within the GridLab project [1] [10] implements on-line steering guided by performance prediction routines deriving results from low level, infrastructure-related sensors (CPU, network load).

The sensors are mainly modules that are dynamically linked against monitoring system executables. They are designed to gather data from various sources, e.g., a special type of sensor can collect performance data from an application. When gathered at the lowest-level component, the information is passed to the so-called Main Monitor responsible for the management of the measurement and for providing the information to local users. The information can also be exposed to outside users by a Monitoring Service, which also does authentication and authorisation of users.

GridLab proposed a protocol for high-level producer-consumer communication. The protocol has three types of messages: commands, command responses and metric values. A consumer can authenticate, initiate a measurement, and collect data. Additionally, the GridLab team proposed a standard set of metrics along with their semantics.

However, the approach is limited in its functionality and flexibility. First, it does not support manipulations on the target application. Second, it seems to rely only on full traces, at least at the current state of development. Finally, the predefined semantics of all metrics requires all Grid users to agree on this, which is rather restrictive [11].

4.3   DataGrid

The GRM monitor and the PROVE visualization tool [17], being developed in the DataGrid project [8], originate from the cluster environment, in which they work as part of P-GRADE, an environment for parallel program development. These tools have been separated from P-GRADE and adapted to work on the Grid [12].

The GRM is a semi-on-line monitor which collects information about application and delivers them to the R-GMA [15], a relational information infrastructure for the Grid. Another GRM component gets the information from the R-GMA and delivers them to the PROVE visualisation tool [16]. According to the authors, *semi-on-line* mode means that only observation but not manipulation or data processing is possible, thus it is not a real on-line monitor. On the other hand though, the acquired data is not stored in local files like in off-line approaches, but is just buffered locally.

Monitoring in GRM/PROVE is mainly based on event tracing. However, event tracing has some serious drawbacks, as outlined in Section 2.

While the GRM/PROVE environment is well suited for the DataGrid project, where only batch processing is supported, it is less usable for the monitoring of interactive applications.

First, the R-GMA communication infrastructure used by GRM is based on Java servlets, which introduces a rather high communication latency. However, in order to perform accurate on-line measurements, it is important that the tool is provided with information as soon as possible. This is especially true when monitoring interactive applications.

Second, achieving low latency and low intrusion at the same time is basically impossible when monitoring is based on trace data. If the traces are buffered, the latency increases, if not, the overhead for transmitting the events is too high. This means that a tool will not be able to provide an update rate, which is high enough to meet the requirements of an on-line visualization, especially for interactive applications.

5   Status and Future Work

Currently, we have released a second prototype implementation of the OCM-G. This version has a full support for a grid environment, including a bottom-up start-up, globus-based security, and support for multiple applications. However, the prototype is still limited to work on a single site only.

The future work in the framework of the CrossGrid project, besides support for multiple sites, includes deployment of the OCM-G as a grid service (however, not in the web-services sense), support for multiple users, and a second layer of security which will allow not only for a proper authentication and authorization of users, but will also prevent from forging components of the monitoring system.

Additionally, we currently work on a web-services based interface to the OCM-G which will allow to deploy the system as a grid service.

6   Summary

Monitoring of interactive applications poses high requirements on the monitoring infrastructure. We have pointed out that on-line monitoring is best for this purpose. High efficiency is also very important, as in case of interactive applications a low response time is needed.

The OCM-G was designed with these requirements in mind. We use an efficient communication layer, data reduction and instrumentation techniques to minimize the intrusion of the monitoring system. The flexible set of monitoring services allows the user to define his own metrics, while the standard monitoring interface OMIS enables interoperability of tools.

Similar Grid application monitoring projects exist, but their analysis reveals that they have a focus which is rather different than that of our project.

Acknowledgements. We would like to thank prof. Peter Kacskuk and prof. Zsolt Nemeth for fruitful discussions.

References

1. Allen, G., Davis, K., Dolkas, K., Doulamis, N., Goodale, T., Kielmann, T., Merzky, A., Nabrzyski, J., Pukacki, J., Radke, T., Michael, M., Seidel, E., Shalf, J. , and Taylor, I.: Enabling Applications on the Grid: A GridLab Overview. International Journal of High Performance Computing Applications: Special issue on Grid Computing: Infrastructure and Applications, to be published in August 2003.
2. Baliś, B., Bubak, M., Szepieniec, T., Wismüller, R., and Radecki, M.: OCM-G – Grid Application Monitoring System: Towards the First Prototype. Proc. Cracow Grid Workshop 2002, Krakow, December 2002.

3. B. Baliś, M. Bubak, W. Rzasa, T. Szepieniec, R. Wismüller: Security in the OCM-G Grid Application Monitoring System. To be published in proc. PPAM 2003, 7-10 September 2003, Czestochowa, Poland. Springer.
4. Bubak, M., Funika, W., and Wismüller, R.: The CrossGrid Performance Analysis Tool for Interactive Grid Applications. Proc. EuroPVM/MPI 2002, Linz, Sept. 2002.
5. Bubak, M., Funika, W., Balis, B., and Wismüller, R.: Interoperability of OCM-based On-line Tools. Proc. PVM/MPI Users Group Meeting 2000, LNCS vol. 1908, pp. 242-249, Balatonfüred, Hungary, September 2000. Springer 2000.
6. Wismüller, R, Ludwig, T.: Interoperable Run-Time Tools for Distributed Systems – A Case Study. The Journal of Supercomputing, 17(3):277-289, November 2000.
7. The CrossGrid Project (IST-2001-32243): `http://www.eu-crossgrid.org`
8. The DataGrid Project: `http://www.eu-datagrid.org`
9. The GrADS Project: `http://hipersoft.cs.rice.edu/grads`
10. The GridLab Project: `http://www.gridlab.org`
11. GridLab deliverable 11.3: Grid Monitoring Architecture Prototype. `http://www.gridlab.org/Resources/Deliverables/D11.3.pdf`
12. Kacsuk, P.: Parallel Program Development and Execution in the Grid. Proc. PAR-ELEC 2002, International conference on parallel computing in electrical engineering. pp. 131-138, Warsaw, 2002.
13. Ludwig, T., Wismüller, R., Sunderam, V., and Bode, A.: OMIS – On-line Monitoring Interface Specification (Version 2.0). Shaker Verlag, Aachen, vol. 9, LRR-TUM Research Report Series, 1997. `http://wwwbode.in.tum.de/~omis/`
14. Z. Nemeth: Grid Performance, Grid Benchmarks, Grid Metrics. Cracow Grid Workshop, October 27-29, 2003, Cracow, Poland. Invited talk.
15. R-GMA: A Grid Information and Monitoring System. `http://www.gridpp.ac.uk/abstracts/AllHands_RGMA.pdf`
16. N. Podhorszki and P. Kacsuk Monitoring Message Passing Applications in the Grid with GRM and R-GMA Proceedings of EuroPVM/MPI'2003, Venice, Italy, 2003. Springer 2003.
17. Podhorski, N., Kacsuk, P.: Design and Implementation of a Distributed Monitor for Semi-on-line Monitoring of VisualMP Applications. Proc. DAPSYS 2000, Balatonfured, Hungary, 23-32, 2000.
18. Vetter, J.S., and Reed, D.A.: Real-time Monitoring, Adaptive Control and Interactive Steering of Computational Grids. The International Journal of High Performance Computing Applications, 14 357-366, 2000.

Grid Infrastructure Monitoring as Reliable Information Service*

Petr Holub, Martin Kuba, Luděk Matyska, and Miroslav Ruda

Institute of Computer Science, Masaryk University,
Botanická 68a, 602 00 Brno, Czech Republic
{hopet,makub,ludek,ruda}@ics.muni.cz

Abstract. A short overview of Grid infrastructure status monitoring is given followed by a discussion of key concepts for advanced status monitoring systems: passive information gathering based on direct application instrumentation, indirect one based on service and middleware instrumentation, multidimensional matrix testing, and on-demand active testing using non-dedicated user identities. We also propose an idea of augmenting information provided traditionally using Grid information services by information from the infrastructure status monitoring which gives verified and thus valid information only. The approach is demonstrated using a Testbed Status Monitoring Tool prototype developed for a GridLab project.

1 Introduction

A large-scale heterogeneous Grid is subject to frequent changes and service disruptions of some of the huge number of components that constitute this environment. Grid management requires on-line monitoring of the resources to determine their state and availability. The less dynamic data about the Grid resources are usually published by the resources themselves using information services (e. g. Meta Directory Service from Globus package [2]), while the highly dynamic data are usually published via different means (some implementation of the general Grid Monitoring Architecture, GMA [1]). The information provided by both of these approaches is used by other Grid services for discovery of elements of the environment and the ways these elements can be used.

The general Grid monitoring covers two complementary areas: application monitoring and infrastructure monitoring. Both can be subdivided into performance monitoring and status monitoring. Application performance monitoring, application status monitoring, and infrastructure performance monitoring are out of scope of this paper. We are dealing with Grid infrastructure status monitoring, which will be called *status monitoring* for brevity. Status monitoring covers infrastructure sanity checks, availability and interoperability of computers, other components, as well as web services and Grid services [5].

---

* This work is supported by the European Commission, grant IST–2001–32133 (Grid-Lab).

In this paper we introduce an idea of augmenting the information service by the status monitoring service. The augmentation is performed by verifying the information provided by the information service using the data from the status monitoring, and allowing validated results only. Such model is ready for testing within the GridLab project where GridLab Testbed Status Service [3] will be used as one of information sources. A description of GridLab Testbed Status Monitoring Tool prototype is also covered by this paper. Roughly, the primary goal for the information service augmentation is a provision of enough data supporting production-quality Grid management; another goal is a verification and correction of static data provided by the "classical" information services.

2 Infrastructure Status Monitoring

Classical infrastructure status monitoring uses so called active tests, run by the monitoring service itself. These tests are fully under the control of the status monitoring service, but they pose additional load on the monitored resources (some sensors must run on the resources, the monitoring data are transmitted over the network, etc.). The alternative is passive monitoring[1] that gathers monitoring data directly from the users' applications running on the Grid (e. g. large data transfers). This passive monitoring poses only negligible additional load on the Grid but it is irregular and of very heterogeneous nature. Therefore, a perfect status monitoring system should complement the passive monitoring with active tests in cases where enough data are not available (e. g. due to longer period of user inactivity).

Both monitoring approaches use sensors as the primary data sources (generators). They can be run either in "push" mode, when sensor continuously sends data to any subscribed monitoring service, or in "pull" mode when the sensor is polled each time the data is required by monitoring service.

Passive monitoring model was based on an idea of an application instrumentation, i. e. a specific code is incorporated into the applications to report monitoring data. With the monolithic application model this means that developers themselves must include the instrumentation calls into their own code. Use of instrumented libraries linked at compile time or even better at run time is a step toward less obtrusive monitoring. With the increased use of service-based or middleware-based applications the instrumentation calls can be hidden within the service code or in the middleware and the application developers or the users do not have to be even aware of the fact that the whole program or its specific run is instrumented. The application based instrumentation (either directly in the application code or within the higher layers of the service code) has one major advantage – it can serve as a source of very complex monitoring data. The successful completion of a high-level application request (e. g. a service or even a set of services) is simultaneously a proof of proper function of all the services used as well as the lower middleware layers. A simple message about

---

[1] For the sake of clarity we don't use word "test" in the context of passive information gathering in this paper and we reserve it for active tests.

successful service call covers a success of many related (lower) services, increasing substantially scalability of the monitoring by allowing the system to omit individual tests that are implicitly successful. On the other hand, a failure can immediately trigger more detailed status tests of called services, thus leading to very fast failure discovery.

Traditionally status monitoring has been performed on machine oriented basis: either the machines sent continuously some data, or machine by machine was tested whether all required and advertised services are running. Introduction of widely deployed services within the Open Grid Services Architecture [5] framework leads to the necessity to perform also the service oriented monitoring to check that all services are running properly. Most services run in a machine independent way, i. e. they are not tightly associated with a particular machine and can run in several instances simultaneously or can be easily re-started on any machine from a subset of Grid machines. This means that a service – not a machine – must be tested. Testing of a service means that the service must be found (discovered), connected to and actually tested (run) dynamically, with no stored (cached) information about the placement of the service.

For many services it is important to test availability on N-to-N or M-to-N basis (where M might be subset of N or it might be completely different and independent set) instead of 1-to-N basis. For instance data transfer service may be required to be capable of transferring data from any node to any node (or even a set of nodes). Or a user may be required to be able to login from any node within a selected subset of Grid nodes to any node from different subset. As a first step towards more complex solution, we have introduced matrix tests that perform either M-to-N or N-to-N tests to cover such cases.

Another important aspect of the status monitoring is whether the tests run using some dedicated testing identity (e. g. using dedicated service certificate) or whether the tests are run using ordinary users' identities. While the second option is rather automatic for instrumented checks, it must be ensured that similar way is possible for active checks as well. It is also desirable to be able to run active tests on demand under specific user identity as this provides means for looking for a cause of a problem encountered by particular users only.

3   Monitoring Services as Information Services Augmentation

Information services traditionally advertise information about resources available on the Grid (machines and their capabilities, job submission mechanisms, services etc.). Owners of the resources or directly the resources usually publish such information about the resources into information service without any validation, and therefore obsolete or invalid information can be easily advertised.

Status monitoring can augment traditional information services by taking information published in them, checking validity and then publishing results in form of verified and thus authoritative information about resources using interface common to information services.

Another problem with the Grid information services is that the most common information service – Globus MDS – also shows serious performance bottleneck when too many non-homogeneous information providers are subscribed to it (especially with high percentage of "problematic" ones, like information providers behind firewalls or incompatible versions of software clients). Status monitoring service can mitigate these problems by providing "cached" and valid only data from such service.

4   Prototype Implementation

GridLab Testbed Status Monitoring Tool prototype [3] has been designed to test availability and sanity of Grid environment (this system is not used for performance monitoring as this is covered by Mercury [4], which is other part of the GridLab project). Very first version of this tool was based on monitoring tool available from TeraGrid Project [6]. This monitoring tool comprised a single threaded Perl script performing all tests in sequential order, making this solution not scalable. Also adding new tests was not easy and decreased the scalability even further. Based on the experience gained with this and similar tools we created new design of the testbed monitoring tool.

Current prototype has a core written in Java language and uses clean layered architecture shown in Fig. 1. We not only made testing independent of other parts, we also split a storage of results from the presentation, providing very high system flexibility. System is easily configurable using XML language. This architecture is scalable enough for small to medium size Grids, with at most few hundreds of nodes. The system may need to be enhanced with hierarchical distributed setup for larger Grids, or with robust features from peer-to-peer networks if fault tolerance is of a high concern.

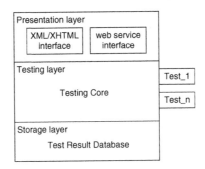

Fig. 1. GridLab testbed status monitoring architecture

Testing layer. The current GridLab testbed status monitoring is still a centralized activity, which means all the tests are initiated from one site and all the results are gathered there. While the sequential run of individual tests is inefficient, the fully parallel run of all tests is also impossible for larger Grid infrastructure (with fifty or more resources in the testbed). The fully parallel run may not only overload the testing machine, it may also pose an unacceptable load on the whole Grid infrastructure. Therefore, we use thread pool of configurable size to perform tests in a limited configurable parallel setup providing us compromise between load on both testing and tested infrastructure and scalability needed.

The testing layer is exposed through a language independent interface which makes it possible to implement new tests in virtually any programming language. For example current tests based on Globus 2 protocols have been written either using Java CoG or using small C wrapper for executing binaries written in other languages. The wrapper takes care of timeouts for hung-up jobs and clean-up for incorrectly finished ones, making the monitoring tool prototype resistant to failures. Especially hang-ups caused by firewalls incorrectly discarding packets showed to be a constant problem in Grid environment.

Test dependencies have been implemented that allow skipping of tests for which some mandatory prerequisite has failed. This decreases the unnecessary load on the tested Grid infrastructure. A language for general description of more complex dependencies is under development. We plan to use the same approach for the passive monitoring based on service and application instrumentation (the description of dependencies is crucial in such environment).

The architecture also supports a user triggered on-demand tests. These tests run under users' own identities and provide valuable data for problem and bug tracking.

Storage layer. The regular tests are run periodically and their results are stored by the storage layer. As the history must be made available for inspection, the data are stored in a database. While currently a PostgreSQL database is used, any other relational database can be easily substituted since JDBC database interface is employed.

Presentation layer. The presentation layer supports both static and dynamic web pages creation. For static results presentation, the test results are converted to XML and then transformed to a static XHTML page using XSLT processing. The XHTML page mimics the original TeraGrid tests layout and provides good general overview of the current infrastructure status in the form of a full matrix of colored boxes.

For dynamic results presentation integrated in a Grid portal, GridSphere [7] portlet based interface with multi-lingual capabilities has also been implemented. This interface supports browsing through status data history.

Test results are available via web service interface as well which allows for using this monitoring service as an information service by other services on the Grid. This specific web service uses SOAP transport protocol with GSI security and the implementation is moving towards OGSA compliance (now lacking few of the required Grid service interfaces).

4.1   Incorporated Tests

While all currently implemented tests use active pull model, our general status monitoring framework supports easy integration of passive monitoring as well.

Active tests were chosen because of faster and easier implementation compared to passive monitoring and especially applications, services and middleware instrumentation. At this stage of the development, the "production" application runs are still a minority on the GridLab testbed, which means that passive monitoring can not yet be a major source of monitoring information. All tests are run on regular scheduled basis with possible activation on demand by users using their own identities.

Simple tests. A test from the simple test category produces a scalar value for each tested machine. The prototype currently incorporates all tests available in the original TeraGrid software and adds also several new tests:

- Globus-2 tests: GRIS, GSI-FTP, Gatekeeper, GSI-SSH, and GIIS,
- availability of MPI C and MPI Fortran compilers,
- job manager tests: tests all job managers advertised in information services, whether they can run both normal and MPI jobs,
- GridLab specific tests: check on accepted CAs (whether compliant to Grid-Lab requirements), check whether required software is installed and really working (C, C++, CVS, F90, GNU make, Perl, Java), check whether grid-mapfile contains all required users, check GridLab Mercury [4], and GridLab MDS Extensions and MDS web service [8].

Except for GIIS which is tested once per GIIS server (in the case of GridLab only once for the whole testbed since there is only one GIIS server in the testbed), all other tests run on per machine basis.

The simple tests on GridLab testbed currently take about 15 minutes to test all of 17 services on all 19 machines using 6 concurrent threads. The time is spent mostly in waiting for response due to delays in network communication and in waiting for timeouts, because the widespread use of firewalls leaves no way to distinguish a slow responding service from unavailable service other than waiting for a timeout. The only notable CPU load is due to authentication and encryption in GSI communication.

Service tests. With OGSA model that is generally seen as the next generation model for the Grid environment, Grid services become cornerstones of Grid infrastructure. Therefore service oriented tests are appropriate solution for monitoring infrastructure based on this paradigm. Services may run on various Grid nodes and the important issue is whether service is running correctly and not whether the service runs on one particular machine. Another fact supporting approach different from machine oriented tests is that different machines will run different subsets of services and eventually the matrix of host and services may become quite sparse.

All the services produced by GridLab are persistent GSI-secured web services. It means they are accessible using HTTPG protocol (HTTP over GSI). Invocation of the web service methods by the testing tool is implemented using either Java CoG or C program using gSOAP tool [9] with GSI plug-in. The services support Grid security features, however to full OGSA compatibility they lack `portType` inheritance, because most of them are implemented in C, and there is no C server-side implementation of OGSA available yet.

In the first stage the service status monitoring checks whether the service is responsive. We could not rely on all services's API being inherited from a single `portType`, so we require that each GridLab service must provide an operation called `getServiceDescription()` returning a string containing service description. The responsiveness of a service is checked by calling this operation.

We have developed first stage tests for the following GridLab web services: GRMS, Adaptive service, Meta-data service, Replica Catalog, Data Movement, Data Browsing, Authorization, Message Box Service, and Testbed Status.

Second stage is aimed at verifying whether service is operational and performs as expected. Actual tests differ largely from service to service. Up to now second stage tests for Data Movement service and GRMS have been implemented.

The service tests on GridLab testbed currently take just several seconds to test all 9 services.

Matrix tests. Up to now two matrix tests have been implemented for GridLab infrastructure: Data Movement service test and GSI-SSH tests. The first one checks correct operation of Data Movement service between all pairs of nodes in an N-to-N fashion thus forming two-dimensional matrix of results. The test can be also easily extended to third dimension accommodating the possibility that data transfer can be initiated from a third node, i. e. node that is neither source nor target of the data being transferred. This example demonstrates problem with extreme load growth imposed on underlying infrastructure when complex active measurements and tests are put in use.

The GSI-SSH test checks whether it is possible to login from one node to another node. The test can work in either full N-to-N or in M-to-N fashion since only a selected subset of Grid nodes can be allowed to initiate SSH connection to the rest of the Grid.

While the matrix tests are not scalable, they provide invaluable information about the "real" Grid status. The current history of use of the data movement test had shown that it is almost perfect source of monitoring information about node mutual interoperability (as opposed to the 1-to-N centralized tests which check just interoperability between the testing machine and each node). The matrix tests reflect much better the actual situation users encounter when using a Grid and are able to find very specific and subtle problems (e. g. various incompatible firewall configurations). These tests have also character of complex tests that are similar to high level application tests (see Sec. 2), which means that if the test passes correctly all lower layers and services are verified as well. If failure of such test is experienced, specific lower level tests can be immediately triggered to identify precise source of the problem. For example Data Movement matrix tests will not run without firewalls set up correctly, `grid-mapfile` installed properly etc. This complex property allows to omit a lot of other tests thus compensating the scalability issue to some extent.

The matrix tests on GridLab testbed currently take about 2 hours to test a full matrix of 17×17 data transfers among all 17 machines, most of the time is again spent waiting for timeouts caused by firewalls.

We expect that most of the inter-node tests required by full matrix setup could be replaced by the passive monitoring information when the Grid is used for "real" production (the applications will become actual data sources). This will add the necessary scalability to this kind of tests.

5   Future Work

Current status monitoring prototype tool mostly implements active tests in bottom-up fashion, i. e. testing starts from low level tests and proceeds to higher levels only if lower level prerequisites are successfully tested. For future work we are targeting opposite approach in which tests of lower level services and layers will be triggered only when higher level test fails to allow more precise identification of source of problems. This approach will be enabled by employing high degree of passive monitoring based on instrumentation of applications, services, and various middleware layers resulting in lower load on Grid infrastructure induced by monitoring itself. Heavier use of push mode sensors goes hand in hand with deployment of passive monitoring model which results in far more scalable and inobtrusive monitoring solution.

We plan to extend the Grid Application Toolkit [10] (the specific middleware layer connecting transparently applications with lower layers of Grid infrastructure) which is developed within the GridLab project with instrumented interfaces that will allow use of applications as monitoring data providers. In the same time we plan to use this instrumented layer to develop a monitoring worm that will "travel" autonomously through he Grid, gathering the monitoring information from used middleware components and nodes and sending this information (probably in a digested form when no error is to be reported) to some central site. The travel of the worm will be accomplished in close collaboration with all the middleware components (resource discovery, resource brokerage, job submission service etc.), thus testing extensively the Grid environment as a whole. The combination of active tests and passive monitoring with the data provided by the (regular, random or user triggered) worm reports should cover the whole Grid with a minimal obtrusive overhead. Understanding the interactions of these monitoring components will be subject of our future study.

We also want to build a database of typical problems occurring in the Grid environment. It will be used to produce better explanation of problems detected, thus improving understanding of the test results by end users.

6   Conclusions

A Grid infrastructure status monitoring system is an essential component of any Grid that aims to provide a usable working environment. Such a system is also a core of the Grid management, including information provision and validation for resource management on the Grid. The status monitoring system being developed within the EU GridLab project is one of the most comprehensive status monitoring systems currently deployed on a really large scale heterogeneous

Grid. As not only individual components, but also emerging Grid services are permanently monitored, it represents a preliminary version of an OGSA compliant status monitoring system. Another advantage of this system is its use as information service augmentation and verification tool, providing a guarantee for a reliable information provided by a general information service (like the MDS).

The ability to define test dependencies in the monitoring system decreases monitoring overhead on the Grid infrastructure through elimination of the tests known in advance to fail. As a complement to this approach, we introduced some very high level tests whose successful completion signalizes that all the lower layers are working and eliminates necessity of individual tests. An example of such higher level tests that is already used on the GridLab testbed is the Data Movement service test. Even the N^2 complexity of this test is not prohibitive as it can potentially replace a large bunch of simpler, but also obtrusive tests. These will be needed only for a targeted inspection when the higher level tests fail.

The passive, service instrumentation based monitoring is another part of the whole Grid monitoring system. While not discussed in this paper to much extent, they may eventually replace most of the active (monitoring system triggered) tests and thus keeping the overhead of the Grid monitoring to the acceptable level even in very large Grids.

References

1. Tierney, B., Aydt, R., Gunter, D., Smith, W., Swany, M., Taylor, V., Wolski, R.: A Grid Monitoring Architecture. GGF Technical Report GFD-I.7, January 2002. http://www.gridforum.org/Documents/GFD/GFD-I.7.pdf
2. Czajkowski, K., Fitzgerald, S., Foster, I., Kesselman, C.: Grid Information Services for Distributed Resource Sharing. In Proceedings of the 10th IEEE International Symposium on High-Performance Distributed Computing (HPDC-10), IEEE Press, August 2001.
3. Holub, P., Kuba, M., Matyska, L., Ruda, M.: GridLab Testbed Monitoring – Prototype Tool. Deliverable 5.6, GridLab Project (IST–2001–32133), 2003. http://www.gridlab.org/Resources/Deliverables/D5.6.pdf
4. Balaton, Z., Gombás, G.: Resource and Job Monitoring. In the Grid. Proc. of the Euro-Par 2003 International Conference, Klagenfurt, 2003. 404–411
5. Foster, I., Kesselman, C., Nick, J., Tuecke, S.: The Physiology of the Grid: An Open Grid Services Architecture for Distributed Systems Integration. Open Grid Service Infrastructure WG, Global Grid Forum, June 22, 2002. http://www.globus.org/research/papers.html#OGSA
6. Basney, J., Greenseid, J.: NCSA TestGrid Project: Grid Status Test. http://grid.ncsa.uiuc.edu/test/grid-status-test/
7. Novotny, J., Russell, M., Wehrens, O.: GridSphere: A Portal Framework for Building Collaborations. 1st International Workshop on Middleware for Grid Computing, Rio de Janeiro, June 15 2003.
8. Aloisio, G., Cafaro, M., Epicoco, I., Lezzi, D., Mirto, M., Mocavero, S., Pati, S.: First GridLabMDS Release. Deliverable 10.3, GridLab Project (IST–2001–32133), 2002. http://www.gridlab.org/Resources/Deliverables/D10.3c.pdf

9. van Engelen, R. A., Gallivan, K. A.: The gSOAP Toolkit for Web Services and Peer-To-Peer Computing Networks. In the proceedings of IEEE CCGrid Conference 2002.
10. Allen, G., Davis, K., Dolkas, K. N., Doulamis, N. D., Goodale, T., Kielmann, T., Merzky, A., Nabrzyski, J., Pukacki, J., Radke, T., Russell, M., Seidel, E., Shalf, J., Taylor, I.: Enabling Applications on the Grid: A GridLab Overview. International Journal of High Performance Computing Applications: Special issue on Grid Computing: Infrastructure and Applications, August 2003.

Towards a Protocol for the Attachment of Semantic Descriptions to Grid Services

Simon Miles, Juri Papay, Terry Payne, Keith Decker, and Luc Moreau

School of Electronics and Computer Science,
University of Southampton,
Southampton, SO17 1BJ, UK
{sm,jp,trp,ksd,L.Moreau}@ecs.soton.ac.uk

Abstract. Service discovery in large scale, open distributed systems is difficult because of the need to filter out services suitable to the task at hand from a potentially huge pool of possibilities. Semantic descriptions have been advocated as the key to expressive service discovery, but the most commonly used service descriptions and registry protocols do not support such descriptions in a general manner. In this paper, we present a protocol, its implementation and an API for registering semantic service descriptions and other task/user-specific metadata, and for discovering services according to these. Our approach is based on a mechanism for attaching structured and unstructured metadata, which we show to be applicable to multiple registry technologies. The result is an extremely flexible service registry that can be the basis of a sophisticated semantically-enhanced service discovery engine, an essential component of a Semantic Grid.

1   Introduction

Service discovery is a difficult task in large scale, open distributed systems such as the Grid and Web, due to the potentially large number of services advertised. In order to characterise their needs, users typically specify the complex requirements they have of a service, including demands on its functionality, quality of service, security, reputation etc. These requirements cannot be fully expressed in the constrained information models provided by existing service registry technologies such as UDDI (the de facto standard for Web Services registry), the OGSA Registry [7] or the Jini lookup service [1].

More demandingly, user requirements may contain information that assumes an understanding of particular application domains and that is meant to effect the outcome of the discovery process. For example, a bioinformatician may search for services that process "expressed sequence tags" but also that operate on "nucleotide sequences". The knowledge that the latter biological concept is a more general form of the former is known by the user, but is unlikely to be expressible in either the query or standard published descriptions of any of the potentially useful services.

On the other hand, there may be information that could be utilised in the discovery process, but is not be published by the service provider. For example,

M. Dikaiakos (Ed.): AxGrids 2004, LNCS 3165, pp. 230–239, 2004.
© Springer-Verlag Berlin Heidelberg 2004

recommendations about which services to use may come from one member of an organisation, and could be used by collaborating members of that organisation.

Finally, there are functional entities other than services that need to be publicised. For example, *workflow scripts* describe how to compose services together to get a useful composite behaviour. They are location-independent descriptions of service use and should be publishable in the same registries as services since they provide comparable function, i.e. they are invocable, take inputs and return outputs (this equivalence is recognised explicitly in DAML-S [6]).

Given the plethora of services and sophistication of user requirements, many have advocated the use of semantic descriptions that qualify functional and non-functional characteristics of services in a manner that is amenable to automatic processing [3, 6, 14]. Against this background, we have designed a system that allows the attachment of semantic information so as to provide a solution to the shortcomings of existing registry technologies. These developments are part of the architecture developed by the myGrid project (www.mygrid.org.uk). In this paper, we report on our experience of designing such a system, specifically focusing on the following contributions.

- We have developed a protocol for attaching metadata to registered service descriptions, and for querying over service descriptions and their metadata.
- We have implemented a UDDI-compatible service registry that allows metadata to be attached to various parts of the service description, such as the services themselves, their operations, their inputs and their outputs (as specified in WSDL documents describing service interfaces).
- A programmatic interface (API) provides clients with an easy way to access this information, whether held in a remote Web Service or locally.
- We demonstrate with a common information model that our attachment methodology applies to multiple discovery technologies in a single registry, including UDDI, DAML-S and BiOMOBY.

In this paper we will first examine the limitations of existing approaches (Section 2), then look at how we overcome these by providing a metadata attachment mechanism (Section 3). We then examine the protocol by which a client can register and query over metadata (Section 4), and in Section 5 we discuss how our services overcome some of the problems mentioned above. Finally, we discuss implications of our work and its current and future developments in Section 6.

2 Limitation of Existing Approaches

The UDDI service registry (Universal Description, Discovery, and Integration) [12] has become the de-facto standard for service discovery in the Web Services community. Service queries are typically white or yellow pages based: services are located using a description of their provider or a specific classification (taken from a published taxonomy) of the desired service type. Service descriptions in UDDI are composed from a limited set of high-level data constructs (Business Entity, Business Service etc.) which can include other constructs following a rigid schema. Some of these constructs, such as tModels, Category Bags and Identifier

Bags, can be seen as metadata associated with the service description. However, while useful in a limited way, they are all very restrictive in scope of description and their use in searching the registry. In particular, services are not the only entities that need to be classified, e.g. classifications could also be defined for individual operations or their argument types. It is not convenient to use searching mechanisms for services that are distinct from those for their argument types. Likewise, a tModel's reference to an external technical specification, such as a WSDL file describing a service interface, also implies that a different mechanism is required for reasoning over service interfaces. These are clear restrictions of the facilities offered for attaching metadata to entities in UDDI service descriptions.

Related to this, some uses of WSDL, the interface definition language of Web Services, suffer from limitations, as illustrated by Figure 1 displaying the interface of an existing bioinformatics service called BLAST. BLAST is a widely used analysis tool that establish the similarity of a DNA sequence of unknown function to already annotated ones to help the biologist gain an understanding of its possible function. We use BLAST in a data-intensive bioinformatics Grid application, which aims to make an educated guess of the gene involved in a disease and to design an experiment to be realised in the laboratory in order to validate the guess. The BLAST service is invoked, as part of a workflow enacted over the Grid, on a large number of sequences without user intervention.

The interface of Figure 1 identifies a portType composed of one operation, which takes an input message comprising two message parts in0 and in1. These parts are required to be of type string, but the specification does not tell us the meaning of these strings: sequences, for which many formats are supported. This example was chosen because it precisely illustrates limitations of some existing service descriptions. While this interface specification could easily be refined by using an XSD complex type [4], it is unrealistic to assume that all services in an open Grid environment will be described with the appropriate level of detail. Moreover, should it be so, we cannot expect all service providers to always use type definitions expressed with the terms of reference adopted by a given user.

Other problems related to the rigid nature of UDDI and WSDL, and the lack of metadata attachment capabilities, can be seen when looking at the uses to

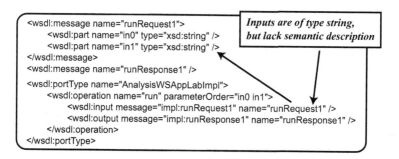

Fig. 1. Basic Local Alignment Search Tool (BLAST) Interface Excerpt

which they are put. A UDDI query typically returns a list of available services, from which a subset may conform to a known and/or informally agreed upon policy and thus can be invoked. Such approaches work well within small, closed communities, where a priori definitions of signatures and data formats can be defined. However, across open systems such as the Grid, no assumption can be made about how desired services are described, how to interact with them, and how to interpret their corresponding results. Additionally, service providers typically adopt different ways to model and present services, often because of the subtle differences in the service itself. This raises the problem of *semantic inter-operability*, which is the capability of computer systems to meaningfully operate in conjunction with one another, even though the languages or structures with which they are described may be different. *Semantic discovery* is the process of discovering services capable of semantic inter-operability.

Also, UDDI provides no data structures to represent either the abstract or concrete details contained within a WSDL document, but only a standard way to express that a service implements a particular WSDL interface. A new proposal allows tModels to reference specific bindings and port types [5]. However, this extension still does not provide access to, or queries over, operations or messages, which would allow the discovery of services capable of specific operations.

DAML-S attempts a full description of a service as some process that can be enacted to achieve a goal. First, by its nature, the DAML-S ontology may be sub-classed to provide new information about services such as, e.g. the task performed by a service, as discussed in [14]. DAML-S provides an alternate mechanism that allows service publishers to attach semantic information to the parameters of a service. Indeed, the argument types referred to by the profile input and output parameters are *semantic*. Such semantic types are mapped to the syntactic type specified in the WSDL interface by the intermediary of the service grounding. We feel that such a mechanism is a step in the right direction, but it is convoluted (in particular, because the mapping from semantic to syntactic types involves the process model, which we did not discuss). It also has limitations since it only supports annotations provided by the publisher, and not by third-parties; furthermore, a profile only supports one semantic description per parameter and does not allow multiple interpretations. Finally, semantic annotations are restricted to input and output parameters, but not applied to other elements of a WSDL interface specification.

3   Extending Service Descriptions

Having discussed the limitations of existing technologies, we now focus on the capabilities of our service registry. This allows for extension of service descriptions by adding *metadata attachments*. A metadata attachment is a piece of data giving information about an existing entity in a service description, and is explicitly associated with that entity. Entities to which metadata can be attached include the service itself, an operation supported by the service, an input or output type of an operation invocable on the service. The metadata is attached by calls to the registry after publishing, with reference to the entity to which the metadata will be attached. To establish that this mechanism is generic, we have applied it to service descriptions supported by UDDI, WSDL, DAML-S and BioMOBY, which we encode within a common information model.

We have adopted RDF triples [11] to represent all descriptions of services. RDF (Resource Description Framework) is an XML data format for describing Web and Grid resources and the relations between them. Triples are simple expressions of the relations between resources, consisting of a subject, a relation and an object. All our triples are stored in a triple store, which is a database whose interface and implementation are specially designed to hold such triples. Specifically, we rely on the Jena implementation [8] of such a triple store.

To illustrate our general mechanism, we consider different kinds of metadata attachment, for which we found practical uses in our Grid application:

1. attaching ratings to services;
2. attaching functionality profiles to services;
3. attaching semantic types to operation arguments.

Ratings can provide users with assessments from experts on the value of a particular service; functionality profiles can be used to both refine and broaden a search to exactly those services that are relevant; and semantic types allow clients to ask whether services are applicable to the type of data they have (so overcoming the limitations of WSDL described above). Our presentation is based on examples that were generated by dumping the contents of our registry; it is in N3 format [2], which we have chosen for readability. For example, in Figure 2, we show the representation of a service annotated by two numerical ratings, with different values, provided by different authors at different times. The service is described by many pieces of information from the standard UDDI model such as its service key (the value to the right of uddi:hasServiceKey), and by two pieces of metadata attached to it (under uddi:hasMetadata). Each piece of metadata has a type (in this case, both are of type mygrid:NumericRating), a value (the rating itself) and two pieces of provenance information. The provenance information is the time and date at which the metadata was published and the name of the publisher. Such information is particularly useful in a registry

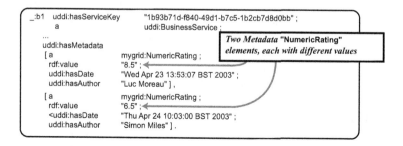

Fig. 2. Rating Attachment (N3 Notation)

allowing third parties to attach ratings as it can be used to identify the origin of an annotation.

In myGrid, we describe services by a service profile [14] specifying which particular type of process a service uses to perform its task (uses_method), which application domain specific task they perform (perform_task), which resources they use (uses_resources) and what application they are wrapping (is_function_of). A relevant excerpt of the registry contents is displayed in Figure 3, b1 denoting a service and Pe577955b-d271-4a5b-8099-001abc1da633 the "myGrid profile". This is useful because it presents clients with information that is concise but matches their knowledge of the service's application domain (bioinformatics in this case), and can be reasoned about by other semantic technologies using expert knowledge on the application domain available on the Grid.

```
mygrid:Pe577955b-d271-4a5b-8099-001abc1da633
      mygrid:uses_resources       mygrid2:nucleotide_sequence_database ;
      mygrid:uses_method          mygrid2:mygrid_bioinformatics_primitive_service_operation;
      mygrid:performs_task        mygrid2:pairwise_local_aligning ;
      mygrid:is_function_of        mygrid2:blastn .          myGrid service profile

_:b1  uddi:hasServiceKey          "e577955b-d271-4a5b-8099-001abc1da633" ;
      a                           uddi:BusinessService ;
      uddi:hasName
           [ rdf:_1               "testService" ;
             a                    uddi:NameBag ] ;          MetaData Attachment
      uddi:hasMetadata
           [ a                    mygrid:Profile ;
             uddi:hasDate         "Wed Apr 23 15:06:23 BST 2003" ;
             rdf:value            mygrid:Pe577955b-d271-4a5b-8099-001abc1da633 ;
             uddi:hasAuthor       "Luc Moreau" ] .
```

Fig. 3. Attachment of a myGrid profile (N3 Notation)

In Figure 4, we show a semantic description of parameter in0 declared in the interface of Figure 1. The node rdf:_1 denotes the message part with name in0. It is given a metadata attachment, mygrid2:nucleotide_sequence_data, which again refers to a term in the ontology of bioinformatics concepts [14]. In scientific application areas, the scientists often wish to ask which services are available to analyse the data they have obtained from experiments. We showed that the description of input and output syntax, given for example by XSD definitions in WSDL, is not always adequate to determine whether the service is applicable for consuming or producing data of a particular semantic type.

4 Service Registry Protocol and Implementation

Protocol. The protocol to publish metadata and discover services according to metadata was designed in a similar style to the UDDI protocol, so that UDDI clients could easily be extended to support such features. It is not possible to present the complete protocol in this paper. Instead, we refer the reader to

```
rdf:_3 [ a      wsdl:Message ;                    ┌─────────────────────────────────┐
         wsdl:hasMessagePart                       │ Semantic Description of in0     │
         [ rdf:_1                                   │ rdf:_1 denotes its message part │
                [ a                          wsdl:MessagePart ;
                 wsdl:hasName                "in0" ;
                 wsdl:hasTypeName
                        [ a                  wsdl:QName ;
                         wsdl:hasNameSpace   "http://schemas.xmlsoap.org/xsd/" ;
                         wsdl:hasLocalName   "string" ] ;
                 uddi:hasMetadata
                        [ a                  mygrid:semantic_type ;
                         uddi:hasDate        "Fri Aug 22 11:12:29 BST 2003" ;
                         rdf:value           mygrid2:nucleotide_sequence_data ;
                         uddi:hasAuthor      "Luc Moreau" ];
     ] ; ... ] ] ;
```

Fig. 4. Attachment of Semantic Types to Arguments (N3 Notation)

`www.ecs.soton.ac.uk/~sm/myGrid/Views/` for the full set of commented interfaces. As an illustration, Figure 5 shows some of the methods that allow the attachment of metadata, respectively to a business service, to a business entity and to a message part. All these methods not only attach some metadata to the respective entity, but also add the aforementioned provenance information such as author and date of creation. Symmetrically, services can be discovered by using a metadata filtering mechanism. An example of metadata-based search method appears in Figure 5. Given some metadata, the `findServiceByMetadata` function returns the list of services that are annotated with such a metadata.

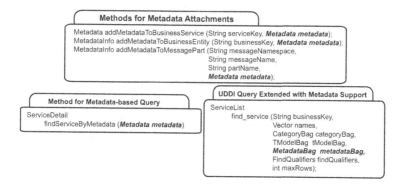

Fig. 5. Metadata Attachment Methods

The benefit of our approach is the ability to extend some existing interfaces in an incremental manner, so as to facilitate an easier transition to semantic discovery for existing clients. For instance, we have extended the UDDI `find_service` method to support queries over metadata that would have been attached to published services. In the method specification of Figure 5, `metadataBag`, a new

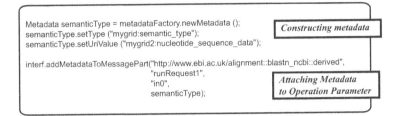

Fig. 6. Registering a parameter semantic type

criterion for filtering services is introduced, which contains a set of metadata that a service must satisfy.

API. We also provide a client-side library, or API, that makes it easy to use the protocol to communicate with the registry. Figure 6 illustrates how our API can be used to attach a semantic description to the first input of the **runRequest1** operation of Figure 1. The arguments of the **addMetadataToMessagePart** are the namespace of the service interface (an excerpt of which appears in Figure 1), the operation name (**runRequest1**), the parameter name (**in0**), and an object of type **Metadata**, whose type and values have been initialised to **semantic_type** and **nucleotide_sequence_data** respectively.

As all the information is represented in a triple store, a more direct interface to the triple store allows users to query the registry using the RDQL query language [8]. An API that allows users to store triples in the triple store is also provided. Several interfaces currently provide access to our general information model. Some of them preserve compatibility with the existing UDDI standard, and ensure inter-operability within the Web Services community. Others, such as the interface to the triple store, directly expose the information model, and offer a powerful and radically different way of discovering services through the RDQL interface. While such functionality is very useful, its radically different nature does not offer a smooth transition for clients implementors wishing to adopt semantic discovery.

Implementation. We have implemented the protocol in a registry, within which all service descriptions and metadata attachment are expressed as RDF triples and stored in the Jena triple store. We have designed and implemented a set of interfaces to the Jena triple store in order to offer a registry functionality. A registry implements a series of factory methods to create instances of interfaces to the triple store. The triple store is passed as argument to the factory methods and is itself created by a store factory; different implementations of a store may exist, in memory or in a relational database [8].

5   Discussion

We can now return to the initial Grid service discovery requirements presented in the introduction, and show how the work presented above addresses each.

Automated Service Discovery. Using our registry, arbitrary metadata can be attached to service descriptions and then programmatically discovered. Metadata can be simple strings and URIs referring to other resources, such as ontological concepts. It can also be arbitrarily structured by giving typed relations between pieces of metadata using triples. This can be attached to service descriptions using the methods and technologies discussed in Section 4.

Recommendations and Personal Opinions. Recommendations regarding services, and opinions on their suitability from users can be attached as metadata to service descriptions and used in discovery. Clearly, this information may not be appropriate for storing in the public registries in which services are published. We are currently working on a factory to create "views" over existing registries.

Publishing of Other Process Descriptions. Workflow scripts and other location-independent processes can be published and discovered in our registry. Because they can be discovered and executed using the appropriate tools, they are directly comparable to services invocation. In terms of interfaces, workflows and parameterised queries both take inputs and provide outputs, each of which may be semantically annotated to enhance discovery.

6   Conclusion

In this paper, we have presented a protocol to publish semantic descriptions of services to promote semantic inter-operability. Our approach uses a mechanism capable of attaching metadata to any entity within a service description. Such metadata may be published by third parties rather than the service providers. Our design extends standard UDDI to provide semantic capabilities, offering a smooth transition to semantic discovery for UDDI clients. We have used these facilities to register service descriptions specified by the myGrid ontology [14]. Our future work will focus on providing service descriptions to Grid Services. This has extra demands on top of those for Web Services, due to Grid Services being created by factories, having lifetimes and server-side metadata. Grid Service factories require extra information to be stored in a service registry to allow clients to identify them as such and be informed as to how to use them to create the Grid Services they need.

Acknowledgements. This research is funded in part by EPSRC myGrid project (reference GR/R67743/01). Keith Decker from the University of Delaware was on sabbatical stay at the University of Southampton when this work was carried out. We acknowledge Carole Goble, Phillip Lord and Chris Wroe for their contributions to discussion on the work presented in this paper.

References

1. Arnod et al. *The Jini Specification*. Sun Microsystems, 1999.
2. Tim Berners-Lee. Notation 3. http://www.w3.org/DesignIssues/Notation3, 1998.

3. Tim Berners-Lee, James Hendler, and Ora Lassila. The Semantic Web. *Scientific American*, 284(5):34–43, 2001.
4. Paul V. Biron and Ashok Malhotra. Xml schema part 2: Datatypes. `http://www.w3.org/TR/xmlschema-2/`, May 2001.
5. John Colgrave and Karsten Januszewski. Using wsdl in a uddi registry (version 2.0). `http://www.oasis-open.org/committees/uddi-spec/doc/draft/uddi-spec-tc-tn-wsdl-20030319-wd.htm`, 2003.
6. DAML-S Coalition. DAML-S: Web Service Description for the Semantic Web. In *First International Semantic Web Conference (ISWC) Proceedings*, pages 348–363, 2002.
7. Ian Foster et al. The Physiology of the Grid — An Open Grid Services Architecture for Distributed Systems Integration. Technical report, Argonne National Laboratory, 2002.
8. Jena semantic web toolkit. `http://www.hpl.hp.com/semweb/jena.htm`
9. Phillip Lord et al. Semantic and Personalised Service Discovery. In W. K. Cheung and Y. Ye, editors, *WI/IAT 2003 Workshop on Knowledge Grid and Grid Intelligence*, pages 100–107, Halifax, Canada, October 2003. Department of Mathematics and Computing Science, Saint Mary's University, Halifax, Nova Scotia, Canada.
10. Simon Miles et al. Personalised grid service discovery. *IEE Proceedings Software: Special Issue on Performance Engineering*, 150(4):252–256, August 2003.
11. Resource Description Framework (RDF). `http://www.w3.org/RDF/`, 2001.
12. Universal Description, Discovery and Integration of Business of the Web. `www.uddi.org`, 2001.
13. MD Wilkinson and M. Links. Biomoby: an open-source biological web services proposal. *Briefings In Bioinformatics*, 4(3), 2002.
14. Chris Wroe et al. A suite of daml+oil ontologies to describe bioinformatics web services and data. *International Journal of Cooperative Information Systems*, 2003.

Semantic Matching
of Grid Resource Descriptions*

John Brooke[1,2], Donal Fellows[1,2], Kevin Garwood[1], and Carole Goble[1]

[1] Department of Computer Science, University of Manchester,
Oxford Road, Manchester, M13 9PL, UK
j.m.brooke@man.ac.uk
http://www.sve.man.ac.uk/General/Staff/brooke
[2] Manchester Computing, University of Manchester, UK

Abstract. The ability to describe the Grid resources needed by applications is essential for developing seamless access to resources on the Grid. We consider the problem of resource description in the context of a resource broker being developed in the Grid Interoperability Project (GRIP) which is able to broker for resources described by several Grid middleware systems, GT2, GT3 and Unicore. We consider it necessary to utilise a semantic matching of these resource descriptions, firstly because there is currently no common standard, but more fundamentally because we wish to make the Grid transparent at the application level. We show how the semantic approach to resource description facilitates both these aims and present the GRIP broker as a working prototype of this approach.

1 Introduction

We describe here a semantic based approach to resource description which is becoming increasingly important in the area of establishing standards for interoperability in Grid middleware systems. Much work has been done in setting up Grids for particular purposes, e.g the various Particle Physics DataGrids [1], Grids on heterogeneous architectures [2],[3]. Such Grids have independently developed schemas to describe the resources available on their Grids so as to enable higher-level functions, e.g resource brokers, to discover resources on behalf of their clients. Now within any Grid or Virtual Organisation (VO) there is often a great deal of implied knowledge. Since this is known and defined as part of the VO, it is possible to use this knowledge implicitly in writing workflows and jobs which have to be brokered. On the other hand, on a Grid uniting several organisations in a VO where the hardware and software may be heterogeneous, it is not possible to rely on assumptions such as software version numbers, performance of applications, policies and location of different parts of file systems (temporary storage, staging areas etc). In this latter case such knowledge has to

---

* The work described here was supported by two EU Framework 5 Projects in the IST Programme, EuroGrid, IST-1999-20247 and GRIP, IST-2001-32257.

M. Dikaiakos (Ed.): AxGrids 2004, LNCS 3165, pp. 240–249, 2004.

be made explicit at the local rather than VO level and must be interrogated by brokers and other high level agents.

The work described was developed in the Grid Interoperability Project[4] to create a broker which could interrogate on behalf of its clients two different resource schemas. One schema is the GLUE [5] schema used to provide a uniform description of resources on the Data Grids being developed in the US and Europe and to enable federation of VOs in those projects for global analysis of data from particle physics experiments. The other schema is provided by the Unicore framework [6], in particular the software model used to create local Incarnation Data Base (IDB) entries, used to 'ground' or 'incarnate' Abstract Job Objects (AJO), which are composed on behalf of client applications and sent around the Grid as serialised Java objects. The incarnation process provides the translation of the grid-level AJO into the particular terminology of the local resource descriptions. The motivation for providing interoperability between these two systems is that both are widely deployed in Europe (now also in the Asia-Pacific region) and federating Grids on a European level will ultimately face the problem of interoperability between them.

We need to introduce a Semantic Grid approach [7] for two reasons. One is that there is currently no agreed framework for Resource Description on Grids, although this issue is being investigated by the CIM and CRM working groups at GGF. As we show below, the MDS-2 framework used by Globus (GT2 and GT3) [8] is conceived differently from the resource descriptions of the Unicore Incarnation Data Base (IDB). The second and more fundamental reason is that the semantics of the request for resources at an application level needs to be preserved in some manner in order that appropriate resources can be selected by intermediate agents such as brokers and schedulers. We describe this in more detail in Section 2. Our approach is in line with the Open Grid Services Architecture (OGSA) [9] and we intend to move to a full OGSA service for the interoperability functionality.

The structure of the paper is as follows. In Section 2 we describe the background of our semantic analysis and its relation to the problem of designing an interoperable broker. In Section 3 we describe an integration of a semantic translation service with the architecture of the GRIP resource broker. In Section 4 we discuss how we abstracted ontologies for both Unicore and the GLUE schema. In Section 5 we describe how we obtain a mapping between these two ontologies. In Section 6 we draw some tentative conclusions and outline future work.

2   Foundations of Semantic Translation

In [10] there is an analysis of the difference between Grid computing and previous work on distributed computing, mainly on computational clusters. Behind the formalism proposed is the notion that the essence of a Grid is the virtualization of resource and the virtualization of the concept of a user. The user virtualization is most usually provided by a digital certificate, while the question of resource virtualization is addressed by OGSA. Currently, however, the OGSA services are only just beginning to be defined, therefore applications currently have to work with pre-OGSA Grid systems. Essentially we compare Globus Toolkit (GT2 and GT3) with Unicore, since these systems are the ones currently deployed for large-scale Grid computing, they have both had to address the problem of resource virtualization and have tackled the problem in different ways. A comparison between them can shed light on the issues that need to be tackled by OGSA.

The Grid resource problem we address can be summarised thus: we have a user who wishes to perform various tasks (computation, data storage, data transfer, database access etc) on some Grid which provides access to shared heterogeneous resources. The user needs to compose a request for such resources *without* knowing the details of the resources on which their work will run. If they do know the details of the resources, they are running in a pre-Grid mode since conventional distributed computing has addressed such problems. How can we match the users request to the universe of resources and how can we check that the users request will run successfully prior to the user's committal of their work? We suggest that if this pre-committal check cannot be performed, the Grid is in effect unusable, certainly as a "virtual machine". This requirement has also been described as "Uniform Access" [12].

The Globus project addresses this question by proposing protocols for resource description and resource discovery. Servers close to the resource describe its characteristics (GRIS, Grid Resource Information Servers) and higher level index servers (GIIS, Grid Indexed Information Servers). In GT2, this hierarchy is described as a Meta-Directory Service (MDS-2) and is implemented using LDAP. MDS-2 describes how the information is to be published and accessed, but it does not describe what information is to be provided. The DataTAG project has addressed the issue of describing metacomputing environments across the various Virtual Organisations involved mainly in Grid projects centred around the requirements of particle physics and has produced the GLUE (Grid Laboratory Uniform Environment) schema which can be implemented in MDS-2. Resource brokers can be developed (e.g. in the DataGrid project) to seek resources on behalf of clients. GLUE implemented under MDS-2 is thus an important step to virtualization of resource.

Unicore represents a very different approach, that of modelling the universe of workflows that users might conceivably wish to submit to a Grid. Whereas in Globus resource discovery is conceptually separated from the language in which the actual workflows and scripts are submitted (RSL, Resource Specification Language), in Unicore they are almost exactly the same thing. The tasks to be implemented are described as abstractions encapsulated in a hierarchy of Java classes, serialised and sent across the internet to the resources on the Grid (as an AJO, Abstract Job Object). Each resource on the Grid is represented by it virtualization as a Vsite. The Vsite has an Incarnation Data Base (IDB) associated with it which contains the necessary information to translate the abstractions in the AJO into concrete resource descriptions. The tasks of the AJO are also translated into Perl scripts for local job submission via the TSI (Target System Interface). For more details of this process and for a fuller description of the Unicore architecture see [6].

UoM Broker Architecture

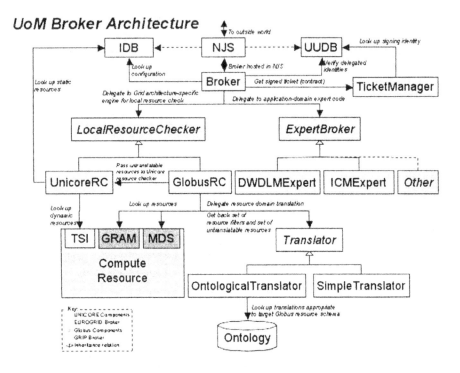

Fig. 1. The architecture of the resource broker with a translator whose role is to map from a Unicore Abstract Job Object (AJO) to an LDAP search of the MDS-2 information services

The Unicore and Globus approaches are to some extent complementary, since the information encapsulated in the IDB can *theoretically* be recovered from the Globus MDS-2 service. One of the aims of the GRIP project was to see if this could be done in practice, by providing a translator service that can map AJO descriptions to the various schema implemented via MDS-2. In this paper we chose the GLUE schema because of its wide usage in inter-Grid projects spanning major US and European Grid Projects.

3   Architecture for the Translation Service

In Figure 1 we show how the first prototype of the translator service fits into the architecture of the GRIP resource broker. This was built around the technology developed for a resource broker in the EuroGrid project ([2]) since this broker has been tested in a highly demanding heterogeneous environment consisting of a Grid of European HPC centres hosting machines with multiple and complex architectures.

The broker component associated with the virtualized resource (Vsite) can receive requests for resource discovery either in AJO form using the Network Job

Supervisor (NJS) acting as a service for AJOs or else via some other Resource Discovery service. In the first prototype released early 2003 it could either evoke the EuroGrid brokering technology (left hand side of the diagram) or else it could translate the AJO into a filter for an LDAP search on MDS-2. At this stage the translator was essentially hand-coded to do this for a very limited set of resource description terms. The aim was to replace this hand-coding with an Ontology Engine that could automate the translation. We now describe how we developed this Ontology Engine. This lead to a search down the right-hand route of the diagram, both sides converge on a Resource Discovery service, albeit provided by different mechanisms, either Unicore or Globus. We believe this is the first implementation of a broker designed explicitly to invoke multiple Grid resource discovery mechanisms.

4   Constructing and Mapping the Ontolgies

As noted above, this transation approach has not been attempted before in a Grid context. We therefore adopted the following procedure. Since the Unicore abstractions are expressed in a hierarchy of Java classes we could extract an initial ontology from the JavaDocs that encapsulates the semantics in the classes and inheritance tree. We then applied the same approach to the documentation provided by the GLUE schema.

We needed a knowledge capture tool to construct the initial ontologies. We investigated the possibility of using a full Ontology Editor such as DAML-OIL [13], [14]. However this would have involved too much complexity for the scope of the GRIP project. We expected that the ontologies would change rapidly as we started to look at the process of mapping. Also, we considered that we needed to supplement what was in the documentation with the implicit knowledge of the developers which would have to be extracted via structured interviews. We decided to use the PCPack tool from Epistemics Ltd. It allowed us to rapidly compose the ontology, to express the provenance of the terms that we employ and to capture the mappings that we make in XML format. As these mappings are adjusted by the tools graphical interface, the XML is automatically updated. The XML files derived from the knowledge capture process will be used by the Ontology Engine in Figure 1. We show a part of the Unicore AJO structure captured by PCPack in Figure 2.

When we came to examine the GLUE schema we found a fundamental difference of philosophy to the Unicore approach. GLUE models the physical resources available and their dynamic capabilities (loading etc). This dynamic information is not currently provided in the Unicore IDB, it would have to be requested by the resource broker by launching an AJO that queried the status of the queues for example. On the other hand the GLUE schema we examined does not have a description of software resource which may be required in a Grid where many different applications will be run. The intersection of the Unicore resource description universe with the GLUE resource description universe is represented in very schematic form in Figure 3.

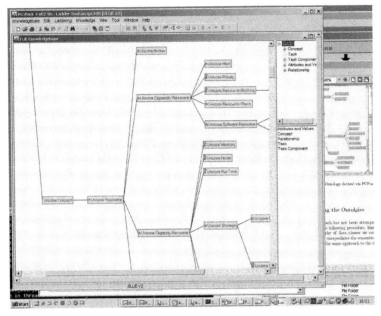

Fig. 2. Part of the Unicore Ontology derived via PCPack

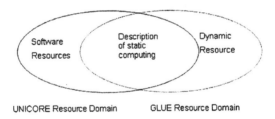

UNICORE Resource Domain   GLUE Resource Domain

Fig. 3. Diagram showing the intersection of the Unicore and GLUE resource domains

We derived an ontology from the GLUE schema documentation using PC-Pack. We then added provenance for each of the leaves in the tree. This shows how we can justify our semantic definitions in terms of the original GLUE schema. PCPack allows us to restructure the documentation of Unicore and Grip in the form of two ontologies. Although they refer apparently to the same universe, namely the resources available on the Grid, they have different structures for two main reasons. One is that the ontology picks up the structure of the tools used to construct them, in Unicore Java classes, in GLUE implemented in MDS-2, a meta-directory structure. The second reason is that the Unicore AJO describes resources from the point of view of the requesting user, GLUE describes resources from the point of view of the resource providers so that the users of the Grid can search accordingly. We now investigate the mappings between these two partial ontologies as a first step towards an ontology engine for resource translation.

5   Ontology Mapping Between Unicore and GLUE

5.1   Scope of Mapping

In Table 1 we illustrate a subset of the mappings between Unicore and Globus. These refer to the memory available for a programme and illustrate the difference in approach of two systems. Unicore models the users request, by checking the maximum memory that they can request on the resource. Note that this may not be the maximum machine memory since there may be policy restrictions (as imposed by queue limits for example). GLUE provides a metadata model of the machine, the policy limits have to be either described as machine limits (which confuses two potentially different quantities) or else have to be checked in some other way. We consider that until efforts in mapping ontologies are attempted, such questions will not be examined, since within the universe of each system all is consistent (for well-constructed systems).

Table 1. Comparison of some terms used in Unicore (left) and GLUE (right) that can be mapped to each other. Note this mapping is not trivial since a request is not the same as a resource available

Unicore Ontology	Globus Ontology
Maximum Memory Capacity Request	Host Virtual Main Memory Available
Maximum Memory Capacity Request	Subcluster Virtual Main Memory Available
Minimum Memory Capacity Request	Host RAM Main Memory Available
Minimum Memory Capacity Request	Subcluster RAM Main Memory Available
Priority Value	Priority

To illustrate some of the questions about an ontology, we take the case of a parallel machine or workstation cluster. The term "Main Memory" can be used at several places in the description of the cluster, processor memory, node memory aggregated memory for the cluster, aggregated memory for a collection of clusters in a hierarchical structure. The semantics of "Main Memory" vary according to how it is located in this hierarchy, which is essentially what GLUE is attempting to model. From the programmer or application perspective, "Maximum Memory Capacity Request" refers to the upper limit that the application or programme can used and is again relative to the programming model (MPI, OpenMP, threads etc).

5.2   Implementation of the Ontological Mappings

We mapped as many terms as we could and then incorporated them into the Ontological Translator (Figure 1). The method described the translation from Unicore to GT3 (this is similar to the translation process for GT2, which is also based on GLUE).

1. We implement a set of scripts that compile the ontology mappings from PCPack into a compacted XML format.

2. The translation engine loads the compacted format and builds an in-memory version of it.

3. The general strategy is to compile a Unicore resource check into an XPath query for a GT3 Index Service, that will have a non-empty result precisely when the resource check is satisfiable.

4. For each Unicore Resource, we look it up and, if a mapping for that resource exists, generate a constraint on the XPath query that corresponds to satisfaction of that resource within the Unicore IDB.

5. Resources without translation are collected together and, if the search of the Index Service succeeds, are checked against the Unicore IDB for the virtual resource (Vsite). This stage is necessary because the set of matchable terms is very incomplete.

In Figure 4 we show a screenshot of a graphical representation of the mapping process that is intended to be used in discussions between the developers of Unicore and GLUE to promote discussion and to widen the range of mappable terms. On the left we have the Unicore native terms and immediately to the right of these the derived ontology. On the right we have the equivalents for the GLUE schema. Essentially the procedure of the Ontological Translator is an automation of the mappings arrived at in these discussions. The XML description that it utilises has the following structure.

1. An outermost <translator> element with no attributes.

2. Child elements are <mapping> and <domain> in any order. We need to have a minimum of one <mapping> and two <domain> elements.

3. <mapping> has **name**, **from** and **to** attributes. The **name** says what the mapping is and the **from** and to state what domain we are going from and to (e.g from Unicore to GLUE).

4. <mapping> contains an arbitrary number of <map> elements.

5. <domain> has a **name** attribute (for matching against a <mapping>'s **from** or **to** attribute.)

6. <domain> contains an arbitrary number of <element> elements.

7. <element> contains an arbitrary number of <attribute> attributes.

8. <attribute> contains no elements.

9. Both <element> and <attribute> have the same attributes. They are **name** (an ontological name for the entity) **id** (a unique number to the entity) and **native** (which gives a "native" name for the entity). **native** is optional, but the other two are required.

10. <map> elements have two required attributes and one optional attribute. **from** and **to** are required and specify the entity (by matching against id number) within the **from** and **to** domains we are giving a mapping between.

Note that overall mappings are generally many-to-many; no uniqueness checks are applied.

6   Conclusions and Future Work

The work here is only a start, only very small subsets of Unicore and GLUE can be immediately mapped in this way. However, it is a necessary start, and opens

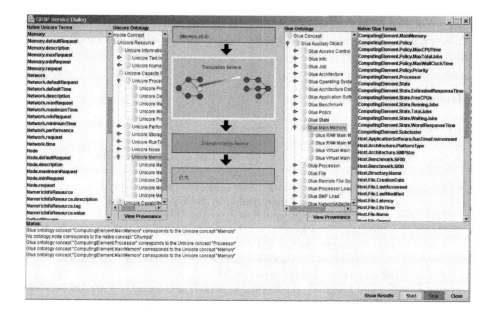

Fig. 4. The translator service. On the left is the Unicore ontology terms, on the right the GLUE ontology and the translation workflow is in between

important issues for theoretical discussion and experimental implementation. There are multiple ways of describing a Grid resource and they are all valid in different contexts. The development of a Grid Resource Ontology will transform services such as resource brokerage and resource discovery. For scalable and dynamic Virtual Organisations these are essential tools. At present we can only achieve any sort of Grid scaling by imposing homogeneity of resources on a VO. Thus in the EU DataGrid and Cern LCG (probably the largest production grids currently operating) the VO policy in terms of operating system, versioning of Grid software, hardware deployment and architecture is prescribed. This is a valuable experiment in scaling but it is not the future of Grid Computing, whose particular domain is the seamless integration of heterogeneous resources.

We believe that the work described here shows that the application level description of resource needs to be preserved as we move to the search for the physical resources needed to run an application. This is because some general description of a compute node in terms of peak FLOPs rating, load, memory usage etc does not give sufficient information to provide a broker with the answer to the question "Can my clients job run on this particular resource".

Research is needed into ways in which Grid Resource Descriptions can be made sufficiently general that sysadmin tools which automatically update these databases when new software or users are added to the resource. The ontology tools we have described provide a first step to this, since they automatically output XML descriptions in line with the terms of the ontology. In this way they can provide an OGSA service for joining Grids together, even if they are running different underlying middleware for the description, control and monitoring of resources.

References

1. The EU DataGrid project, http://www.datagrid.org
2. The EU EuroGrid Project, http://www.eurogrid.org
3. UK Level 2 Grid, information available from the UK National eCentre, http://www.nesc.ac.uk
4. Grid Interoperability Project, http://www.grid-interoperability.org
5. Andreozzi, S.: Glue schema implementation for the LDAP model, available at http://www.cnaf.infn.it/ sergio/publications/Glue4LDAP.pdf
6. Erwin, D., Snelling, D.: Unicore: A Grid Computing Environment LNCS 2150, Euro-Par 2001, Springer, pp 825-834.
7. Goble, C.A., De Roure, D.: Semantic Grid: An Application of the Semantic Web. ACM SIGMOD Record, 31(4) December 2002.
8. Czajkowski K., Fitzgerald, S., Foster, I., and Kesselman, C.: Grid Information Services for Resource Sharing. in Proceedings of HPDC-10, IEEE Press, 2002.
9. Foster, I, Kesselman, C., Nick, J., and Tuecke, S.: The Physiology of the Grid. GGF Document available at http://www.ggf.org/ogsa-wg
10. Németh, Z., Sunderam, V.: Characterizing Grids: Attributes, Definitions, and Formalisms. Journal of Grid Computing, 1(1), p9-23, 2003.
11. Access Grid: an environment for advanced collaborative working, http://www.accessgrid.org
12. Johnston, W., Brooke, J.M.: Core Functions for Production Grids, GGF GPA-RG discussion document, http://grid.lbl.gov/GPA
13. Horrocks,I.: DAML+OIL: a reason-able web ontology language. Proc. of EDBT 2002, March 2002.
14. Ankolenkar, A., Burstein, M., Hobbs, J.R., Lassila, O., Martin, D.L., McDermott, D., cIlraith, S.A., Narayanan, S., Paolucci, M., Payne, T.R., and Sycara, K.: DAML-S: Web Service Description for the Semantic Web. The First International Semantic Web Conference (ISWC), Sardinia (Italy), June 2002.

Enabling Knowledge Discovery Services on Grids*

Antonio Congiusta[1], Carlo Mastroianni[2], Andrea Pugliese[1,2],
Domenico Talia[1,2], and Paolo Trunfio[1]

[1] DEIS, University of Calabria,
Via P. Bucci 41C, 87036 Rende, Italy
{acongiusta,apugliese,talia,trunfio}@deis.unical.it
[2] ICAR-CNR,
Via P. Bucci 41C, 87036 Rende, Italy
mastroianni@icar.cnr.it

Abstract. The Grid is mainly used today for supporting high-performance compute intensive applications. However, it is going to be effectively exploited for deploying data-driven and knowledge discovery applications. To support these classes of applications, high-level tools and services are vital. The Knowledge Grid is a high-level system for providing Grid-based knowledge discovery services. These services allow professionals and scientists to create and manage complex knowledge discovery applications composed as workflows that integrate data sets and mining tools provided as distributed services on a Grid. This paper presents and discusses how knowledge discovery applications can be designed and deployed on Grids. The contribution of novel technologies and models such as OGSA, P2P, and ontologies is also discussed.

1 Introduction

Grid technology is receiving an increasing attention both from the research community and from industry and governments. People is interested to learn how this new computing infrastructure can be effectively exploited for solving complex problems and implementing distributed high-performance applications [1]. Grid tools and middleware developed today are larger than in the recent past in number, variety, and complexity. They allow the user community to employ Grids for implementing a wider set of applications with respect to one or two years ago. New projects started in different areas, such as genetics and proteomics, multimedia data archives (e.g., a Grid for the Library of Congress), medicine (e.g., Access Grid for battling SARS), drug design, and financial modeling.

Although the Grid today is still mainly used for supporting high-performance compute intensive applications in science and engineering, it is going to be effectively exploited for implementing data intensive and knowledge discovery applications. To succeed in supporting this class of applications, tools and services for data mining and knowledge discovery on Grids are essential.

* This research has been partially funded by the Italian FIRB MIUR project "Grid.it" (RBNE01KNFP).

Today we are data rich, but knowledge poor. Massive amount of data are everyday produced and stored in digital archives. We are able to store Petabytes of data in databases and query them at an acceptable rate. However, when humans have to deal with huge amounts of data, they are not so able to understand the most significant part of them and extract the hidden information and knowledge that can make the difference and make data ownership competitive.

Grids represent a good opportunity to handle very large data sets distributed over a large number of sites. At the same time, Grids can be used as knowledge discovery engines and knowledge management platforms. What we need to effectively use Grids for those high-level knowledge-based applications are models, algorithms, and software environments for knowledge discovery and management.

This paper describes a Grid-enabled knowledge discovery system named Knowledge Grid and discusses a high-level approach based on this system for designing and deploying knowledge discovery applications on Grids. The contribute of novel technologies and models such as OGSA, P2P, and ontologies is also discussed. The Knowledge Grid is a high-level system for providing Grid-based knowledge discovery services [2]. These services allow researchers, professionals and scientists to create and manage complex knowledge discovery applications composed as workflows that integrate data, mining tools, and computing and storage resources provided as distributed services on a Grid (see Figure 1). Knowledge Grid facilities allow users to compose, store, share, and execute these knowledge discovery workflows as well as publish them as new components and services on the Grid.

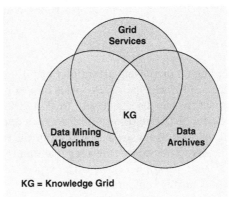

Fig. 1. Combination of basic technologies for building a Knowledge Grid

The knowledge building process in a distributed setting involves collection/generation and distribution of data and information, followed by collective interpretation of processed information into "knowledge." Knowledge building depends not only on data analysis and information processing but also on interpretation of produced models and management of knowledge models. The knowledge discovery process includes mechanisms for evaluating the correctness, accuracy and usefulness of processed data sets, developing a shared understanding of the information, and filtering knowledge to be kept in accessible organizational memory. The Knowledge Grid provides a higher level of abstraction and a set of services based on the use of Grid resources to support all these phases of the knowledge discovery process. Therefore, it allows end users to concentrate on the knowledge discovery process they must develop without worrying about Grid infrastructure and fabric details.

This paper does not intend to give a detailed presentation of the Knowledge Grid (for details see [2] and [4]) but it discusses the use of knowledge discovery services and features of the Knowledge Grid environment. Sections 2 and 3 discuss knowledge discovery services and present the system architecture and how its components can be used to design and implement knowledge discovery applications for science, industry, and commerce. Sections 4 and 5 discuss relationships among knowledge discovery services and emerging models such as OGSA, ontologies for Grids, and peer-to-peer computing protocols and mechanisms for Grids. Section 6 concludes the paper.

2   Knowledge Discovery Services

Today many public organizations, industries, and scientific labs produce and manage large amounts of complex data and information. This data and information patrimony can be effectively exploited if it is used as a source to produce knowledge necessary to support decision making. This process is both computationally intensive and collaborative and distributed in nature. Unfortunately, high-level tools to support the knowledge discovery and management in distributed environments are lacking. This is particularly true in Grid-based knowledge discovery [3], although some research and development projects and activities in this area are going to be activated mainly in Europe and USA, such as the Knowledge Grid, the Discovery Net, and the AdAM project.

The Knowledge Grid [2] provides a middleware for knowledge discovery services for a wide range of high performance distributed applications. Data sets and data mining and data analysis tools used in such applications are increasingly becoming available as stand-alone packages and as remote services on the Internet. Examples include gene and protein databases, network access and intrusion data, and data about web usage, content, and structure.

Knowledge discovery procedures in all these applications typically require the creation and management of complex, dynamic, multi-step workflows. At each step, data from various sources can be moved, filtered, and integrated and fed into a data mining tool. Based on the output results, the analyst chooses which other data sets and mining components can be integrated in the workflow or how to iterate the process to get a knowledge model. Workflows are mapped on a Grid by assigning nodes to the Grid hosts and using interconnections for implementing communication among the workflow nodes.

The Knowledge Grid supports such activities by providing mechanisms and higher level services for searching resources and designing knowledge discovery processes, by composing existing data services and data mining services in a structured manner. Designers can plan, store, validate, and re-execute their workflows as well as manage their output results.

The Knowledge Grid architecture is composed of a set of services divided in two layers:

- the *Core K-Grid layer* that interfaces the basic and generic Grid middleware services and
- the *High-level K-Grid layer* that interfaces the user by offering a set of services for the design and execution of knowledge discovery applications.

Both layers make use of repositories that provide information about resource metadata, execution plans, and knowledge obtained as result of knowledge discovery applications.

In the Knowledge Grid environment, discovery processes are represented as workflows that a user may compose using both concrete and abstract Grid resources. Knowledge discovery workflows are defined using a visual interface that shows resources (data, tools, and hosts) to the user and offers mechanisms for integrating them in a workflow. Information about single resources and workflows are stored using an XML-based notation that represents a workflow (called *execution plan* in the Knowledge Grid terminology) as a data-flow graph of nodes, each representing either a data mining service or a data transfer service. The XML representation allows the workflows for discovery processes to be easily validated, shared, translated in executable scripts, and stored for future executions. Figure 2 shows the main steps of the composition and execution processes of a knowledge discovery application on the Knowledge Grid.

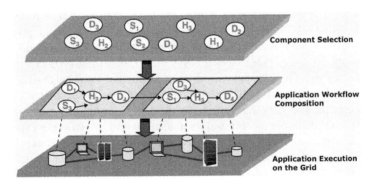

Fig. 2. Main steps of application composition and execution in the Knowledge Grid

3   Knowledge Grid Components and Tools

Figure 3 shows the general structure of the Knowledge Grid system and its main components and interaction patterns. The High-level K-Grid layer includes services used to compose, validate, and execute a parallel and distributed knowledge discovery computation. Moreover, the layer offers services to store and analyze the discovered knowledge. Main services of the High-level K-Grid layer are:

- The *Data Access Service* (*DAS*) allows for the search, selection, transfer, transformation, and delivery of data to be mined.
- The *Tools and Algorithms Access Service* (*TAAS*) is responsible for searching, selecting, and downloading data mining tools and algorithms.
- The *Execution Plan Management Service* (*EPMS*). An execution plan is represented by a graph describing interactions and data flows among data sources, extraction tools, data mining tools, and visualization tools. The Execution Plan Management Service allows for defining the structure of an application by building the corresponding graph and adding a set of constraints about resources. Generated execution plans are stored, through the RAEMS, in the *Knowledge Execution Plan Repository (KEPR)*.
- The *Results Presentation Service* (*RPS*) offers facilities for presenting and visualizing the knowledge models extracted (e.g., association rules, clustering models, classifications).

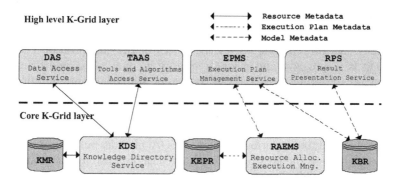

Fig. 3. The Knowledge Grid general structure and components

The Core K-Grid layer includes two main services:

- The *Knowledge Directory Service* (*KDS*) that manages metadata describing Knowledge Grid resources. Such resources comprise hosts, repositories of data to be mined, tools and algorithms used to extract, analyze, and manipulate data, distributed knowledge discovery execution plans and knowledge obtained as result of the mining process. The metadata information is represented by XML documents stored in a *Knowledge Metadata Repository (KMR)*.
- The *Resource Allocation and Execution Management Service* (*RAEMS*) is used to find a suitable mapping between an "abstract" execution plan (formalized in XML) and available resources, with the goal of satisfying the constraints (computing power, storage, memory, databases, network performance) imposed by the execution plan. After the execution plan activation, this service manages and coordinates the application execution and the storing of knowledge results in the *Knowledge Base Repository (KBR)*.

The main components of the Knowledge Grid have been implemented and are available through a software environment, named *VEGA* (*Visual Environment for Grid Applications*), that embodies services and functionalities ranging from information and discovery services to visual design and execution facilities [4].

The main goal of VEGA is to offer a set of visual functionalities that give the users the possibility to design applications starting from a view of the present Grid status (i.e., available nodes and resources), and composing the different stages constituting them inside a structured environment.

The high-level features offered by VEGA are intended to provide the user with easy access to Grid facilities with a high level of abstraction, in order to leave her free to concentrate on the application design process. To fulfill this aim, VEGA builds a visual environment based on the component framework concept, by using and enhancing basic services offered by the Knowledge Grid and the Globus Toolkit.

Key concepts in the VEGA approach to the design of a Grid application are the *visual language* used to describe in a component-like manner, and through a graphical representation, the jobs constituting an application, and the possibility to group these jobs in *workspaces* to form specific interdependent stages. A consistency checking module parses the model of the computation both while the design is in progress and prior to execute it, monitoring and driving user actions so as to obtain a correct and consistent graphical representation of the application. Together with the workspace concept, VEGA makes available also the *virtual resource* abstraction; thanks to these entities it is possible to compose applications working on data processed/generated in previous phases even if the execution has not been performed yet. VEGA includes an *execution service*, which gives the user the possibility to execute the designed application, monitor its status, and visualize results.

Knowledge discovery applications for network intrusion detection and bioinformatics have been developed by VEGA in a direct and simple way. Developers found the VEGA visual interface effective in supporting the application development from resource selection to knowledge models produced as output of the knowledge discovery process.

4   Knowledge Grid and OGSA

Grid technologies are evolving towards an open Grid architecture, called the *Open Grid Services Architecture* (*OGSA*), in which a Grid provides an extensible set of services that virtual organizations can aggregate in various ways [5].

OGSA defines a uniform exposed-service semantics, the so-called Grid service, based on concepts and technologies from both the Grid computing and Web services communities. Web services define a technique for describing software components to be accessed, methods for accessing these components, and discovery methods that enable the identification of relevant service providers. Web services are in principle independent from programming languages and system software; standards are being defined within the World Wide Web Consortium (W3C) and other standards bodies.

The OGSA model adopts three Web services standards: the *Simple Object Access Protocol (SOAP)*, the *Web Services Description Language (WSDL)*, and the *Web Services Inspection Language (WS-Inspection)*.

Web services and OGSA aim at interoperability between loosely coupled services independently from implementation, location or platform. OGSA defines standard mechanisms for creating, naming and discovering persistent and transient Grid service instances, provides location transparency and multiple protocol bindings for service instances, and supports integration with underlying native platform facilities. The OGSA model provides some common operations and supports multiple underlying resource models representing resources as service instances.

OGSA defines a Grid service as a Web service that provides a set of well-defined WSDL interfaces and that follows specific conventions on the use for Grid computing. Integration of Web and Grids will be more effective with the recent definition of the the Web Service Resource Framework (WSRF). WSRF represents a refactoring of the concepts and interfaces developed in the OGSA specification for exploiting recent developments in Web services architecture (e.g., WS-Addressing) and aligning Grids services with current Web services directions.

The Knowledge Grid, is an abstract service-based Grid architecture that does not limit the user in developing and using service-based knowledge discovery applications. We are devising an implementation of the Knowledge Grid in terms of the OGSA model. In this implementation, each of the Knowledge Grid services is exposed as a persistent service, using the OGSA conventions and mechanisms. For instance, the EPMS service implements several interfaces, among which the notification interface that allows the asynchronous delivery to the EPMS of notification messages coming from services invoked as stated in execution plans. At the same time, basic knowledge discovery services can be designed and deployed by using the KDS services for discovering Grid resources that could be used in composing knowledge discovery applications.

5   Semantic Grids, Knowledge Grids, and Peer-to-Peer Grids

The Semantic Web is an emerging initiative of World Wide Web Consortium (W3C) aiming at augmenting with semantic the information available over Internet, through document annotation and classification by using ontologies, so providing a set of tools able to navigate between concepts, rather than hyperlinks, and offering semantic search engines, rather than key-based ones.

In the Grid computing community there is a parallel effort to define a so called *Semantic Grid* (www.semanticgrid.org). The Semantic Grid vision is to incorporate the Semantic Web approach based on the systematic description of resources through metadata and ontologies, and provision for basic services about reasoning and knowledge extraction, into the Grid. Actually, the use of ontologies in Grid applications could make the difference because it augments the XML-based metadata information system associating semantic specification to each Grid resource. These services could represent a significant evolution with respect to current Grid basic services, such as the Globus MDS pattern-matching based search.

Cannataro and Comito proposed the integration of ontology-based services in the Knowledge Grid [6]. It is based on extending the architecture of the Knowledge Grid with ontology components that integrate the KDS, the KMR and the KEPR. An ontology of data mining tasks, techniques, and tools has been defined and is going to be implemented to provide users semantic-based services in searching and composing knowledge discovery applications.

Another interesting model that could provide improvements to the current Grid systems and applications is the peer-to-peer computing model. P2P is a class of self-organizing systems or applications that takes advantage of distributed resources – storage, processing, information, and human presence – available at the Internet's edges. The P2P model could thus help to ensure Grid scalability: designers could use the P2P philosophy and techniques to implement nonhierarchical decentralized Grid systems. In spite of current practices and thoughts, the Grid and P2P models share several features and have more in common than we perhaps generally recognize. Broader recognition of key commonalities could accelerate progress in both models. A synergy between the two research communities, and the two computing models, could start with identifying the similarities and differences between them [7].

Resource discovery in Grid environments is based mainly on centralized or hierarchical models. In the Globus Toolkit, for instance, users can directly gain information about a given node's resources by querying a server application running on it or running on a node that retrieves and publishes information about a given organization's node set. Because such systems are built to address the requirements of organizational-based Grids, they do not deal with more dynamic, large-scale distributed environments, in which useful information servers are not known a priori. The number of queries in such environments quickly makes a client-server approach ineffective. Resource discovery includes, in part, the issue of presence management – discovery of the nodes that are currently available in a Grid – since specific mechanisms are not yet defined for it. On the other hand, the presence-management protocol is a key element in P2P systems: each node periodically notifies the network of its presence, discovering its neighbors at the same time.

Future Grid systems should implement a P2P-style decentralized resource discovery model that can support Grids as open resource communities. We are designing some of the components and services of the Knowledge Grid in a P2P manner. For example, the KDS could be effectively redesigned using a P2P approach. If we view current Grids as federations of smaller Grids managed by diverse organizations, we can envision the KDS for a large-scale Grid by adopting the super-peer network model. In this approach, each super peer operates as a server for a set of clients and as an equal among other super peers. This topology provides a useful balance between the efficiency of centralized search and the autonomy, load balancing, and robustness of distributed search. In a Knowledge Grid KDS service based on the super-peer model, each participating organization would configure one or more of its nodes to operate as super peers and provide knowledge resources. Nodes within each organization would exchange monitoring and discovery messages with a reference super peer, and super peers from different organizations would exchange messages in a P2P fashion.

6   Conclusions

The Grid will represent in a near future an effective infrastructure for managing very large data sources and providing high-level mechanisms for extracting valuable knowledge from them [8]. To solve this class of applications, we need advanced tools and services for knowledge discovery.

Here we discussed the Knowledge Grid: a Grid-based software environment that implements Grid-enabled knowledge discovery services. The Knowledge Grid can be used as a high-level system for providing knowledge discovery services on dispersed resources connected through a Grid. These services allow professionals and scientists to create and manage complex knowledge discovery applications composed as workflows integrating data sets and mining tools provided as distributed services on a Grid.

In the next years the Grid will be used as a platform for implementing and deploying geographically distributed knowledge discovery [9] and knowledge management platforms and applications. Some ongoing efforts in this direction have recently been initiated. Examples of systems such as the Discovery Net [10], the AdAM system [11], and the Knowledge Grid discussed here show the feasibility of the approach and can represent the first generation of knowledge-based pervasive Grids.

The wish list of Grid features is still too long. Here are some main properties of future Grids that today are not available:

- *Easy to program* – hiding architecture issues and details,
- *Adaptive* – exploiting dynamically available resources,
- *Human-centric* – offering end-user oriented services,
- *Secure* – providing secure authentication mechanisms,
- *Reliable* – offering fault-tolerance and high availability,
- *Scalable* – improving performance as problem size increases,
- *Pervasive* – giving users the possibility for ubiquitous access, and
- *Knowledge-based* – extracting and managing knowledge together with data and information.

The future use of the Grid is mainly related to its ability to embody many of these properties and to manage world-wide complex distributed applications. Among these, knowledge-based applications are a major goal. To reach this goal, the Grid needs to evolve towards an open decentralized infrastructure based on interoperable high-level services that make use of knowledge both in providing resources and in giving results to end users. Software technologies as knowledge

Grids, OGSA, ontologies, and P2P will provide important elements to build up high-level applications on a World Wide Grid. They provide the key components for developing Grid-based complex systems such as distributed knowledge management systems providing pervasive access, adaptivity, and high performance for virtual organizations in science, engineering, industry, and, more generally, in future society organizations.

Acknowledgements. We would like to thank other researchers working in the Knowledge Grid team: Mario Cannataro, Carmela Comito, and Pierangelo Veltri.

References

1. I. Foster, C. Kesselman, J. M. Nick, and S. Tuecke, The Physiology of the Grid: An Open Grid Services Architecture for Distributed Systems Integration, technical report, *http://www.globus.org/research/papers/ogsa.pdf*, 2002.
2. M. Cannataro, D. Talia, The Knowledge Grid, *Communications of the ACM*, 46(1), 89-93, 2003.
3. F. Berman, From TeraGrid to Knowledge Grid, *Communications of the ACM*, 44(11), pp. 27-28, 2001.
4. M. Cannataro, A. Congiusta, D. Talia, P. Trunfio, A Data Mining Toolset for Distributed High-Performance Platforms, *Proc. 3rd Int. Conference Data Mining 2002*, WIT Press, Bologna, Italy, pp. 41-50, September 2002.
5. D. Talia, The Open Grid Services Architecture: Where the Grid Meets the Web, *IEEE Internet Computing*, Vol. 6, No. 6, pp. 67-71, 2002.
6. M. Cannataro, C. Comito, A Data Mining Ontology for Grid Programming, *Proc. 1st Int. Workshop on Semantics in Peer-to-Peer and Grid Computing*, in conjunction with WWW2003, Budapest, 20-24 May 2003.
7. D. Talia, P. Trunfio, Toward a Sinergy Between P2P and Grids, *IEEE Internet Computing*, Vol. 7, No. 4, pp. 96-99, 2003.
8. F. Berman, G. Fox, A. Hey, (eds.), *Grid computing: Making the Global Infrastructure a Reality*, Wiley, 2003.
9. H. Kargupta, P. Chan, (eds.), *Advances in Distributed and Parallel Knowledge Discovery*, AAAI Press 1999.
10. M. Ghanem, Y. Guo, A. Rowe, P. Wendel, Grid-based Knowledge Discovery Services for High Throughput Informatics, *Proc. 11th IEEE International Symposium on High Performance Distributed Computing*, p. 416, IEEE CS Press, 2002.
11. T. Hinke, J. Novotny, Data Mining on NASA's Information Power Grid, *Proc. Ninth IEEE International Symposium on High Performance Distributed Computing*, pp. 292-293, IEEE CS Press, 2000.

A Grid Service Framework for Metadata Management in Self-e-Learning Networks*

George Samaras, Kyriakos Karenos, and Eleni Christodoulou

Department of Computer Science, University of Cyprus
{cssamara,cs98kk2,cseleni}@ucy.ac.cy

Abstract. Metadata management is critical for Grid systems. More specifically, semantically meaningful resource descriptions constitute a highly beneficial extension to Grid environments that started to gain significant attention. In this work we contribute to the effort of enhancing current Grid technologies to support semantic descriptors for resources – termed also the *Semantic Grid*. We use a *Self e-Learning Network (SeLeNe)* as the testbed application and propose a set of services that are applicable in such a case in alignment to the *Open Grid Services Architecture (OGSA)*. We concentrate on providing services for the utilization of Learning Objects' (LO)[1] metadata, the basic of which, however, are generic enough to be utilized by other Grid-based systems that need to make use of semantic descriptions. Different service placement scenarios produce a number of possible architectural alternatives.

1 Introduction

Grid Technology has found uses in a wide area of applications that usually address large scale, process and data intensive problems. Our effort is to bring data-centric services adjusted to the Grid environment and to expand its functionality in the area of resource sharing using e-Learning as the testbed application. As we elaborate in section 2, we consider metadata management (viewed as semantically meaningful resource descriptions of learning material), crucial especially as the Grid expands to be supplemented with capabilities towards supporting (and incorporating) technologies from the Semantic Web, termed the "Semantic Grid" [1] under the guidelines of the Global Grid Forum (GGF) [2].

Our work derives from our IST project SeLeNe: The SeLeNe Project is aiming to elaborate new educational metaphors and tools in order to facilitate the formation of learning communities who require world-wide discovery and assimilation of knowledge. To realize this vision, SeLeNe is relying on semantic metadata describing educational material. SeLeNe offers advanced services for the discovery, sharing, and collaborative creation of learning resources, facilitating a syndicated and personalised access to such resources.

---

* This work has been supported by the E.U. Project "SeLeNe: Self e-Learning Networks", IST-2001-39045.
[1] A LO is generally defined as an artifact in *digital* form utilized during the learning process.

M. Dikaiakos (Ed.): AxGrids 2004, LNCS 3165, pp. 260–269, 2004.
© Springer-Verlag Berlin Heidelberg 2004

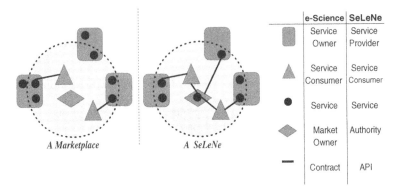

Fig. 1. SeLeNe and the Semantic Grid

Service-based educational systems open new ways in the usability of the Grid as their primary requirements include the provision of adequate services for sharing, syndicating heterogeneous resources and relevant content discovery. Efforts are already under way: In [3] an attempt is made to provide an infrastructure for future eScience. Of our interest in this work, is the adoption of a service-based perspective to meet the needs of a global and flexible collaborative system for educational purposes. The Grid is described as a collection of service providers and service consumers brought together in a "marketplace", initiated and managed by a "marketplace owner". We parallelize the "marketplace" to a SeLeNe (Fig.1) and the "marketplace owners" to the system point of entry, which provides reliability in accessing the system. These we later refer to as Authority sites.

It is envisioned that the SeLeNe service layering will enable generic services to be provided which will support the high level Application-specific services. OGSA GridService [4] can be adapted to the requirements of an e-learning environment as it provides a process-oriented model on which our data-oriented model services will be based. However, the various services – as described in the OGSA Layers – need not be deployed within every physical site. Each node may create and offer different services to the system, included in a predefined set. It is apparent, also, that services may require the collaboration of many sites (e.g. a query service) functioning in a distributed manner.

An educational environment such as the one envisioned by SeLeNe, however, exceeds the requirement of a standard client-server Grid model. Firstly, information sharing must be extended to the semantic level. The semantic extension of the SeLeNe-offered services will aim to address the diversity among consumers and producers of LO descriptions (in addition to services) in terms of ontological contexts. These requirements would require high coupling among services and the ability for the combination of these services towards the completion of specific e-learning tasks. In addition, the need for personalization - which requires each participating learner or site to be viewed as individual - and for collaboration - which requires for a global view of the SeLeNe components' interaction – impose a model that should functionally allow for the handling of both cases.

Although we do view the problem through Grid lenses, we identify the need to incorporate techniques from both Grid and P2P technologies. Efforts have already been initiated towards the incorporation of P2P capabilities to the OGSA framework by the GGF community. Although currently efforts are still at an early draft stage, one can clearly see the practical need for P2P-usable OGSA [5].

To this end, the most relevant work to SeLeNe is done within the SWAP project [19], which combines P2P and Semantic Web technologies to support knowledge sharing. Web Services technologies [20] provide an excellent infrastructure on which SeLeNe services can be build. However we also consider other alternatives, especially in the light of P2P/Grid requirements mentioned earlier. The JXTA project framework [21] offers a purely Java-based services core and concentrates on a P2P-oriented model. On the other hand the Globus project [17] provides a range of basic services for the construction of Grid-based systems. These technologies have been studied extensively as part of a number of previous works [19, 16, 18]. Herein, we provide the definition of the required services and the architectural model that would suit the user requirements, assigning much less weight on the possible future implementation alternatives.

It is important to note that some vital services need to be available at all times (e.g. registration, mediated querying etc) as well as the fact that we need to provide some method for information integration. Therefore we propose that "authority" sites should be present that will be more reliable and may acquire the role of mediator (e.g. to interconnect related sites by clustering) or coordinator (e.g. to support ontology mappings when and if necessary).

2   An OGSA-Guided, Metadata-Centric Architecture

It has already been mentioned that SeLeNe is concentrating on the management of LO metadata having in mind. Based on the OGSA service layering we construct, in this section, a corresponding layered set of services required for a SeLeNe[2].

Management and manipulation of LO metadata is at least as important and critical as LO management itself. In an educational system, content descriptions are crucial in order to provide a uniform method for the discovery of LOs relevant to the user's queries and for combining multiple such descriptions to realize specific tasks that lead, eventually, to supporting the learning objectives. Additional requirements such as personalization support, change notification and automatic/semi-automatic metadata generation are only indications of the demanding nature of metadata management. When addressing large data set services in OGSA layering, metadata handling is usually present at the Resource and Collective layers. In our case, as metadata is the actual shared resource and due to the mentioned requirements we believe that it is required to provide metadata services covering all layers. For example there exists the need for descriptions of LOs to be accessed, manipulated and stored in an RDF repository

---

[2] User Requirement Analysis for Self e-learning Networks is available in [8] as further work in the SeLeNe project.

(i.e. the Repository's API). This is suitable to be included to the Fabric layer services since a number of different storage alternatives may be present. On the other hand there exist high-level services that will support Trails and Personalization of LO descriptions (i.e. adaptation of the learning material based on specific user profiling and paths followed in the LO space during the learning process) that need to be placed at the Application layer.

Table 1. SeLeNe Services

	Service Name	Core	OGSA Layer
	Presentation		
	Collaboration		
	Trails & Personalization		Application
App. Specific	User Registration		
	LO Registration		
	View		
	ECA		
	Query	X	Collective
	Update		
	Syndication		
Generic	Locate		Resource
	Information	X	
	Sign-on		Connectivity
	Communication	X	
	Access	X	Fabric

2.1 Service Classification

It is understandable that not all services can be deployed at each and every SeLeNe-participating site. However, we feel that it is a requirement that there should be an as-small-as-possible set of specific services that each SeLeNe site will assume present in all other SeLeNe sites. The basic reason for this is to make sure that at least communication and discovery of available services will be possible as soon as a single SeLeNe site is identified as an entry point. These services, we can call *Core Services*. Additional *Appended Services* will be present in order to complete the larger percentage of SeLeNe functionality.

One can clearly see that the proposed interfaces in OGSA (GridService, Notification, Registry, Factory, HandleMap [6, 4]) are, to a major degree, process-centric. In SeLeNe, however, RDF metadata is the actual resource and for this reason we should provide additional or adapted interfaces to meet a, to a large extent, data-oriented system.

What we are envisioning is that the set of proposed services will be possible to be deployed in alignment to the OGSA guidelines (and possibly over widely used grid technologies such as Web Services and Globus) but also extended to provide additional functionality that is missing from today's Grids but required by an e-learning network (i.e. P2P support and expanded semantic (RDF) metadata usage). In this sense, as proposed in section 3.2, existing infrastructure can be utilized to mediate the underlying service functionality described below but targeting to support RDF descriptions as the requested resource (i.e. instead of computation cycles, storage, large data objects etc.). As argued next, generic RDF services can then be adopted by other grid systems. Besides characterizing services as being either core or appended, one other important distinctive factor for offered services is whether a service is generic or application specific (i.e. SeLeNe specific). *Generic* services will reside at the "hourglass neck" of the OGSA layers. These services will be usable for other applications or systems that require or make use of RDF. Examples of generic services include RDF view creation and change notification. On the other hand, *application specific* services concentrate on the specifics within the SeLeNe with respect to the e-learning requirements such as trail management and personalization services. In the following subsections we will describe the high level functionality for each of the proposed services.

2.2 Core Services

Access Service. This service is located at the lower layer of the Grid Architecture (Fabric). This service provides the direct access API to the local RDF Repository. It includes access methods for local requests as well as appropriate manipulation of locally stored descriptions (i.e. insert, delete and update of the repository content) irrespective of its low-level implementation. The actual storage repository can be realized over a number of implementation alternatives such as Sesame RDF Repository [9], Jena toolkit [11] and the ICS-FORTH RDFSuite [10].

Communication Service. This service provides the basic communication mechanisms for exchanging data. Current protocols may be used on which communication links can be established (such as TCP/IP) but we should also consider creating a simple "SeLeNe specific" communication service (i.e. for the exchange of specific types of messages e.g. task request submission.) Possible example technologies that can support this "SeLeNe specific" communication service are SOAP [12] and RPC techniques (e.g. Java RMI), however the message content and structure is not part of our current investigations. RPC is generally more appropriate for more formalized and concrete (e.g. local) communications and can be used in a local SeLeNe (e.g. installed at a single institution). On the other hand SOAP addresses incompatibility problems among multiple communicating and possibly remote groups.

Information Service. The Information service provides the capabilities of acquiring descriptive information on some SeLeNe site. Informally, it will be able to answer questions of the form: "what does this node understand in terms of metadata?" It provides the profile of the site (not the user). Put in another way, it provides metadata on metadata and more specifically the Namespaces used and the RDF Schema(s) for that specific site. The Information service is built on top of the Access service. It does not raise any new research issues for us.

Query. The Query Service is of great importance: we need to define a powerful query language that will allow for the extraction of results from multiple, local RDF repositories. The Query Service should be distributed and should allow for search message routing in order to forward sub-queries to sites that can provide answers. It may also need to call the Syndication service to translate queries expressed against one RDF taxonomy to sub-queries expressed against different local taxonomies. It then passes a subquery to the Access service supported by a particular peer, expressed in terms of that peer's local RDF Schema. Another issue is the exploitation of the semantic meaning of our data to relate users of similar interests. A good, super-peer based technique is provided in [13] where a clustering technique is used to mediate heterogeneous schemas. Authority sites can become responsible for keeping semantically meaningful indexes about other neighboring sites.

2.3   Appended Services

Sign-On. A site is able to register to the SeLeNe in order to advertise its content and services. Also, in this way, it should be able to make its presence known to other sites. Sign-on allows for the update of the indexes of neighbors as well as the directly connected authority site(s).

Locate. This service relates to the OGSI GridService and makes requested service lookup possible. As soon as a site is connected, it should be able to discover where there are services that will be used, along with any required parameters that these services will need. We assume for now standard registry techniques depending on the architectural deployment of SeLeNe. A distributed cataloging scheme could suffice in this case (e.g. UDDI [15].) Semantic service descriptions is an issue not addressed within SeLeNe for now although it does pose an interesting future research issue for the evolution and expansion of the proposed set of services.

Syndication. The Syndication service is responsible for the translation between different RDF schemas. This is accomplished by using the user-supplied mappings between heterogeneous schemas. This implies both data-to-data and query-to-query translations. Syndication issues are also of high importance.

Update. The Update Service is used to appropriately transfer updates to descriptions expressed in diverse schemas. By analogy to the Query service, this service will take an update request for Peer 1 expressed in some RDF_Schema_2 and translate it into the equivalent update expressed in terms of RDF_Schema_1 by using the Syndication service. The Update Service would then request for the invocation of the appropriate operation of the Access service at Peer 1 to enact the actual update on its local RDF repository.

Event-Condition-Action (ECA). LO descriptions are gradually updated and enhanced due to the ongoing learning process. Users should be able to register their interest to receive changes when they occur that are relevant to metadata that are of their interest. This feature should be provided by the ECA Service, which will propagate updates and notifications to registered sites.

View. The View Service provides the functionality of creating personalized views by structuring (and re-structuring) virtual resource descriptions among the SeLeNe LO descriptions' space. By this way we allow for the user to actually built-up her own virtual learning environment which she can navigate and expand. The View Service will can be realized over RVL that is able to, additionally, allow the definition of virtual schemas and thus amplifies the personalization capabilities of the SeLeNe system.

LO Registration. This service provides the API for submitting a new LO by providing its description to the SeLeNe. Storing LO descriptions is handled by the use of the Access service. The registration process makes use of the Syndication service and allows the registration of both atomic and composite LOs.

User Registration. The user will be registering to a SeLeNe in order to create and later use her profile and thus acquire a personalized view of the system. User descriptions are also stored using the Access service. Issues of costing are not considered at this moment as we focus mainly on the personalization/profile creation aspect of the User.

Trails & Personalization. The Trails & Personalization Service is related to a specific user or group of users. It is concentrated on the educational characteristics of the user and provides the API to extract user-profiling information. It is proposed that this service should run as a user-side agent when possible while trails could be formed and managed by message exchanging of the participating person or group agent or agents.

Collaboration. A Collaboration Service should allow the communication between users and groups of users and it is proposed that this is mediated by a central authority site. At least two sites should request the creation of a collaboration session and others may be added later. Collaboration services may include already available systems such as Blackboards, Message Boards, CVS (for collaborative code writing) or e-mail and instant messaging services. The SeLeNe Collaboration Service lies above these services in order to provide connections to other SeLeNe services.

Presentation. Based mainly on the user profile, the Presentation service should be able to produce graphical visualization of metadata. This could, for example, be a RDF graph. It could also be produced locally or via a web-based engine. Since visualization and presentation are highly related to the learning experience itself, there is no simplified methodology for it and will most possibly require much work.

3   Approaches to Service Placement

3.1   Architectural Models

In Figure 2 three models are shown: Continued lines represent direct connections between sites while discontinued lines represent possible connections established

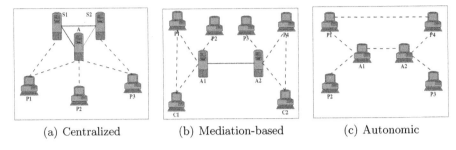

    (a) Centralized   (b) Mediation-based   (c) Autonomic

Fig. 2. Service Placement Approaches

due to service calls. Detailed interaction flows among site service calls with respect to the services proposed can also be found in [22].

One first approach is to take a look at the *Centralized* scheme. In such an architecture, a number of "fixed" service providers exist which are highly available and powerful enough to accommodate a large number of services. The centralisation has to do with the fact that the greater percentage computation and the totality of the RDF descriptions storage are found at a centralised location.

Provider servers are connected and together they provide a service provision cluster. Clients (or consumers) connect to the cluster via a specific entry point or an Authority. Metadata located at consumer sites need to be registered at any cluster server. In this sense, servers act as metadata repositories for LOs. Query and Integration/Mediation services are provided for metadata among the servers and replies are sent back to the requester. Since all tasks are handled within the group of servers, consumer sites are not actually aware of each other. This strategy is similar to a brokering system such as EducaNext/Universal [7].

In a *Mediation-based scheme*, consumers and producers (of both LOs and Services) are logically clustered around mediators/brokers that in our case will be taking the role of Authorities. This is also similar to the Consumer-Broker-Producer model (in terms of services) and also resembles the super peer scheme (in terms of content). The reason for this model to be named Mediation-based is due to the fact that its functionality is primarily facilitated by mediator machines, similar to "Brokers"/"Authorities." Authorities are affiliated with a number of "Providers" that become known to them. Sites may be both LO producers and providers but need to register their content to a broker which will provide the means for communication with other sites by creating logical communities. This last characteristic is highly desirable in SeLeNe. Edutella [16] is a mediation-based educational system built on the the JXTA infrastructure.

An *Autonomic* system is characterized by the fact that each site is autonomous in terms of service provision (i.e. each site may provide any number of services). In such cases, a core services requirement is the existence of a Service Discovery protocol (such as the previously described Discovery Service), which should be completely distributed. Metadata is maintained at each site and there is no centralization. Therefore, a distributed and possibly partially replicated

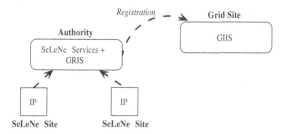

Fig. 3. An example of SeLeNe Services over Globus Information Services

metadata catalog should exist to address intermittent connectivity issues. One such autonomic (P2P) approach is found in the SWAP project. The core difference however is that SWAP is component-based, not service-based.

It is noted that extensive support for P2P environments will require a new global infrastructure [5]. Therefore, in addition to these efforts it is expected that the new version of the Globus Toolkit (GT3) [17] will adopt open protocol standards also applied in Web Services technologies. An improved OGSA specification in combination with GT3 support for standard technologies will bring this goal closer to realization.

3.2 Proposed Initial Globus Integration

The most relevant components to resource discovery and Grid services' information are the Globus *Information services* [14] or *Monitoring and Discovery Service (MDS)*. We omit description of this service due to space limitations.

Although SeLeNe services are self-contained (providing registration, query, syndication, adaptation service), still, it is extremely difficult to claim the replacement or even direct integration of semantic resource descriptions with Globus MDS. One alternative could be implementing SeLeNe services as completely independent entities, i.e. as additional Grid Application, OGSI-compliant Services. Below we provide a possible set up, depicted in Fig. 3.

- SeLeNe sites act as Information Providers, (IPs) where Information are the descriptions available at the local repositories. It is assumed that Core SeLeNe services run on these sites including Information and Access services, essential for this functionality.
- The Grid Resource Information Server (GRIS) runs on Authority sites. SeLeNe IPs register resource descriptions to the Authorities. Note that Authorities can be providers themselves. Authorities, thus act as "gateways" to the rest of the Grid.
- GRISs Register with *any* available Grid Information Index Server (GIIS). In this way SeLeNe services are made accessible to external users by queering the GIIS.

4 Conclusion

The usage of semantic metadata resource descriptions can highly benefit Grid technology. In our work within the SeLeNe project we have proposed a set of core and appended services that allow for the query, access and syndication of heterogeneous RDF-based descriptions and propose the incorporation of such services to the current Grid Infrastructure. We use an educational e-learning application as a testbed and find that the usability of such a service set can be applied to multiple architectural models. We believe that semantic metadata for the Grid constitutes a critical extension towards the realization of the Semantic Grid vision.

References

1. The Semantic Grid Community Portal. Available at `www.semanticgrid.org/`
2. Global Grid Forum (GGF). Available at `www.gridforum.org`
3. D. De Roure, N.R. Jennings, N.R. Shadbolt. The Semantic Grid: A Future eScience Infrastructure. National e-Science Centre. Univ.of Edinburgh, *UK. UKeS 2002.*
4. I. Foster, C. Kesselman, J. Nick, and S. Tuecke. The Physiology of the Grid: An open grid services architecture for distributed systems integration. *Technical report, Open Grid Service Infrastructure WG, GGF, Jun. 2002.*
5. The OGSAP2P Group. Available at `www.gridforum.org/4-GP/ogsap2p.htm`
6. Ian Foster, Carl Kesselman, Steven Tuecke. The Anatomy of the Grid Enabling Scalable Virtual Organizations. *International J. Supercomputer Applications, 2001.*
7. EducaNext (Universal) Project. Available at `www.educanext.org`
8. K. Keenoy, G. Papamarkos, A. Poulovassilis, M. Levene, D. Peterson, P. Wood, G. Loizou. Self e-Learning Networks - Functionality, User Requirements and Exploitation Scenarios, *SeLeNe Project Del. 2.2*, Aug. 2003.
9. Sesame Open Source RDF Schema-based Repository and Querying facility. Available at `sesame.aidministrator.nl`
10. ICS-FORTH RDFSuite. High-level Scalable Tools for the Semantic Web: Available at `http://139.91.183.30:9090/RDF/index.html`
11. Jena Semantic Web Toolkit. Available at `www.hpl.hp.com/semweb/jena.htm`
12. Simple Object Access Protocol (SOAP). Available at `www.w3.org/TR/SOAP`
13. Leonidas Galanis, Yuan Wang Shawn, R. Jeffery David J. DeWitt. Processing XML Containment Queries in a Large Peer-to-Peer System. *CAiSE 2003*
14. K. Czajkowski and S. Fitzgerald and I. Foster and C. Kesselman, Grid Information Services for Distributed Resource Sharing, *HPDC 2001.*
15. The Universal Description, Discovery and Integration Protocol. Available at `www.uddi.org`
16. Edutella Project. Available at `edutella.jxta.org`
17. Globus Toolkit. Available at `www.globus.org`
18. OntoWeb: Available at `www.ontoweb.org`
19. The SWAP System. Available at `swap.semanticweb.org/public/index.htm`
20. Web Services at W3C. Available at `www.w3.org/2002/ws`
21. Project JXTA. Available at `www.jxta.org`
22. The SeLeNe Consortium. An Architectural Framework and Deployment Choices for SeLeNe. *SeLeNe Project Del. 5.0. Dec. 2003.*

Author Index